The Degradation of Work?

Skill, deskilling and the labour process

The Degradation of Work?

Skill, deskilling and the labour process

Edited by
Stephen Wood

Hutchinson
London Melbourne Sydney Auckland Johannesburg

Hutchinson & Co. (Publishers) Ltd
An imprint of the Hutchinson Publishing Group
17–21 Conway Street, London W1P 6JD

Hutchinson Group (Australia) Pty Ltd
30–32 Cremorne Street, Richmond South, Victoria 312
PO Box 151, Broadway, New South Wales 2007

Hutchinson Group (NZ) Ltd
32–34 View Road, PO Box 40–086, Glenfield, Auckland 10

Hutchinson Group (SA) (Pty) Ltd
PO Box 337, Bergvlei 2012, South Africa

First published 1982

© Stephen Wood 1982

Set in Times by A-Line Services,
Saffron Walden, Essex

Printed in Great Britain by The Anchor Press Ltd
and bound by Wm Brendon & Son Ltd
both of Tiptree, Essex

British Library Cataloguing in Publication Data
The degradation of work?
    1. Industrial sociology
    I. Wood, Stephen
    306'.3   HD6955
ISBN 0 09 145400 X

Contents

Acknowledgements

I would like to thank the following for their help and encouragement in the development of this book: Sally Alexander, Veronica Beechey, Rosemary Crompton, Tony Elger, Andrew Friedman, Patrick Fridenson, John Foster, Stephen Hill, Bryn Jones, John Kelly, Tony Lane, David Lee, Craig Littler, Gavin MacKenzie, Charles More, Howard Newby, Theo Nichols, Roger Penn, Stuart Reid, Ceridwen Roberts, Michael Rose, and Jill Rubery. The discussions I had with Tony Elger, Stephen Hill, Craig Littler, David Lee, Charles More, and Jill Rubery were especially valuable.

I would also like to thank Rab MacWilliam of Hutchinson and Howard Newby for their considerable editorial assistance, and the Nuffield Foundation for a grant which helped the authors to meet to discuss the ideas which have been developed in this book.

Stephen Wood
March 1981

Contributors

Stephen Wood (editor) gained his BSc. in behavioural sciences from Aston University in Birmingham and his Ph.D from Manchester University. He was a research associate at Manchester University from 1973 to 1974, and has been a lecturer in industrial relations at the London School of Economics from 1974 to date. He is co-editor (with Keith Thurley) of *Management Strategy and Industrial Relations* (Cambridge University Press 1982). He is currently completing work on redundancy, and is involved in co-operating with the International Institute of Management in Berlin on a comparative study of employers' hiring practices.

Veronica Beechey gained her BA in sociology from Essex University in 1968. She had a studentship at Nuffield College, Oxford, from 1968 to 1970 and from 1972 to 1973. She is a lecturer in sociology at Warwick University and is currently working at the Open University on a new women's studies course. She has also taught in America and on adult shop stewards' courses in Coventry. She is currently doing research into part-time women's employment in the Coventry labour market.

Rosemary Crompton gained her BSc. in sociology from Bedford College, London University, in 1964, and has been a lecturer in the School of Economic and Social Studies at East Anglia University from 1968 to date. She is joint author (with Dorothy Wedderburn) of *Workers' Attitudes and Technology* (Cambridge University Press 1972) and (with Jon Gubbay) of *Economy and Class Structure* (Macmillan 1977). She is currently completing a SSRC-financed project on the contemporary work situation of clerical employees.

Tony Elger gained his BA in sociology and psychology from Hull University, and is currently a lecturer in sociology at Warwick

University. He is an active member of the Conference of Socialist Economists, and his research, teaching and political interests focus on the politics of production and work place industrial relations.

Bryn Jones worked for the Department of Health and Social Security for several years before taking a sociology degree from the London School of Economics in 1973. He was subsequently a research student in sociology at Liverpool University, working for a doctoral thesis on the influence of Marxist and sociological theories of class and social stratification in the study of the British working class. Since 1978 he has been a SSRC-financed research fellow, and a lecturer in sociology at Bath University. The essay in this book arose from case study investigations of the process of occupational change in the automation of the British engineering industries. He is currently working with Dr Michael Rose at Bath University on a SSRC-sponsored study of the changing 'industrial relations' strategies of employers and trade unions over 'work reorganization' schemes in different sectors of British industry.

John Kelly gained his BSc. from Sheffield University in 1973 and his Ph.D from London University in 1979. He was a postgraduate student at the London School of Economics from 1974 to 1977, a research associate in social and applied psychology at the Research Unit, Sheffield University, from 1977 to 1980, and has been a lecturer in industrial relations at the London School of Economics from 1980 to date. He is co-editor (with C. W. Clegg) of *Autonomy and Control at the Workplace* (1981) and author of *Scientific Management, Job Redesign and Work Performance* (forthcoming). He is currently writing up research on the steel strike.

David Lee gained his BSc. in economics from the London School of Economics and a diploma in industrial sociology from Liverpool University. He was a research associate at Birmingham University, where he gained his Ph.D, a research fellow and lecturer in sociological studies at Sheffield University from 1963 to 1969, and a lecturer in sociology at Essex University from 1969 to 1977. In 1977 he became a senior lecturer.

Craig Littler gained his BSc. and Ph.D from London University. He is a consultant lecturer in industrial relations at City University, London, and a research fellow at the Open University. He is the author of *Control and Conflict: The Development of the Labour Process in Britain, Japan and USA* (Macmillan 1981). He is currently working on a book on recent trends in job design and is doing research in China.

Charles More gained his MA from Oxford University and his MSc. and Ph.D from London University. He taught in schools for several years, and then did postgraduate work in economic history at the London School of Economics. He has published a book, *Skill and the English Working Class 1870–1914*, based on his thesis. He is currently a lecturer in economic and social history at the College of St Paul and St Mary in Cheltenham.

Roger Penn gained his BA from Cambridge University and his MA from Brown University. He did postgraduate research in social and political sciences at Cambridge. He was a lecturer in sociology at Essex University from 1976 to 1977, and has been a lecturer in sociology at Lancaster University from 1977 to date.

Stuart Reid gained his BA from Cambridge University, and did postgraduate research in the Social and Political Sciences Committee, Cambridge, from 1976 to 1979. He was senior research associate at East Anglia University from 1979 to 1980, and has been a lecturer in sociology at Brunel University from 1980 to date. The essay with Rosemary Crompton in this book arises partly from his postgraduate studies of the effects of computers on clerical employees.

1 Introduction

Stephen Wood

This book is about the nature and importance of skill. It is concerned with such questions as: has there been a general deskilling and routinization of jobs? Are 'skilled' jobs really any different from semi- or un-skilled ones? Is the skill of the skilled worker essentially artificial, socially constructed in order to maintain differentials in wages and status? Have particular groups been able to resist encroachment by management into their traditional craft autonomy? Has working-class pressure itself been able to reverse or counter the 'deskilling trend' or has it influenced managements to do so? Are attempts to humanize work simply cosmetic or doomed to fail? What of the new technology – computers, micro-processors, numerically controlled machines: do they deskill jobs further?

Such questions have taken on a new theoretical significance since the publication in 1974 of Braverman's *Labor and Monopoly Capital*. This book has been widely acclaimed by British social scientists and has certainly aroused a great deal of interest and discussion (see, for example, MacKenzie, 1977; Coombs, 1978; Zimbalist, 1979). Its essential thesis is that there has been a general and progressive deskilling of jobs in the twentieth century, that there is a long-term trend for jobs to be increasingly devoid of intrinsic content, routinized and mechanical. Linking the organization of work to class analysis, Braverman argues that the working class has become increasingly homogeneous, as Marx and Engels claimed in the *Communist Manifesto*. His analysis of deskilling challenges a conventional view of America as having experienced an upgrading of work in the last decades and contests the distinctions that are conventionally drawn between types of workers, such as blue/white-collar, traditional and new working-class, clerical and factory.

The book was especially welcomed because of its attempt to bring the labour process into the arena of radical debate as part of the general renewal and development of Marxist analysis. Its wide-ranging concerns – for example, its attempt to relate the content of work to wider questions of class, its redefinition of the relationship between office and factory work, its concern with women's work – were particularly appreciated. Nevertheless, most of the commentators on *Labor and Monopoly Capital* levelled some criticisms at Braverman, some of which have important implications for his work. For example, it is argued that his thesis relies too heavily on an assumed universal and unproblematic adoption by management of Taylor's 'scientific management', and that he neglects the ways in which workers may resist managerial initiatives and managements may opt for strategies which provide workers with some autonomy. Such weaknesses may imply more fundamental criticisms, particularly that Braverman's work may be constrained by his deliberate concentration on the objective content of class – and indeed some commentators recognized this. However, most reviewers in the 1970s concluded that, on balance, the book should be judged positively.

Such conclusions have fuelled what perhaps might be seen as an excessive enthusiasm for Braverman in Britain. This is an over-reaction, based partly on the book's polemical content and apparent political significance but, above all else, on the widespread accept-ance of its overall thesis, the deskilling argument.

This over-reaction was perhaps justified to some extent, for by the early 1970s debate in sociology had become largely programmatic, concerned with 'high' and abstract Marxist structuralism or the extreme subjectivism of ethnomethodology. Furthermore, this reaction was indirectly encouraged by Braverman, who argued that there had been little or no concern for, or analysis of, the labour process in the twentieth century, and that this reflected the 'extraordinary thoroughness and prescience with which Marx per-formed his task' (Braverman, 1974, p.9). However, this over-reaction reflects a certain insularity and lack of development in British social science, for in several European countries there had long been a debate about the nature of skill; in France and Germany (Gottschalch and Ohm, 1977: Mickler, Mohr and Kadritzke, 1977), for example, empirical programmes had been devised to examine the changing constitution of the occupational structure and the skill content of jobs. As Rose (1979) implies, for the French sociologist, for instance, there must have been a sense of *déjà vu* about Braverman's work, as Naville, Friedmann and others had long been concerned with such questions and had contributed to the definition of Taylorism as a 'social problem' which has itself spawned further research.

Nevertheless, there has been some concern in Britain about the nature of skill, and indeed More (1978) shows that towards the end of the last century there was a controversy over the processes and consequences of specialization, not dissimiliar to the Braverman debate, involving writers such as Hobson, Tawney and others. It could be argued that from Adam Smith onwards a concern about the division of labour has underlain just about all social science, and that much twentieth-century work has been written against a background of increasing mechanization. Major schools, including human relations and the British tradition of industrial relations theory, for example, have all developed against a background of certain assumptions about the way in which the skill content of jobs has changed. Furthermore, many of the studies of industrial sociology have been concerned with the impact of, and reactions to, technological change (Scott *et al.*, 1956; Woodward, 1966). Most Marxists have, in fact, shown some concern for deskilling; Gramsci (1971, p. 279) explicitly wrote about Taylorism and Fordism, and a central assumption of the Frankfurt school is the increasingly degrading and one-dimensional nature of modern employment. But in all such work there has been a failure to consider in depth the real nature and content of jobs, and this is even true of the empirical study of technology and alienation by Blauner (1964).

It is not clear that even Braverman examines such issues in the kind of detail that may be required or with the thoroughness that many reviewers attribute to him. The basis of Braverman's argument is that work, at least in capitalism, is geared to the creation of profit rather than the satisfaction of man's needs. This creates a fundamental conflict of interest between workers and capitalists, and thus in order that capital can realize the full potential of the labour it employs, control is necessary, for workers cannot be relied upon to work in the best interest of capital in a context of antagonistic relations. The importance of Taylorism to both Braverman's theory and his perception of the twentieth century lies in the fact that Taylor was the first management theorist to recognize the vital importance of control. The essence of scientific management, Braverman stresses, is its divorce of conception from execution, such that management is totally responsible for the planning and design of work tasks and workers are restricted to simple manual operations. Manual and mental labour should be separated, he argues, and all autonomy, discretion and 'brain work' should be removed from the shop floor and monopolized by management. This represents the deskilling to which Braverman refers; work is progressively degraded, as all elements of knowledge, responsibility and judgement are taken from the worker and his tasks become totally programmed, routinized and specialized. Primacy, in Braverman's account of the development of skill in the twentieth century, is given to Taylorism. Technology is of secondary importance, though Braverman does imply that increasingly control is incorporated into the machine. Accordingly, mechanization goes hand in hand with the advance of Taylorism, even though Braverman argues that there is no need to accept any connection between technical innovations and managerial strategies for control. Taylorism is concerned with the control of labour at any given level of technology, and its importance is independent of the 'advance of technology' so Braverman tells us (Braverman, 1974, p. 110). It is central to the development of capitalism precisely because it represents capitalist rationality; it is the 'explicit verbalization of the capitalist mode of production'. Accordingly, other management theorists, such as Mayo and Herzberg, are for Braverman essentially ideologists, since the changes they prescribe, such as job enrichment, are cosmetic and function simply to 'habituate the worker' to deskilled jobs.

A great deal of Braverman's account of the changing nature of work is based on Taylor's prescriptions and on what subsequent writers have said should happen or, in some cases, has happened. Consequently, he treats as unproblematic, both historically and theoretically, the implementation of Taylorism. Braverman presents as the essence of the twentieth century a particular rationality of its dominant class, a rationality which is all pervading, so that all parts of society function smoothly to reproduce the totality. In effect, the capitalist class is treated unquestionably as, in Marxist terms, a class 'for itself', fully conscious of its economic interests and organized and conspiring to realize them.

Braverman's main focus, then, is capitalist rationalization. He admits in his introduction that he does not attempt to deal with the modern working class on the level of its consciousness, organization or activities. He thus sees himself as imposing a justifiable and methodologically valid limitation on his study, which for him is 'about the working class as a class *in itself*, not as a class *for itself*' (Braverman, 1974, pp. 26–7). But this limitation, which is discussed at greater length in the next chapter, in a sense does not matter. For in Braverman's analysis the consciousness of the working class is in effect a reflection of objective conditions created, almost conspiratorially, by capital. Indeed, one of the main criticisms that has been levelled at Braverman is his rendering of the working class as passive, inert, living 'in accordance with the forces which act upon it' (Coombs, 1978; Schwarz, 1977; MacKenzie, 1977; Stark, 1980). He thus neglects the way in which the working class has created its own organizations, the trade unions and political parties; associates workers' knowledge simply with that required to perform given jobs; and underplays the differences between sections within the working class. By contrast, he treats the dominant class as a totally organized, omniscient and united force.

Braverman appears to regard his self-imposed limitation as a licence to work principally with Taylorism and to describe the objective side of capitalist development simply in terms of managerial strategy. Many of the problems of Braverman's work arise from his use of Taylor. For he takes the logic of Taylorism to be the logic of capitalism,[1]* which, in Braverman's terms, is the necessity of ensuring that control over the labour process passes into the hands of management. Thus he assumes that prior to Taylorism control was not in the hands of management, but was rather a kind of management by neglect (the *laissez-faire* method, as Taylor called it), in which workers knew more than managers. In fact, he offers no real historical analysis of what Taylorism was assumed to be attacking and superseding, the craft tradition. Furthermore, Braverman draws his two key concepts, the conception and execution of work, from Taylor, and consequently at all times works with an individualistic and task-centred notion of skill and the labour process. Finally, in his treatment of Taylorism he neglects the importance of elements other than those relating to the individual labourer and overlooks Taylor's concern for increasing the efficient flow of materials. What could be regarded as the progressive side of Taylorism – its attempt to systematize work and to move beyond oral traditions and rules of thumb – is thus accorded no significance.

Above all else Braverman builds into his analysis an assumption that, having consciously designed the organization of work to further capital accumulation, managements inevitably get their own way. This assumption is derived, in effect, from his uncritical acceptance of Taylor's ideology, for the power of capital is taken to triumph by

*Superior figures refer to the Notes on pages 201–12.

virtue of the new managerial and scientific technology at its disposal. Consequently, as I have already suggested and as Stark (1980, p. 92) articulates, 'It is not unfair to argue that Braverman portrays the capitalist class as veritably omniscient and the working class as infinitely malleable.' Much research[2] into the organization of work since Braverman has attempted to counter this view, to allow for the possibility and reality of workers' resistance to management initiatives. Friedman (1977a, 1978) and Edwards (1979) have both emphasized the opposition to Taylorism and the way in which managements, at least in certain circumstances, have had to develop fresh alternative strategies to control the labour process. Friedman, for example, argues that managements have often adopted what he terms responsible autonomy strategies which have avoided the direct control inherent in Taylorism.

For Friedman the issue of workers' resistance is more than simply a problem of gaining compliance with managerial systems, for it can be highly organized and strategic. Thus by concentrating on Taylorism, Friedman argues, Braverman is isolating capital's solution to the control problem from the struggle which necessitates such 'solutions'. For Braverman management's use of Taylorism is simply designed to avoid the autonomy that individual labourers have, whereas Friedman and Edwards highlight the fact that, at least in the twentieth century, managements have had to confront organized labour and what Edwards (1979, p. 16) terms 'chronic resistance to their effort to compel production'. Consequently, managements 'have attempted to organize production in such a way as to minimize opportunities for resistance and even to alter workers' perceptions of the desirability of opposition. Rather than placing emphasis on Friedman's responsible autonomy strategies, Edwards argues that managements have attempted to maintain control through the use of industrial relations procedures, through bureaucratic rules which channel conflict into manageable and acceptable ways and especially through the use of internal labour markets and dual labour markets which divide and segment the working class.

The danger inherent in the approach adopted by Friedman and Edwards is that it does not go far enough, that it may still present management as omniscient, conspiratorial and able, at least for a certain period of time, to get its own way – that is, to solve successfully its problem of control. The perspective underlying this book places more emphasis on the way in which the production system is created out of the relationship between management and labour. It is accepted that a major problem raised by Braverman's account is the way he 'presents the reorganization of the labour process as the outcome of a conscious design rather than as the product of the struggle of contending groups' (Stark, 1980, p. 92).

For while it may be necessary to have hierarchical modes of management and specialized divisions of labour, strategic groups of workers often play a crucial role both in the determination of the structure of these hierarchies and in the division of labour. Moreover, the struggle is not simply a battle between the autonomous and free-floating policies of managements and workers, for these policies themselves are forged out of the changing technological and market opportunities available to enterprises. As Zeitlin (1979) points out the balance of forces between capital and labour is itself conditioned by the market: it creates pressures for change, and sets limits to the relationship between management and labour, and, furthermore, influences relations *within* the ranks of both workers and managers. This implies the need to abandon simple, unilinear models of capitalist development and to undertake detailed historical and empirical studies of the interaction of the relations and forces of production in specific industrial contexts. Such work will not view work organization as a simple reflection of management strategy; it will examine the independent role of product and labour markets, technology and trade unionism in the process of the struggle and negotiation which constitutes the labour process.

A consideration of workers' resistance opens up the issue of the social construction of skill – that is, the question of whether certain workers or jobs are labelled skilled even though the content of their work is largely unskilled. Two extreme versions of the argument that skill is socially constructed are possible. First, one might stress the way in which the labels attached to certain jobs are created or maintained by managements as a way of coping with worker resistance, as they are used to segment and reduce the power and cohesion of the working class. Alternatively, labels might be seen as the direct result of workers' resistance or initiatives: strongly organized groups of workers might secure for themselves a level of wages normally or previously associated with apprenticeship-trained workers and may even create and control their own apprenticeship system, designed to reinforce exclusive unionism rather than to provide a necessary and comprehensive training.

Braverman is aware that labelling goes on, but his analysis stresses the reality of deskilling as an economic technique initiated by management and the largely illusory nature of such labels. Braverman's aim is to demystify such labels and thus to argue that basically the working class is one. He shows that it is important to distinguish between the actual nature and content of work and the job definitions applied by government statisticians in censuses, for example. But he uses this distinction merely for the purpose of disclosing a false ideology, a belief that there are real differences between basically similar degraded jobs. Consequently, as Phillips and Taylor (1978, p. 5) point out, 'he fails to take account of the sense in which job definitions are established in the process of struggles around the organization of work, and hence are as much part of the contemporary reality of capitalist production as the jobs they refer to.' In sociological terms, all skills are socially constructed, since even 'genuinely' skilled jobs are not simply derivatives of a god-given technology. The issue hinges on the basis on which the jobs and skills are constructed, and whether the criteria by which workers are differentiated and jobs defined are relatively independent of the real or 'technical' skill content of jobs. For example, is the process by which jobs become defined as women's work as opposed to men's independent of the changing nature of jobs and a way of maintaining male privilege or of 'making jobs which are in some senses becoming more alike into genuinely non-comparable tasks' (Phillips and Taylor, 1978, p. 7)?[3]

The main thrust of what follows points away from a crude social construction thesis, which in effect accepts Braverman's contention that the real content of jobs has been deskilled, albeit without denying the importance of job distinctions. It also rejects vulgar Marxism and unilinear theories of history and points to the need for detailed, concrete study of the specific problems involved in any discussion of skill. The implication is that the quest for general trends, such as a progressive deskilling of the work force, or general conclusions about the impact of new technologies are likely to be both theoretically and practically in vain.

Certainly, a crude deskilling thesis must be rejected. True, there may be specific cases, as Crompton and Reid suggest in Chapter 9, in which modern technology may deskill certain jobs. But equally new skills may be created, as they have no doubt been in the twentieth century, particularly through the enormous growth of electronics. Furthermore, both managements and unions may take steps to counter such effects, and certainly, as Friedman stresses, the possibility of alternative modes of management to Taylorism should be admitted. In any long-term comparison there is always the danger of what one takes as, and how one constructs, one's benchmark. In Braverman the benchmark seems, as Elger suggests in Chapter 2 and Littler in Chapter 7, to be a fully fledged artisan, the implication being that he personifies the dominant mode of employment prior to Taylorism. There is clearly a romanticism underlying Braverman's work, for not only did such workers not constitute the majority of workers in the nineteenth century, but also the majority of workers until only a century ago lacked basic skills such as literacy, which are now, mistakenly perhaps, taken for granted and all too often neglected in discussion of the development of the working class and the prerequisites for skilled work.[4]

In this book original materials are presented on theoretical, methodological and empirical questions surrounding the whole debate about skill and the labour process. Chapter 2 contains what is perhaps the most thorough and comprehensive evaluation of Braverman's main ideas to date. Drawing out Braverman's concentration on Taylorism and neglect of worker's resistance Elger suggests ways in which we might move beyond *Labor and Monopoly Capital* and points to the need to examine in quite specific detail, and historically, changes in the labour process. He especially emphasizes the need to locate both management and worker strategies in relation to the process, exigencies and contradictions of capital accumulation.

Beechey in Chapter 3 focuses particularly on an evaluation of Braverman's analysis of the sexual division of labour which, she argues, up until now most general critiques have largely ignored. She shows, for example, that Braverman's concept of the development of the family is simplistic, being based on a romanticized view of its pre-industrial form. She develops a more adequate account and also discusses the way in which deskilling arguments are of relevance to questions of female wage labour. Beechey stresses that we must consider the different forms of both labour and the labour process and should not isolate the family from the labour process. She concludes that this would provide the basis for an approach which links the sexual division of labour more centrally with class analysis.

Wood and Kelly in Chapter 4 take Braverman's over-reliance on Taylorism as their starting-point and look at weaknesses in both Braverman's and Friedman's work. They go further than other critiques by suggesting that built into Braverman is a particular reading of Taylorism in practice. The applications of Taylorism have not been uniform, nor as thorough or widespread as is often implied. But strategies such as Friedman's 'responsible automony' cannot be treated unproblematically as alternatives to Taylorism; they must be viewed in relation to it and its limits, as well as to the way in which industrial relations strategies extend beyond the simple task level. There is thus a need, so Wood and Kelly argue, for detailed, concrete work which both links questions of control at the job level with overall management strategy and which is comparative and historical.

In Chapter 5 Penn, drawing on empirical material from the engineering and textile industries, attacks directly the argument that employers were able to deskill craft work. In effect, workers resisted the move and were able through their organization to develop strategies of exclusion which maintained the privileges of skill and even, in some cases, created skill. Their ability to do this does not necessarily mean that there was an underlying technical deskilling, as in the 'social construction of skill' thesis, for successful exclusion is related to the trade union organization prior to mechanization and to the strategic importance of skill in the industry's overall production process.

More, in another historical survey, shows in Chapter 6, that while the 'politics of the work place' is important in determining who does what and who earns the label 'skilled', it is not a dominant influence. Drawing on fresh material related to the apprenticeship system in the nineteenth century, he suggests that those who possessed the label of 'skilled' for the most part exercised qualities which were necessary for the efficient functioning of industry. The implication he draws from this is that skill demands in industry today must be derived at least in part from technological imperatives, and that the latter in turn do not necessarily have a deskilling tendency.

In Chapter 7 Littler concentrates on two crucial issues: the modes of labour control in nineteenth-century industry and the influence and implementation of Taylorism in Britain. Littler attempts to develop more adequate conceptions of the structures of control in the nineteenth century and stresses the importance of the contract system as opposed to romanticized notions of craft control. Focusing on British industry during the 1880–1939 period, he argues that the transformation of the work place was far more complex than is implied by Braverman's conceptualization of a simple transition from craft to Taylorite forms of organization. In particular, an empirical investigation of the influence of Taylorism shows that there were waves of rationalization in Britain, of which some were Taylorite and others were uninfluenced by Taylorism.

In Chapter 8 Lee stresses, in similar fashion, the need to distinguish between deskilled jobs and the deskilling of individual workers. He develops important distinctions which enable us to discuss different ways in which deskilling may take place. In particular, he shows the way in which any global deskilling of the population which can be discerned is a consequence more of changes in the economy – recessions, for example – than of direct changes in the nature of jobs. In advancing this and other views, Lee is able to relegate the argument about craft control to a less central position than the one which it has been given in much discussion about deskilling, both before and since Braverman. He also takes the argument back to questions of class, as Braverman does, and suggests that the relationship between changes in class structure and labour processes may be very much more complex, and more indirect, than the Braverman analysis implies.

In the final two chapters contemporary changes are examined. Crompton and Reid in Chapter 9 focus on the computer and particularly on its effects on clerical work. Drawing on empirical work, they conclude that there is a technical deskilling process in operation but make the point that Braverman's analysis underestimates the importance of the relocation of capitalist control in the overall deskilling process. They also conclude that he considers in insufficient detail the possibility of any counterbalance or reaction to deskilling. In Chapter 10 Jones scrutinizes one sector of the British engineering industry to examine the adoption of numerical control (NC). He shows that there is considerable variation between firms, and that this confirms the decisiveness of product and labour markets, organizational structures and trade unions' positions as independent influences on the forms of skill deployment. He argues that there is 'nothing sufficiently "inherent" in the hardware of NC or its concept to allow the deskilling, control and surveillance' assumed by both theorists of the labour process and publicists for NC installation. He thus argues against general deterministic theories of deskilling in favour of an approach in which emphasis is placed on the variation of relevant social and economic conditions from enterprise to enterprise.

Taken overall, the contributions to this book support the importance of Jones's conclusions. Above all else, they suggest that to cope with the kinds of omission which critiques of Braverman have highlighted in his analysis involves fundamental questions: to incorporate worker resistance, labour and product markets and extra-economic factors involves more than simply extending one's analysis; it amounts to a theoretical reconsideration. This book clearly points to the need for future work to link the 'micro', 'politics of the work place' focus to the more 'macro' approach adopted by Lee and More in particular. Its great strength is that, taken together, the chapters do not merely question the deskilling thesis: more important, they suggest that the deskilling which has occurred must be located in a context which is far broader than Taylorism, and certainly more complex than a straight managerial conspiracy.

2 Braverman, capital accumulation and deskilling[1]

Tony Elger

Braverman's work has served as both a point of reference and an inspiration for many contemporary Marxist analyses of transformations in the labour process, the structure of employment and class composition in the era of 'monopoly capitalism'. Indeed his contribution is reminiscent of that of his mentors, Baran and Sweezy, in the ways in which it has confronted some of the major orthodoxies of social science and has provided a focus for the renewal and development of Marxist studies.

The scope and significance of Braverman's analysis can be characterized in terms of the following features. First, it reinstates the imperative of capital accumulation as the fundamental dynamic determining the 'incessant transformation' and 'tendential degradation' of labour in capitalist societies. Second, it attempts to locate specific aspects of such transformation and degradation within the totality of developments in capitalist production set in motion by capital accumulation. In relation to this concern with the totality of capitalist production Braverman is centrally concerned to grasp the interrelations of the whole complex of features which appear to characterize 'monopoly capital': the rise of oligopolistic competition among giant corporations; the process of rationalization of production; the elaboration of the administrative apparatus of corporate capital; the encroachment of capitalist commodity production into enclaves of non-capitalist production; changes in the character and composition of the industrial reserve army; and the consequent relationships between the modes of organization of the labour process in different sectors.

Two particularly notable features of Braverman's work are integral to this attempt to grasp the totality of production relations of monopoly capitalism. One is the attention he gives to analysing changes in the labour process in the 'new' service industries and occupations. The other is his recognition of the importance of the sexual division of labour in the changing structure of employment of different sectors of production.

These achievements have been recognized by the wide and appreciative audience gained for Braverman's work and must be sustained in any critical assessment. In this paper I do not attempt to provide a comprehensive critique but instead limit myself to a consideration of the manner in which Braverman conceptualizes the relationship between capital accumulation and the degradation of work, and the manner in which he characterizes and periodizes transformations in the organization of production.

General criticism of *Labor and Monopoly Capital (LMC)*

Two dominant themes emerge from many of the Marxist critiques of Braverman.[2] The first concerns the inadequacy of his objectivist conceptualization of the working class, which fails to address the manner in which class struggle is integral to the course of development of the capitalist labour process.[3] The second focuses on the implication, in the structure and discourse of LMC, that analyses of both the obstacles confronting the accumulation process and their resolution in the reorganization of the labour process can be divorced from analysis of broader forms of political domination and struggle.[4]

The first criticism focuses on the much quoted self-denying ordinance announced by Braverman in his introduction: 'no attempt will be made to deal with the modern working class on the level of its consciousness, organization or activities. This is a book about the working class as a class *in itself*, not as a class *for itself*' (Braverman, 1974, p. 27). However valuable this disclaimer may be in relation to much conventional subjectivist sociology or other vague discussions of class-consciousness, it is evident that this conceptualization remains seriously disabling.

It warrants a treatment of the working class as an object of capital, which, while underlining the capacity of capital to reorganize the labour process, degrade the labourer and propel her/him from sector to sector, forgets that the working class remains an active agency in the capital relation. As Schwarz (1977, p. 162) remarks, Braverman's approach fails to recognize 'the working class as an active and problematical presence within the mechanism of accumulation'.

The second criticism is closely bound in with the first because it is primarily (though not exclusively) in relation to the problematical character of class relations in production that the critical significance of political relations and state institutions in reconstructing class relations has become a major focus of contemporary Marxist discussion of capitalist hegemony. In relation to such debate Braverman notices the central significance of economistic trade unionism for the character of working-class accommodation with advanced capitalism. He implies however that this mode of accommodation arises directly out of the forms taken by capital accumulation and the capitalist labour process in the era of monopoly capitalism, rather than being a complex and contradictory product of the interrelations between such developments and the organization of politics and state activity in capitalist society.[5]

These criticisms do not merely suggest that Braverman's discussion is incomplete, for the boundaries marked out by such criticisms delineate a quite coherent project: the underlying theme of LMC is indeed that in monopoly capitalism capitalist control and domination is secured in a *thoroughgoing* fashion *within* production. For Braverman the process of degradation of work and the disciplining effect of the reserve army of labour together appear to produce a virtually inert working class, unable to pose any substantial problems for capital either within production or beyond it. This interpretation is, in my view, supported by the terms of Braverman's rejoinder to some of his critics – his response to the critique of objectivism focuses on the ultimate emergence of a revolutionary consciousness under the spur of 'an enormous intensification of the pressures which have only just begun to bear upon the working class', with minimal recognition of the need to explore the complex relations between current problems of accumulation and forms of class struggle and such a possible future (Braverman, 1976, p. 124).[6]

Of course, this in no way denies the significance of an analysis of the development of the capitalist labour process, but it does argue that such an analysis must (a) locate the forms of class struggle, characteristic of specific phases in the transformation of the capitalist labour process, as integral features of that transformation, and (b) remain sensitive to the complex relationships between class relations in production and broader forms of political domination and struggle. If the structure of Braverman's analysis enables him to foreclose such crucial questions, it is important to go beyond a reassertion of their importance to examine the features of his account of the capitalist labour process which facilitate this closure, and to consider alternative conceptualizations which do not have similar consequences. In accordance with this objective, I will now turn to an examination of Braverman's analysis of the transformation of the capitalist labour process, and to a consideration of alternative accounts.

The degradation of craft work

The most sustained theme of LMC concerns the degradation of craft work into common detailed labour as the capitalist labour process is 'rendered independent of craft, tradition and the workers' knowledge' (p. 113). Braverman's most vivid passages depict the process – or more often the capitalist theorization of the process – of the abrogation of established 'rounded' craft expertise by capital and its transformation into a body of principles and practices from which the worker is excluded and through which she/he is thoroughly subordinated to the imperatives of capital accumulation. This theme provides the focus of the discussion of 'scientific management' but is also central to the discussion of machinery and to the analysis of the degradation of clerical labour. Thus in the latter case Braverman notes that while 'clerical work in its earliest stages has been likened to a craft' (p. 298), the increasingly predominant form of office labour is routinized, mechanically paced paper-processing, in many ways analogous to other forms of routinized manual labour within manufacturing industry.

Braverman's treatment of the degradation of craft work focuses upon two central imperatives of the capitalist organization of the labour process. The first is the concern to cheapen labour: in Marxian terms, to reduce the value of labour power by substituting simple for complex labour. The second and more fundamental imperative for Braverman is to guarantee effective capitalist control of the labour process – by dissolving those esoteric skills which underpinned effective craft opposition to the reorganization of production in the hands of capital and its agents.

For Braverman these developments are seen to gain their most significant momentum and their most coherent theoretical expression for capital in the last decades of the nineteenth century, in the 'scientific management' movement, and to achieve unrivalled dominance during the first half of this century, thus constituting the most crucial form of 'the degradation of work in the twentieth century'. The central thrust of this major theme of LMC is succinctly outlined in Braverman's summary of the logic of Taylorism:

Workers who are controlled only by general orders and discipline are not adequately controlled, because they retain their grip on the actual processes of labour . . . [and] they will thwart efforts to realize to the full the potential in their labour power. To change this situation control over the labour process must pass into the hands of management, not only in a formal sense but by the control and dictation of each step of the process, including its mode of performance. [p. 100]

The point of departure for Braverman's analysis of the unity of the labour process and capital accumulation is a restatement of the classical Marxist account of the exchange between capital and wage labour:

The worker enters into the employment agreement because social conditions leave him or her no other way to gain a livelihood. The employer, on the other hand, is the possessor of a unit of capital which he is endeavouring to enlarge. . . . In everything that follows therefore we shall be considering the manner in which the labour process is dominated by and shaped by the accumulation of capital. [p.53]

This formulation does not, significantly, lead to any extensive discussion of the forms of extraction of surplus value and exigencies of accumulation which have dominated successive phases of the capitalist labour process. Rather, it is simply accompanied by general references to the character of accumulation as a structural imperative of capitalism. Braverman then proceeds to a general diagnosis of what he sees as the fundamental obstacle confronting capital accumulation. This diagnosis hinges on the manner in which, in the context of antagonistic class relations, the 'infinite potentiality' of labour power may remain inadequately realized because of entrenched working-class routines:

If the capitalist builds upon this distinctive quality and potential of human labour power, it is also this quality, by its very indeterminacy, which places before him his greatest challenge and problem . . . what he buys is infinite in potential but in its realization it is limited by the subjective state of the workers, by their previous history, by the general social conditions under which they work, as well as the particular conditions of the enterprise and by the technical setting of their labour. [p. 57]

The dynamics of the transformation of the labour process are located in a general contradiction between capitalist control of the product of wage labour on one hand and customary and worker-regulated modes of labour (equated with craft skills) on the other.

Thus Braverman establishes the basis for a general and abstract impulsion of capital towards the 'real' subordination of labour and directly identifies this abstract impulsion with a uniform process of degradation of craft skills. I now want to draw out some of the deficiencies of this formulation and relate these to Marx's own discussion.

Capital accumulation and the real subordination of the labour process

The major deficiencies of Braverman's discussion relate on the one hand to the inadequately located character of the impulsion to control imputed to capital and, on the other, to the pre-eminent role attributed to craft skill as an obstacle to capital.

1   A central feature of an adequate analysis of the transformation of the capitalist labour process must be an attempt to locate the forms, and phases of development, of capitalist control over the labour process more precisely than Braverman attempts to do. This is not merely a matter of specifying the discrete conjunctural conditions which affect the general tendencies which he delineates. It involves a commitment to the specification of the relationship between forms of the extraction of surplus value in the process of capital accumulation and phases in the organization of the capitalist labour process. While Braverman acknowledges the distinct forms of appropriation analysed in *Capital* under the headings of absolute and relative surplus value, the relationship between these forms and the development from the 'formal' to the 'real' subordination of the labour process to capital accumulation remains virtually unexplored. In Marx's discussion of the development of 'real' subordination, however, the forms of capitalist reorganization of the labour process are situated in alternative strategies of surplus value production, each with inherent limits and contradictions and characteristic forms of class struggle.[7]

2   There is a strong tendency in Braverman's account to conceptualize the transformation in terms of a switch from thoroughgoing craft controls to pervasive capitalist direction of the labour process. Even when he recognizes that capital faces a recurrent task of re-establishing its control over the labour process, he conceptualizes worker opposition in the inadequate terms of a polarity: either renascent craft expertise or generalized subterra-

nean hostility (for examples, see p. 120n., p. 172 and p. 180n.). As the Brighton Group (1977) have emphasized, such an approach fails to recognize the complex form of the 'real' subordination of the labour process to capital, and in particular fails to appreciate the manner in which forms of specialized expertise and craft competence may be embedded within a complex structure of collective labour effectively subordinated to capital accumulation. In addition, it loses sight of those forms and bases of organized working-class resistance which cannot be understood in terms of rounded craft skills.

3   As the previous point implies, Braverman's conception of the craft worker in opposition to capital equates complex competences, a high value of labour power and effective collective opposition to capitalist initiatives. There is little discussion of the problematic character of this equation where:

(a) complex competences may be thoroughly subordinated to capital and be subjected to both an extended working day and intensification (as in Marx's conception of modern manufacture and domestic industry), or

(b) collective organization may gain increased wages and the status of skilled worker with little evidence of craft expertise.[8]

4   Finally, Braverman's discussion of the organization of the labour process remains for the most part at the level of its theorization by 'management scientists'. His reliance on such programmatic material gives a spurious concreteness to his account of a general impulsion to control directly realized in deskilling. However, a critical consequence is that insufficient consideration is given to the conditions in which such strategies are implemented and, in particular, to the effectiveness of workers' resistance to changes in the labour process.

Having outlined some of the major weaknesses of Braverman's discussion, I now turn to a brief examination of Marx's conceptualization to provide a more coherent indication of the implications of, in particular, the first two of these criticisms.

Marx's discussion of the relationship between the logic of capital accumulation and the reorganization of the capitalist labour process is a complex one, and his treatment of absolute and relative surplus value is developed in the course of separate discussions of the historical development of struggles over the length of the working day on one hand, and of the sequential development of co-operation, the manufacturing division of labour and modern mechanized industry on the other.

Marx's analysis of the extraction of absolute surplus value takes as its point of departure opportunities for valorization open to the capitalist in the context of the given conditions of organization of the labour process which capital inherits from previous modes of production. In this context surplus value is extracted under conditions where the capitalist deploys his market power to extend the length of the working day while the labourer retains some control over the actual process of production. In addition, capital may impose a greater intensity and continuity of labour – what Marx sometimes calls a reduction in the 'porosity' of the working day – without transforming the customary organization of labour.

However, the 'merely' formal subordination of the labour process to capital sets definite limits to extraction of surplus value – limits which are crucially defined by the market power and political organization of capital and labour. In the context of working-class resistance to the lengthening of the working day and to reduced porosity, competing capitals turn increasingly to the extraction of relative surplus value.

The development of co-operation and the manufacturing division of labour constitute the initial phases in this tendency towards the extraction of relative surplus value. The development of a complex organization of specialized labourers, and the intensification and co-ordination of work in that context, constitute the initial transformation of the labour process from its inherited basis into a specifically capitalist mode of production – even though one in which capital exercises its domination subjectively rather than in the objective form of machinery.[9]

In the context of manufacture, and even more in the context of modern industry, capital turns to the extraction of relative surplus value on the basis of the intensification and increasing productiveness of labour, which provides the basis for relatively transitory increments in surplus value while specific capitals enjoy productivity above the social average and, in so far as it cheapens the production of consumption goods, reduces the value of labour power.[10]

Marx's account clearly does not represent a simple transition from absolute to relative surplus value. The era of machine production and modern industry becomes characterized by the pursuit of both, in relationships conditioned by the pressure on the rate of profit unleashed by investment directed at increasing the productivity of labour (summarized in the tendency towards a rising organic composition of capital), and by the specific conditions of class struggle which mediate such pressure (influenced by the development of the reserve army of labour).

In relation to these tendencies the transition from 'formal' to 'real' subordination is seen as a complex process beset with contradictions. Thus the phase of the elaboration of the manufacturing division of labour represents, Marx argues, a distinctively capitalist mode of production, in which the power of capital subsists not merely in the relation of capitalist and property-less wage labourer but further in the necessary dependence of the specialized worker (whether relatively skilled or unskilled) upon the collective organization of the capitalist workshop. At the same time this real subordination of the labour process to capital contains, and is qualified by, the forms of competence which remain embodied in the specialized skills of craft workers, which represent an important obstacle to valorization.

The significance of modern mechanized industry in this context is discussed in terms of the interrelationship between the strategy of relative surplus value production and the deepening of the real subordination of the labour process and the labourer to capital. First, it represents the most substantial advance in the extraction of relative surplus value on the basis of increasing both the productiveness and the intensity of labour, an advance which is guaranteed for individual capitals only through the continual revolutionizing of production, but which confronts its own contradictions and thus threatens to bring about a falling rate of profit. Second, this pursuit of relative surplus value through mechanization forms the bases for the 'completion' of the development of the real subordination of the labour process and the labourer to capital, as capitalist control is objectified in machinery, as technical calculation and organization by capital displaces craft expertise and as the development of the reserve army of labour exerts its discipline on workers in both modern mechanized industry and modern manufacture. However this 'completion' of real subordination is not uniform or entirely coherent – for example, the objectification of capitalist control in machinery, and the augmentation of the reserve army of labour press variously on different sectors and in different phases of the cycle of accumulation – and confronts its own contradictions both in the increasingly general organizations of workers and in the tensions between the specialization and flexibility demanded of workers in modern industry.[11]

Having outlined Marx's discussion of accumulation and the development of real subordination, I do not simply wish to contrast it with Braverman's exposition of the deskilling thesis. Marx's own treatment is ambiguous enough to be susceptible to varied interpretations, and it is quite possible to read him as an exponent of a straightforward deskilling thesis, particularly in his discussions of the relationship between machine and worker. However, I do want to argue that an alternative interpretation is warranted by Marx's discussions and offers a more adequate basis for the analysis of the development of the capitalist labour process and, as one aspect of that development, the tendency towards deskilling. This alternative approach would emphasize first, the complex character of the development of the real subordination of the labour process to capital, as the development of a large-scale collective organization of production which dominates any specific form of labour; second, the importance of analysing the development of the complex organization of collective labour in relation to specific strategies of valorization and accumulation and their characteristic contradictions and forms of class struggle.

These themes have not, of course, gone unnoticed among Marxists, and the Brighton Labour Process Group (1976, 1977), Palloix (1976) and Mandel (1978) in particular have, in different ways, conceptualized the relationship between capital accumulation and the development of the capitalist labour process in a more adequate fashion than Braverman. Their analyses imply that:

1 The development of the real subordination of labour to capital must be interpreted in terms of forms of subordination appropriate to the imperatives of valorization and accumulation. In this sense it is necessary to recognize that the continually revolutionized character of modern mechanized production persistently renders 'incomplete' the subordination of labour to capital (in the sense of total direction and control by capital). On one hand, it creates new skills, competencies and other opportunities for bargaining leverage arising from the complex co-ordination and interdependence of the collective labourer; on the other hand, in phases of rapid accumulation unaccompanied by massive displacement of living by dead labour, it depletes the reserve army of labour and provides the basis for powerful worker organization.

2 Such developments can in no sense be interpreted in terms of a

simple contradiction or non-correspondence between capitalist property relations and the social forces of production – in terms, that is, of the 'merely' formal subordination of labour to capital – since they are embedded within a complex capitalist apparatus of production subordinated to the imperatives of valorization and accumulation. Rather, these features define an arena within which subordination of labour adequate to those imperatives is sought by capital and meets various forms of working-class opposition.

3   This form of argument makes it quite clear that the analysis of the development of the capitalist labour process must be set within an analysis of the organization of capitalist production as a whole. This would eventually involve articulation of the discussion of changes in the labour process with analyses of the relationship of capital and labour as it is mediated by the capitalist state and at the level of class organization and conflict beyond production.

These points suggest that Braverman's account moves too directly from an abstract impulsion to control labour power to the concrete strategy of deskilling, in a way which provides a partial and telescoped view of the development of the capitalist labour process. A more adequate account of the transformation of the labour process would involve a more complex and sustained analysis of the historical development of capital accumulation, the contradictions to which accumulation gives rise and the manner in which such contradictions develop and are resolved in class struggle within and beyond production.

Braverman and 'monopoly capital'

Of course, as the very title of his book emphasizes, Braverman's account is not simply of a uniform trajectory towards the realization of real subordination through deskilling. What he does is to locate the crucial phase of development of such real subordination in relation to the emergence of 'monopoly capitalism', but this association itself radically simplifies a more complex pattern of development. It is at this point that the work of Baran and Sweezy so powerfully, but largely implicitly, structures Braverman's whole analysis. Their work enables him to ignore any exploration of the contradictions and struggles which beset mechanization in the form of the tendency and counter-tendencies to the falling rate of profit, and to take for granted the capacity of capitals to finance the apparatus of 'conception' and control, which constitutes the counterpoint to deskilling, out of a rising surplus. These features follow directly from Baran and Sweezy's analysis of the fundamental determining features of capitalist accumulation in the era of monopoly capitalism: namely, their claim concerning the insignificance of tendencies for the organic composition of capital to rise once transformations are taking place within an already mechanized form of production, and their argument that monopoly capital has the capacity to generate an increasing surplus – since price competition is suspended while investment multiplies productivity and, given solutions to problems of realization, production.[12]

The critics of Baran and Sweezy[13] challenge precisely these assumptions and thus suggest that 'monopoly capitalism' cannot be analysed in terms of such fundamental discontinuities in the logic of capital accumulation. Rather, Mandel and others argue that while oligopolization may tend to create distinct levels of profit in oligopolized and non-oligopolized sectors, this pattern is subject to fundamental processes of both long-term competition among capitals, and tendencies and countertendencies to a falling rate of profit associated with movements in the organic composition of capital. Such criticisms underline the inadequacy of Braverman's treatment of the significance of monopoly capitalism merely in terms of the precipitation or facilitation of a generalized impulsion of capital towards deskilling, and they cohere with the earlier argument for a more complex and historically located analysis of the relations between valorization and accumulation and the development of the capitalist labour process before, during and after the phase of monopolization identified as crucial by Baran and Sweezy, and Braverman.

In the remainder of this paper I attempt to contribute to the development of such an analysis by undertaking a more limited task, that of analysing the transformation of skills and competences characteristic of specific phases in the development of the capitalist labour process, and considering their relationship to both phases of valorization and accumulation, and developments in ideological and political relations beyond production.

Craft and capital in the nineteenth century

As has already been noted, Braverman's major concern is to analyse the degradation of work in the era of 'monopoly capitalism', but his understanding of that process is necessarily underpinned by a view of the earlier phases of capitalist development. Indeed, a major premise of his account appears to be a periodization of the degradation of craft work which emphasizes the initiatives of nascent monopoly capital in the final years of the nineteenth century rather than features of reorganization of the labour process which characterized the development of machinery and modern industry throughout that century. This emphasis underwrites the account of the general deskilling of craft work in the monopoly era and the centrality attributed to Taylorism in that transformation. However, it requires rather serious qualification – both from the point of view of an analysis of the capitalist labour process in the nineteenth century and in terms of the foreshortened perspective it offers on developments in the twentieth century.

Two related problems can be posed in relation to the emphasis of Braverman's account:

1 It fails to grant adequate recognition to the rapid development of the real subordination of the labour process to capital on the basis of mechanization in some of the leading sectors of the capitalist economy of the period – a development which variously bypassed established craft skills, attacked and destroyed them directly to replace them with other forms of organization of labour and expertise, or quite often incorporated them in modified form in a radically transformed organization of the labour process.
2 It tends to portray the craftsmen of the second half of the nineteenth century in terms of the 'artisan ideal', when clearly their positions must be seen as in various ways transitional, marked to a substantial degree by real subordination to capital.[14]

This latter point in particular has been underlined by recent contributions to the 'labour aristocracy' debate, which have been concerned to specify more closely the interplay between changes in the organization of the labour process and the nexus of political initiatives and commitments which have generally been associated with that notion. For example, Foster (1974) in his analysis of class struggle in Oldham, has argued that working-class militancy, within and beyond the work place, together with a crisis of declining profitability, precipitated major efforts to reorganize the labour process of both engineering and spinning. He suggests that skilled workers were placed in a more distinct relation of subordination to capital, while responsibilities for pace-making and direction of non-skilled workers were more explicitly delegated to them. His account also outlines some of the complex interrelations between such changes in the organization of the labour process and the forms of capitalist political initiative concerned to secure local and national political hegemony.

Foster's account dwells overmuch on particular forms of this subordination, such as piecemastering, and it is evident that diverse forms of hierarchy, subordination and relative 'privilege' within production constitute the bases of the political phenomenon of the labour artistocracy. Nevertheless, Foster does demonstrate the importance of changes in the location and subordination of craft skills within the capitalist organization of the labour process. Such considerations have led Stedman-Jones (1975, p. 65) to argue:

even the skilled sectors of modern industry bore only a superficial resemblance to those of handicraft. Such skills were precarious and transformable at the will of the capitalist in a way which those of handicraft had not been. In the cotton industry, the artificial position of the cotton spinner has already been noted. In engineering, apart from a residuum of semi-handicraft skills, the new forms of skill were based upon a quantum of literacy and technical instruction, and often included quasi-supervisory functions. They did not possess the direct purchase over the production process enjoyed by handicrafts, and were unusable except in the factories for which they had been acquired. This is part of what is meant by the 'real' subordination of wage labour to capital. . . . What was decisive was the effect of modern industry upon their technical role in the labour process. It was not so much their privileged position as the vulnerability of that position that changed their industrial outlook.[15]

This account of the reorganization of the capitalist labour process in terms of the increasing subordination and vulnerability of craft skills, coupled with an emphasis on the distinctive forms of hierarchization characterizing different industries (notably the specific significance of the sexual division of labour in cotton) and an insistence on the specifically social and ideological location of the labour aristocracy in relation to those forms, represents an important advance over Foster's preoccupation with pace-makers (and capital exports). However, Stedman-Jones himself misplaces its significance when he formulates the transformation as 'the breach in craft controls and then a restabilization of the labour process which left formal distinctions of status untouched'.

This implies that skills became *purely* artificial and illusory, when to an important though variable extent they were transformed and encapsulated within modern industry in ways which sustained significant forms of expertise. Indeed, such skills became the locus of vigorous organization by elite groups of workers, who, in the context of rapid capital accumulation based on established levels of mechanization, were effective in defending relative privilege and parochial autonomy within the capitalist organization of the labour process. Thus the relationship between 'real' expertise and craft privilege in this phase of development of the labour process was mediated by the specific relation of accumulation and mechanization, by the ideological role of elite groups of workers, and by their established forms of collective organization.

These features clearly characterized the engineering industry during the second half of the nineteenth century, for, as both Foster and Stedman-Jones recognize and Burgess (1969) emphasizes, the transformation of skills in that sector before mid-century (from millwright to more specialized fitters and turners) was followed by a long period in which, with expanding markets and a tendency towards labour-using investment, the newer categories of skilled worker were able, on the basis of powerful collective organization, to sustain wage differentials and job controls which militated against the control of capital. Hinton (1971, ch. 2) suggests that these features of the 'craft tradition' became increasingly precarious, in the forms in which they had become stabilized after the 1850s, as a further wave of capital intensive mechanization was unleashed in the last decades of the nineteenth century.[16]

Engineering represents the outstanding case of the relative stabilization of specialized skills for a significant interval within modern mechanized industry. However, the experience of cotton also reveals the scope for some sections of workers to develop 'skill niches' within modern industry, especially in the context of a phase of labour-using investment following a phase of increasing capital intensity. It is in this context that the historian of the cotton unions can argue that 'few occupations "in the cotton" are intrinsically skilled in the sense that their adequate performance necessarily requires any long preliminary training', but 'several textile occupations that are usually regarded as more skilled, are so because other duties – like the supervision of other operatives, or the maintenance and setting of machinery – have been added to the fundamental task of machine tending', while 'there are cases . . . in which a "skill" has been quite artificially created, by the workers' gradual imposition of labour supply controls on a formerly "unskilled" occupation' (Turner, 1962, pp. 110–12).[17]

Engineering and cotton represent sectors in which the changing forms of the real subordination of wage labour and the labour process to capital encapsulate groups of workers who, albeit on a changing basis, experience some continuity of skilled organization and status. Other sectors exemplify more thoroughgoing trans- formations which nevertheless involve important residual or emer- gent forms of competence and bargaining leverage.

For example, in the British steel industry job hierarchies of limited and plant-specific skills arose from changes in the labour process which involved the extension and dilution of forms of collaborative collective bargaining originating in the capital/subcontractor rela- tion. The resultant mutations of collective bargaining (involving the transmutation of wage and promotion hierarchies, sliding-scale agreements and arbitration machinery) need to be understood in relation to both (a) the increasingly effective domination of capital over the labour process associated with intensive mechanization, signalled by the development of narrow skills within a complex apparatus of collective labour, and (b) the specific phasing of increases in productiveness, levels of unemployment and levels of international competition which conditioned the combativity of labour and capital and hence the organization of the collective labourer.[18]

It is evident that the specialization of labour and the proliferation of semi-skilled workers characteristic of much mechanization in the last decades of the nineteenth century represent major advances in the real subordination of labour to capital. However, it remains important to recognize the residual forms of expertise and skill and the conditions in which they may constitute effective obstacles to capitalist initiative. Hobsbawm's (1964) study of the organization of gas workers focuses attention on some of the possible implications of these developments for worker organization. He traces the manner in which stokers (workers with important but easily replicable expertise and dexterity) constituted a nucleus for the general organization of gas-works labour. This organization was achieved in a boom period following a phase in which capital pursued increasing output primarily through the intensification of labour. It was followed, in the context of increasing competition, by a phase of increasing mechanization which, however, did not destroy the organization. For, Hobsbawm (1964, p. 170) argues:

labour-saving and labour-simplifying devices do not, however, automatically dislodge key groups of workers from their strongholds. They do so only when such groups are unable to maintain their relative indispensibility (i.e. their bargaining strength) during the crucial transition period, and cannot therefore 'capture' the new devices for recognised unionism, the standard rate, and standard working conditions.

In this example the pace of technical advance was relatively slow while the industry was comparatively sheltered and partially municipalized: in these circumstances the semi-skilled stokers sustained their organization and leverage.

The theme of all of these studies of skills and the labour process in the mid to late nineteenth century can be summarized as follows: the 'real' subordination of labour to capital, understood in terms of the adequate conditions for valorization, cannot be simply equated with the thorough going destruction of crafts and skills, but such tendencies for the degradation of work must be related to the specific obstacles to valorization confronted by capital, and to the forms of political and economic domination of labour by capital. In particular, they emphasize (a) the complex interplay between the ideological and immediately productive aspects of relations of hierarchy and privilege in the organization of the collective labourer by capital, and (b) the manner in which forms of worker competence and initiative lodged within the real subordination of the labour process to capital may continue to constitute significant bases of both parochial worker resistance and divisions within the working class.

As has already been argued, it is necessary to locate the specific character of such features in relation to the specific strategies of valorization dominating particular periods and sectors of nineteenth-century capital accumulation. In relation to this task, Samuel (1977a) has recently emphasized that characterizations of the transformation of the labour process in this period *merely* in terms of the advance of mechanization and resultant increases in productiveness are highly misleading. He stresses instead, first, that mechanization was adopted very *unevenly* and was combined with advances in the capitalist domination of the labour process which owed little directly to mechanization but were founded on the further sub-division of labour and upon the existence of a surplus of cheap labour; and, second, that the adoption of mechanization was itself significantly characterized by a *'capital-saving'* bias in the context of relatively cheap labour, so that labour intensity, manual dexterity and expertise remained major features of the reorganized labour process.

Samuel's discussion hints at an important specification of the context within which the developing forms of vulnerability and strategies of counter-control characteristic of skilled and quasi-skilled workers in this period might be analysed. However, as yet his argument remains at the more primitive level of a general emphasis upon the continuing centrality of labour power within the labour process, coupled with a rudimentary recognition of these developing forms. Samuel's argument that 'nineteenth century capitalism created many more skills than it destroyed, though they were different in kind from those of the all-round craftsman, and subject to a wholly new level of exploitation' (1977a, p. 59) now requires further explication along the lines indicated above, if we are to avoid either the romanticization of craft or the imagery of precipitate deskilling which tends to seduce Braverman, whether that imagery is applied to the earlier development of modern industry or the later capitalist offensive constituted by 'scientific management'.

Scientific management

Braverman's analysis of 'scientific management' is the pivotal feature of his whole account of the degradation of work in the twentieth century and represents a fine dissection of the manner in which the capitalist control of the labour process was theorized by some agents of capital. However, this account, while it rests firmly within Braverman's characterization of the long-term tendency of capital to wrest the labour process from craft control, remains unsatisfactory in a number of important respects.

First, as has already been suggested, it fails to provide an adequate account of the pre-existing organizational and political bases of capitalist domination and extraction of surplus value or of the crises which confronted valorization on that basis. Second, it appears to assume that an adequate level of subordination was then secured almost entirely at the level of the reorganization of the labour process, in accordance with the theoretical logic of the Taylorist attack on craft skills.

The inadequate analysis of pre-existing forms of the subordination of the labour process to capital, discussed in the previous section, makes it difficult for Braverman to locate the specific context and targets of 'scientific management'. Thus his discussion of the emergence of Taylorism is couched only in terms of a congeries of enabling features:

The separation of hand and brain is the most decisive single step in the division of labour taken by the capitalist mode of production. It is inherent in that mode of production from its beginnings, and it develops, under capitalist management throughout the history of capitalism, but it is only during the past century that the scale of production, the resources made available to the modern corporation by the rapid accumulation of capital, and the conceptual apparatus and trained personnel have become available to institutionalise this separation in a systematic and formal fashion. [Braverman, 1974, p. 126]

In this account it seems that the immanent tendency of capital to establish real control over the labour process reaches its culmination simply when capital has accumulated sufficient resources. There is little indication of the manner in which scientific management and related initiatives arose out of any crisis in the process of accumulation of capital, of the manner in which capital was compelled to increase its scale and intensify its control over the labour process and create a complex corporate apparatus in an effort – itself not contradiction-free – to transcend these constraints.[19]

Hobsbawm provides an analysis, focused upon the British experience, which constitutes an instructive comparison with Braverman in this respect. In his account the development of major crises in the extraction of surplus value is seen as the underlying context of strategies for the reorganization of production which were concerned with both the intensification of labour and the facilitation of technical reorganization of production:

It was safer if less efficient to stick to the old ways, unless pressure of profit margins, increased competition, the demands of labour or other inescapable facts forced a change. But the periods of major economic adjustment after the Napoleonic Wars and the slump of 1873 subjected employers to just this kind of pressure, and hence led to major modifications in the methods of labour utilization. In the post-Napoleonic period the effect was delayed, since employers first attempted to exhaust the possibilities of cutting labour costs by extending hours and cutting money wage-rates. During the Great Depression (1873–96), new methods tended to be adopted more quickly. Roughly speaking, the mid-century brought the beginning of the substitution of 'intensive' for 'extensive' labour utilization, the latter part of the Great

Depression the beginning of the substitution of rational for empirical 'intensive' utilization, or of 'scientific management'. [Hobsbawm, 1964, p. 356]

Thus Hobsbawm indicates the basis on which valorization had been accomplished in the preceding phase of capital accumulation: mechanization, coupled with the subjection of unskilled labourers to driving discipline and the cultivation of craft workers' reliance on more or less customary wage-effort relationships. However, the development of a crisis of profitability in the last quarter of the nineteenth century – as a consequence of both intensified competition (marked in particular by the emergence of over-capacity) and increasingly effective working class demands – constituted the conditions for the 'efficiency movement' as a major capitalist initiative directed primarily at the increasingly sophisticated intensification of labour.

Two features of this account deserve particular attention. First, Hobsbawm makes a real attempt to locate the crisis of accumulation which prompted these new forms of capitalist initiative. This allows us to address such issues as the uneven international adoption of 'scientific management', where it is evident that the United States was the pioneer in relation to Britain and the rest of Europe. Here Hobsbawm's focus on the Great Depression, together with the earlier discussion of differential wages and capital-intensive mechanization, can be related to Sohn-Rethel's (1976, 1978) discussions of this issue. He suggests that the impact of crisis led US employers to early attempts to reorganize the labour process, as they confronted both higher wages and the competitive disadvantage of a lack of secure imperial markets. In Europe, however, such attempts were retarded, until the First World War, by lower wages and the cushion of imperialism.

In addition, Hobsbawm indicates the cluster of initiatives aimed at the intensification of labour within which the pursuit of deskilling must be located. Thus he recognizes that the most sophisticated schemes were devised against, and fought out with, the organized and most highly paid workers and involved major moves towards fragmentation and specification of labour. However, they formed part of a broader array of techniques of wage payment, aimed at the direct intensification of both skilled and non-skilled labour, and of technical and organizational changes, aimed at increasing productiveness.

I now want to turn to one of the few specific Marxian critiques of

Labor and Monopoly Capital, Palmer's (1975) discussion of the American experience of the 'efficiency movement' between 1903 and 1922. Palmer takes up this theme of the heterogeneity of capitalist initiatives but broadens the analysis in a crucial way by tracing the significance of working-class resistance to Taylorism and by examining the ideological role of 'scientific management' in the pursuit of capitalist hegemony.

He begins by relocating Taylorism within a broad range of technical innovations and systems of wage payment and work rationalization which represented responses to the intensification of capitalist competition in the last decades of the nineteenth century. Thus he queries the adequacy of a discussion of the Taylorist programme which does not relate that programme to the role of technical innovations in generating relative surplus value, and underlines the perversity of Braverman's insistence on the lack of any basic interconnections between technical innovations and strategies for reorganizing the work process.

Within this complex of initiatives the attack on craft and quasi-craft controls is properly seen as a central feature, though one which was rather variably applied because of both the period of war-time boom and the specific exigencies of production in various sectors, and the forms of effective worker resistance developed in these contexts. Thus the pursuit of capitalist control of the labour process adequate to the requirements of valorization led to a major but uneven advance of the practices of intensification of labour and of deskilling.

It is in this context that Palmer's central criticism of Braverman, that he 'is limited in his understanding of the extent to which working-class opposition "defeated" Taylorism and pushed capital to employ more subtle means of control in its quest for authority' (Palmer, 1975, p. 32), must be interpreted. Palmer's attention to working-class opposition, and in particular to the persistence of organized resistance through the second and into the third decade of the twentieth century, is not meant to deny the real importance of the processes of deskilling delineated by Braverman. It does, however, suggest that under certain technical and economic conditions craft workers rather effectively defended their autonomy, while the broader efforts to intensify labour which were intrinsic to the Taylor strategy also met more or less effective organized and unorganized resistance, most obviously during the war boom. It is this pattern of resistance and rebellion which has been debated in greater detail by

Montgomery (1974) and Green (1974), who draw out more fully the conflict over control of the labour process which became an important feature of these struggles, and the predominantly parochial control demands and counter-control strategies which issued from them.

Finally, Palmer uses his discussion of the piecemeal application of Taylorist principles and the reality of working-class resistance as the basis for an appreciation of the significant *ideological* role of Taylorism and the 'efficiency movement' more generally. This he portrays in terms of its significance in undermining a 'populist' conception of labour as the sole creative agent in production and substituting a conception of labour as a passive factor of production. Palmer's discussion of this feature of Taylorism suggests that while it informed and gained credence from developments in the practical degradation of work, it played a more general role, especially in the context of relatively effective parochial working-class resistance. Thus it is to be seen as a key component among a series of 'personnel' and 'welfare' initiatives which strengthened and sustained capitalist hegemony beyond and within production. Thus Palmer poses central questions about the relationship between capitalist initiatives in the reorganization of the labour process and the broader ideological and political conditions of capitalist hegemony and valorization which are glossed over in Braverman's treatment.[20]

The decades spanning the turn of the century, then, marked a period of major capitalist initiatives concerned to secure adequate conditions for valorization and accumulation in the context of intensifying international oligopolistic competition and increased worker organization. A substantial deepening of the real subordination of the labour process to capital, accomplished through a combination of mechanization and Taylorist specialization and simplification of labour, was and remains central to, but not exhaustive of, the strategy of capital. The reorganization of the labour process by capital interplayed with broader ideological and political strategies and with specific attempts to intensify the exploitation of labour power.

Without doubt capital in, for example, the engineering sector substantially advanced its domination of the labour process and of the increasingly specialized worker between the 1880s and the 1920s. Such changes, together with the evident dexterity and competence of significant nineteenth-century 'labouring' occupations, justify Braverman's sharp critique of both the method of construction and the conventional 'upgrading' interpretation of occupational census data trends concerning the increasing prominence of 'semi-skilled' workers. However, Braverman's own discussion of the semi-skilled (coloured as it is by an idealized conception of craft skills to which he assimilates very heterogeneous instances of nineteenth-century labour power) is itself severely inadequate in failing to locate the specificity of 'semi-skilled' work within the process of capital accumulation.

The deepening of the subordination of the labour process to capital associated with Taylorism and the advance of mechanization, did not create a simply homogeneous mass of deskilled labour on the shop floor but involved the elaboration of a complex, internally differentiated apparatus of collective labour which contained an uneven variety of narrow skills and specific dexterities. Hyman offers a valuable glimpse of these features in his account of the growth of a major trade-union organization of semi-skilled workers in Britain in the first decades of the century:

automatic machines could be run by a novice after a minimum of instruction; other, more complex machine tools could be operated by workers without a full craft training. . . . By 1914 they [the semi-skilled] accounted for a fifth of the engineering labour force, covering a wide range of operations; indeed, the gap between such semi-skilled workers as the automatic stamper and the universal driller was far greater in terms of skill than was that between the driller and the fully-skilled turner. . . . The situation of the semi-skilled worker who had become proficient on a complex machine tool was closer to that of the craftsman than that of the labourer; he was difficult to replace quickly, and his employers suffered heavy losses if expensive mechanical plant was standing idle. [Hyman, 1971, pp. 40–1, 70]

Such a form of organization of the labour process by capital cannot be understood merely as some transitional phase in the trajectory of a general process of deskilling; it must be analysed in relation to the conditions of valorization and class struggle characterizing the relevant sector and period. Thus it is necessary to consider the contributions which specific forms of mechanization and semi-skilled labour make to the valorization and accumulation process, in terms of increased productiveness, reductions in the value of labour power and intensification of labour, and the manner in which contradictions among these aspects constitute problems for capital and bases of organization and resistance for sections of the working class. The emergence of new forms of expertise around specific phases of technical innovation may, for example, be tolerated by capital during periods of expansion and valorization predominantly on the basis of increasing productiveness of labour. Certainly, the displacement of organized and costly skilled labour by unorganized and cheaper 'semi-skilled' labour may constitute a major opportunity for increased profitability, but the discovery of bargaining leverage and increasing opposition to speed up by semi-skilled workers will not automatically trigger a fresh round of mechanization aimed at further deskilling. The relations between the advantages and disadvantagès to capital of the specific form of the labour process will be related to the relative significance of the aspects of valorization mentioned above and to the combativity of the labourers, as that is influenced by both the specific manner in which 'skills' or dexterities are lodged within the collective labourer and the broader context of forms of political and ideological domination and struggle.

The contemporary degradation of work

The above argument is of particular importance in relation to Braverman's account of the central role of mechanization in the contemporary degradation of work in factory and office. In that account he effectively challenges orthodox myths concerning the general upgrading of labour associated with, in particular, automation. However, because his analysis is developed at the general level of an abstract compulsion towards the destruction of craft expertise and its replacement by pervasive capitalist control of the labour process, he is unable to address the complex, uneven and contradictory character of the organization of collective labour.

Braverman does not entirely ignore the complex and contradictory role of mechanization and reorganization of the labour process in the process of capital accumulation:

This displacement of labour as the subjective element of the process, and its subordination as an objective element in a production process now conducted by management, is an ideal realised by capital only within definite limits, and unevenly among industries. The principle is itself restrained in its application by the nature of the various specific and determinate processes of production. Moreover, its very application brings into being new crafts and skills and technical specialities which are first the province of labour rather than management. Thus in industry all forms of labour coexist: the craft, the hand or machine detail worker, the automatic machine or flow process. [p. 172]

However, this recognition does not become the basis for an

analysis of the manner in which particular forms of organization of the collective labourer and the labour process arise out of specific exigencies of valorization. Instead, in his discussions of mechanization Braverman tends to assume a general congruence between strategies of valorization and accumulation and deskilling, in which the former is lodged directly within the latter:

In the capitalist mode of production, new methods and new machinery are incorporated within a management effort to dissolve the labour process as a process conducted by the worker and reconstitute it as a process conducted by management [p. 170].

In such an analysis the advance of mechanization ultimately becomes a matter of the evolution of techniques adequate to the deskilling imperative, rather than an outcome of the relation between forms of potential technical transformation and other conditions of the process of accumulation, while working-class struggle is accorded the status of a merely transient or frictional reaction to capital (see for example, LMC, pp. 129, 180, 203), rather than being located as the articulation of contradictions within the forms of valorization dominating a specific period of capital accumulation.

My earlier discussion of semi-skilled work has, in contrast with Braverman's treatment, underlined the importance of analysing the ways in which mechanization, as a strategy of accumulation, might (in conjunction with changes in the reserve army of labour) afford opportunities for relatively effective worker organization and struggle. On the one hand, this would involve an attempt to specify the features of collective labour which arise out of the interrelation of mechanism and labour power required for valorization; both such 'positive' features as the need for labour with narrow expertise and experience, and such 'negative' features as dependence upon a disposition among workers to facilitate (rather than disrupt) the logic of integrated production. On the other hand, it would be necessary to locate the organization of these features as the outcome of conflict between capital and labour.[21]

The limitations which the deskilling discourse imposes upon the analysis of mechanization can be clearly traced in Braverman's critique of conventional interpretations of process production and automation. There it underwrites his reliance on Bright's account of transformations in the worker-machine nexus with the secular advance of mechanization, and overshadows any consideration of specific exigencies of accumulation and their interrelation with the forms of expertise, dexterity, responsibility and leverage embodied in the organization of the collective labourer.

The importance of developing a more complex account of the labour process in process production, in which the latter questions would become central, can be indicated by examining a recent study which, unlike Braverman's, focuses upon worker organization and struggle. Nichols and Beynon (1977) provide an account of the organization of the labour process, capitalist strategy and worker organization in one chemicals complex during the last decade. They, like Braverman, frame their analysis of the labour process in terms of deskilling: both contrast the realities of labour in process production with the real skills of nineteenth-century craftsmen and with the spurious sociological idealizations of the upgrading of skills in process production.

However, in their account of the work place Nichols and Beynon also go beyond the simple conception of deskilling to expose the complex and differentiated character of the apparatus of 'deskilled' collective labour produced by the accumulation strategies of one sector of 'modern industry', and the manner in which contradictory features of that apparatus pose problems for capital at particular junctures in the accumulation process. Their discussion emphasizes the following points.

1   The persistent significance of heavy manual labour in the shadow of highly capital intensive production, conditioned by the trade-off for capital between, on the one hand, the wage levels of the labourers and the capacity of capital to intensify that labour, and on the other the costs of investment and gains in production from further mechanisation.

2   The development of job hierarchies, associated with specific production processes, in which forms of limited expertise and empirical skill are radically subordinated to the demands of valorization. The experience of these workers is summarized thus:

> they know their present job, for all its stresses and problems, is the 'best job I could hope for – being unskilled'. They have escaped the tyranny of the bagging line but they live with the fear that it is a temporary release. . . . The operator who is paid for being able to operate a particular chemical process is well aware of the transient nature of his skills. These skills 'cannot be bought' – it 'takes years to really get to

know one of these plants' – but equally, by their very nature, they are tied to the continuance of a particular chemical process. [Nichols and Beynon, 1977, p. 23]

3 The growing importance, for capital, of engineering an active vigilance, responsibility and initiative among workers on its behalf, as a result of the increasing integration, interdependency, and capital intensity of the production process.

The last requirement gains particular prominence as capital responds to increased international competition by intensifying the process of labour and cutting manning levels. This provides the crucial context for the authors' discussion of such capitalist initiatives as 'job enrichment', which may then be located as complex responses to the specific problems of valorization and accumulation confronting this sector of capital, rather than being seen in generic terms as a qualification of, or retreat from, 'deskilling'.

Nichols' and Beynon's account of the labour process invites an analysis of the manner in which the organization of the apparatus of collective labour articulates with the exigencies and contradictions of accumulation, but they do not pursue the issue very far. They move rapidly on to a discussion of the character of struggle in production defined, on the one hand, by developments in the labour process and, on the other, by the forms of accommodation to capital represented by national trade unionism and the organization and ideology of 'labourism'. Some of the issues which require more systematic discussion in an analysis of the labour process in this sector are suggested by another account of the organization of 'skills', this time in oil refining:

The problem of inter-unit mobility was even more intractable. There was clearly good reason for management to encourage people to develop skills in handling jobs on different units. It made it much easier to cover illnesses, and the manpower shortfalls due to holidays. In each refinery there was a small group of workers that were officially polyvalent, that is to say, whose job was to fill gaps in different teams as the need arose, and they had to possess the range of skills necessary to do this. But the real aim of management was to create a much more general capacity for flexibility among those who were normally attached to a particular unit. This seemed, however, to have run into a number of problems. On the one hand the question of payment for new skills once more raised its head in an even more acute form, on the other there seems to have been some reluctance on the part of older operatives to actually pass on their knowledge to other people. Finally, management itself accepted a considerable degree of responsibility for failing to provide enough time for adequate training. What seemed to have happened is that the size of the workforce had to be reduced to a point at which it was difficult to spare people from their everyday work. [Gallie, 1978, p. 90]

Here the contradictory pressures of capital for the ossification of specialized competencies, for the flexibility and general reliability of labour power, and for the demanning and intensification of work, and the forms of resistance and struggle which workers develop around these contradictions, are sharply focused as capital attempts to respond to a crisis of accumulation. In a period of rapid accumulation on the basis of new technology, capital in this sector had moved towards the organization of the collective labourer as series of specialized job hierarchies comparable with those discussed by Stone (1974) and Wilkinson (1977). However, a phase of increasing international competition has shifted capitalist strategy towards the intensification of labour and the expulsion of workers from the industry. In this context workers' struggles over manning and relocation have gained some limited leverage because of both their command over specific forms of quasi-skills and the more general susceptibility of integrated, highly capital-intensive plant to their non-co-operation or disruption.

Such an analysis of the development of the labour process in chemical process production constitutes an attempt to locate the specific and uneven character of the process characterized by Braverman and others as deskilling in relation to the exigencies of valorization and accumulation. In that sector capital has, for a period, cultivated residual forms of expertise organized in a manner which enhances their subordination to the requirements of accumulation, as well as developing a more general ideological offensive designed to engineer the forms of 'responsibility' required by capital in the context of capital-intensive production.

The development of the labour process in the motor industry represents a somewhat different variant of these features of mechanization and struggle arising from the persistent transformation of the immediate process of production in response to exigencies of valorization and accumulation. There the introduction of flow-line production, adopted throughout the industry during the 1920s and 1930s, had a massive impact in the displacement of skilled by semi-skilled workers during that period, as capital sought to reduce the turnover time of capital, to reduce the value of labour power and to intensify labour. In the post-war period the continuing advance of mechanization and automation in motors has brought increasing productivity and a more tightly integrated flow production without further pronounced effects on the narrow and specialized tasks of the workers:

the replacement of the craftsmen on direct production work by semi-skilled operators was brought about by the mass-production techniques of the 1930s. Consequently, the subsequent mechanization has had little further effect on the composition of the direct labour force. The introduction of transfer machines, for example, has meant that fewer semi-skilled machine operators are required to produce any output desired; but the machines are still tended by semi-skilled operators. [Turner *et al.*, 1967, p. 86]

Thus the post-war valorization and accumulation strategies of capital in motors have not created a totally homogeneous unskilled stratum of workers but a mass of semi-skilled workers embodying a limited heterogeneity of forms of training and experience. This mass of semi-skilled work tasks has constituted a terrain on which major struggles have developed between capital and labour, both around attempts at the intensification of labour and around the structuring and advancement of wages.

The increasing integration and capital intensity of production, as it has interplayed with the intensification of international competition in the industry, has led to recurrent attempts by capital to intensify production. Thus Turner *et al.* argue that

under the less mechanized and integrated production systems . . . superficially scientific methods of labour measurement still allow consider-able room for shop-floor negotiation: the 'allowances' to be added to the 'elements' of which particular operations are composed, the 'effort-rating' of the workers studied, and even the 'elements' themselves may all be adjusted to make a specified work load acceptable. The mechanization of handling, however, combined particularly with the use of automatic data processing and other control devices, has very much reduced the margin of managerial uncertainty in workload assessment – and thus also reduced the area within which the 'effort bargaining', which is a major function of union work-place organization, can operate. At the same time, the high capital costs of the new equipments puts a considerable pressure on management to work it as intensively as possible, so that its own front in bargaining is likely to be stiffened. [Turner *et al.*, 1967, p. 92]

However, it is not merely a question of the reduction of management uncertainty. Such developments, in the context of relatively full employment during the post-war boom, have also generated important sources of leverage for effective work-place worker organizations which can sometimes exploit the integration and capital intensity of the plant effectively to resist intensification and to recover some porosity in the working day. Thus, as Beynon argues in his important study of conflict on the frontier of control at Ford's Halewood plant:

these controls over the job gained the operative a degree of autonomy from both supervision and higher management. Through their steward they were able to regulate the distribution of overtime, achieve a degree of job rotation within the section, and occasionally sub-assembly workers, in particular, were able to obtain 'slack' work schedules. But there were quite precise limits to the way in which workers can run the section. [Beynon, 1973, p. 143]

As Beynon has emphasized, such precarious counter-controls cannot be understood through an analysis of developments in the labour process alone but must be seen in the wider contexts of both the post-war development of work-place union organization and changes in class relations beyond production. One important component of the articulation of transformations in the labour process with these developments concerns the specific character of wages struggles in motors. They have involved attempts by capital to develop forms of grading and wage payment which most effectively compel the exercise of specific dexterity and experience to maximize intensity and productiveness, and attempts by workers, both sectionally and more generally, to adopt the rhetoric of 'skills' to gain skilled wages and conditions on the terrain of semi-skilled mass production.

Conclusion

Braverman's work has not merely 'completed' Baran and Sweezy's analysis of monopoly capitalism by extending it to embrace the labour process but has performed the more substantial service of returning attention more generally among Marxists to the study of the development of the capitalist labour process. My discussion has focussed on deskilling as the major theme of Braverman's own return to that study. I have argued that it is necessary to advance beyond the spurious concreteness of the generic impulse towards deskilling which governs Braverman's account towards a historically located theorization of the transformation of the capitalist labour process within which deskilling may be adequately located as a tendency. Such a theorization, to which this chapter serves only as a preliminary contribution, would explicitly locate the forms of transformation of the labour process in relation to phases of valorization and accumulation and would trace their articulation with class relations beyond production. Only on that basis would it appear to be possible to develop an analysis of the labour process which will be of real value in the formulation of working-class strategy and appropriate forms of political intervention in struggles within production.

3 The sexual division of labour and the labour process: a critical assessment of Braverman[1]

Veronica Beechey

Labor and Monopoly Capital is one of the few texts to have recognized the importance of the sexual composition of the working class in the changing structure of employment in different sectors of production. It is relevant, therefore, to subject Braverman's account of sexual divisions to critical scrutiny, to assess the extent to which the theoretical framework of *Labor and Monopoly Capital* enables Braverman satisfactorily to analyse the sexual division of labour. It is surprising that a book as important as *Labor and Monopoly Capital* has not attracted more feminist discussion and criticism and that most of the general critiques of Braverman's work have largely ignored the important question of Braverman's treatment of the sexual division of labour.

There have, however, been two sorts of feminist criticism of *Labor and Monopoly Capital*. Two papers written by American feminists have criticized Braverman for failing to analyse the ways in which monopoly capitalism has affected the domestic role of the woman as housewife. Baxandall, Ewen and Gordon (1976) criticize Braverman for his failure to examine the relationship between the social division of labour and the detail division of labour. They argue that he ignores women's unpaid work within the family and the activities of the working class outside the work place; that women's specific location in the family *and* the labour process affects their consciousness; that the housewife's role was originally a kind of 'crafts-womanship', which has been degraded as the family has been transformed by monopoly capitalism; and that the family has become an 'internal market' for consumption within monopoly capitalism. The family, the authors argue, has developed a form of labour process which mirrors the social relations of the labour process within monopoly capitalism: the degradation of household labour thus parallels the degradation of wage labour. Weinbaum and Bridges (1976) develop the notion that the family is a unit of consumption in monopoly capitalism and discuss the effects of the family's consumption role upon the housewife. They argue that although Braverman does talk about the role of the family in consumption, he scarcely analyses the role of the housewife. They suggest that a crucial way in which monopoly capitalism has transformed the work of housewives is by organizing 'consumption work' for them. Consumption work, according to Weinbaum and Bridges (1976, pp. 90–1), provides a bridge between 'the production of things and the reproduction of people', between production and the family, such that 'the contradiction between private production and socially determined needs is embodied in the activities of the housewife.'

In Britain Jackie West (1978) has recently taken up Braverman's account of the relationship between the changing occupational structure and the changing class structure. She discusses the question which has been raised by a number of analyses of the contemporary class structure (for example, Braverman, 1974; Poulantzas, 1975; and Carchedi 1975a), of the class position of white-collar labour and is particularly concerned with female white-collar labour. West develops three arguments about Braverman's analysis of class. First, she posits that it is questionable whether the office is analogous to the continuous-flow production process of the factory and asks whether the process of rationalization has replaced the all-round clerical worker by the subdivided detail labour. Second, she argues that Braverman has a simplistic conception of the working class, which does not take sufficient account of differentiations and cleavages within the working class apart from those of sex. Finally, West argues that Braverman's only explanation of the fact that women have been drawn into deskilled occupations as cheap labour is because they comprise an ideal reserve of labour for the new mass occupations, since there are large numbers of women available for employment.

If we turn to non-feminist critiques of Braverman, we find two dominant themes emerging, as Tony Elger has pointed out in Chapter 2. The first set of criticisms concerns the fact that Braverman divorces the analysis of the labour process from the broader forms of class relations and state institutions which are important in the constitution of class relations; that is, he abstracts the labour process from the organization of the mode of production as a whole. Specifically, Braverman can be criticized for failing to distinguish between the strategies of individual capitals in organizing the labour process and the strategy of capital in general, represented in state apparatuses which are involved in organizing the general conditions of production and accumulation and in regulating the supply and conditions of labour. An analogous argument can be made with respect to Braverman's framework for analysing the position of female labour. One of the consequences of abstracting the labour process from the broader forms of class relations is that the inter-relationship between the position of women as wage labourers and as domestic labourers within the family is unexplored. Thus, for example, both state policies, which represent the interests of capital in general and are concerned with the conditions of women's labour and with constituting a particular form of family, and ideological assumptions about a woman's place, which embody complex assumptions about women's working and domestic roles that cannot be reduced simply to the organization of the labour process, are unexplored within *Labor and Monopoly Capital*.

A second set of general criticisms concerns Braverman's objectivist conceptualization of the working class. A number of Braverman's critics (Friedman, 1977a; Palmer, 1975; Schwartz, 1977) have argued that this approach has produced a one-sided picture of the capitalist labour process and has failed to analyse the ways in which the organized sections of the working class in particular can limit capital's possibilities for reorganizing the labour process on the basis of new technologies and for effecting the further subordination of labour to capital. This general criticism, like the first, has particular relevance for attempts to understand the position of female wage labour within the capitalist mode of production, because the entry of women into particular branches of production, industries and occupations is determined not only by the demand for labour of individual capitals (which frequently recruit labour on a gender-differentiated basis) but also by the attempts of the male-dominated trade unions to define certain kinds of jobs as 'men's jobs' or 'women's jobs', thereby leaving a restricted range of occupations open for women.

I have summarized some of the criticisms which others have made of *Labor and Monopoly Capital* as a background to my own critique. I shall refer to some of these arguments in my discussion of Braverman's work. I shall discuss three sets of problems which emerge from *Labor and Monopoly Capital*, which can be summarized under three headings: the universal market; skill and deskilling; and the industrial reserve army of labour. I shall conclude with a brief discussion of Braverman's analysis of the class structure under monopoly capitalism.

The universal market

Braverman (1974, pp. 271–83) argues that in the early stages of capitalism the family remained centrally involved in the production process. However, during the past 100 years industrial capitalism has thrust itself between the farm and the household and has appropriated all the processing functions of both, thereby extending the commodity form to the production of food, clothing, shelter and household articles. Thus:

the capitalist mode of production takes over the totality of individual, family and social needs and, in subordinating them to the market, also reshapes them to serve the needs of capital. [ibid, p. 271]

Braverman discusses the impact of these changes on the family's form and functions, arguing that the family loses its role as an institution of social life and as an agency of production in the period of monopoly capitalism and retains the sole function of being an institution for the consumption of commodities. Even its role in consumption has become individualized, as all family members are involved in wage labour, according to Braverman. Thus the process of erosion of the family proceeds through three stages, as is evident from the following passage from *Labor and Monopoly Capital*:

In the period of monopoly capitalism the first step in the creation of the universal market is the conquest of all goods production by the commodity form, the second step is the conquest of an increasing range of services and their conversion into commodities, and the third step is a 'product-cycle' which invents new products and services, some of which become indispensable as the conditions of modern life change to destroy alternatives. [ibid., p. 281]

Eventually therefore, Braverman laments, all social life becomes atomized and mediated through market relations. A second consequence of these changes is that the housewife moves from producing use values within the domestic economy to producing them as a wage labourer under the direct domination of capital, a process which is hastened, in Braverman's view, by the ease with which commodities can be purchased with the wage (instead of being produced within the family) and by the increasing inability of families to maintain themselves economically upon the male wage.

Braverman's chapter on 'The universal market' is the one chapter of *Labor and Monopoly Capital* in which he discusses the family and the ways in which the family has been transformed under the impact of the development of the capitalist mode of production. Its subject matter is an important one for feminists, since it points to the important processes by which the domestic economy is penetrated by the developing capitalist mode of production, the family and the labour process become separate social institutions, and the specifically capitalist form of labour process and capitalist form of family develop. There are, however, a number of problems with Braverman's account of this process, which I wish to discuss.

Braverman has a glorified conception of pre-capitalist society and of pre-industrial capitalism. His model for the pre-industrial family is based on the farm family which produced sufficient to meet its needs, and in which (he assumes) work was a 'natural' function. This 'Golden Age' conception of the pre-industrial family is both romanticized and ahistorical.[2] Braverman ignores the fact that this form of family, which was based upon peasant agriculture and handicrafts and in which production was primarily for subsistence, had a patriarchal set of social relationships and accepted extremely long hours of arduous labour. The family was a unit which owned the instruments of production; there existed a unity of production, generative reproduction and consumption within the family unit; and all members of the family worked together within the domestic economy. There was, however, a form of sexual division of labour, with men working in the fields and women being occupied with household tasks, which included a wide range of activities, as Alice Clarke (1968) makes clear. The wife's (and children's) labour was organized in co-operation with the husband's labour, and all were essential to the survival of the family unit. However, the male head of the household controlled the labour process within the domestic economy, and women were clearly subordinated to their husband's or fathers' patriarchal authority – a form of subordination which was reflected in legal and property relations and in the dominant ideological assumptions about women. As well as romanticizing the pre-industrial agricultural family form, Braverman fails to make differentiations among the forms of pre-industrial family – between, for example, families engaged in agricultural production and those engaged in crafts, between town and countryside and between different regions.

Braverman's account of the effects of the development of

industrial capitalism on the family is simplistic. He fails to take account of the fact that there were intermediate forms of labour process between peasant agriculture and handicrafts and capitalist manufacture. Marx (1976) analyses these in terms of the developing tendencies within capitalism to extract absolute surplus value and formally to subordinate labour to the control of capital. The most important intermediate process has been the putting-out system organized by merchant capital, in which merchant capitalists put work out to families, and commodities were produced by the family within the domestic economy. Medick (1976) has described this intermediate process as the 'proto-industrial family economy'. Furthermore, the relationship between production within the domestic economy and production within manufacture and large-scale industry is more complicated than Braverman suggests. On the one hand, some forms of production of commodities have been retained within the domestic economy throughout the history of capitalism (for example, in homework). On the other hand, some forms of production of commodities were removed from the domestic economy into manufacturing workshops before the development of large-scale industry. The relationship between the domestic production of commodities and the production of commodities within capitalist manufacture and large-scale industry varied greatly by industry, trade and region. The family was not simply or instantly transformed by the development of industrial capitalism. The fact that the transformation of the family was prolonged, complicated and variable suggests that the effects of the development of industrial capitalism on the family cannot be deduced abstractly from a general analysis of the penetration of the family by capitalist production, nor from the functional requirements of capitalism for a market for its commodities. It suggests that an adequate analysis must show the ways in which the concrete forms of family have been transformed in the course of the historical development of the capitalist mode of production.

A further set of problems raised by Braverman's account of the universal market is related to his view that women were taken from the household to become part of the industrial reserve army of labour, and that ex-housewives produce the same use values under the direct domination of capital as they previously produced within the family. In this part of his analysis Braverman telescopes three processes into one. These are, first, the transformation of the domestic economy; second, the creation of an industrial reserve army of labour and the drawing of women into wage labour; and third, the production of use values by ex-housewives under the direct domination of capital. Both the transformation of the domestic economy and the creation of an industrial reserve army of labour were extremely uneven and prolonged historical processes. Although large numbers of women were forced, throughout the history of capitalism, into various forms of casual and seasonal employment both within agriculture and in the towns, it is only since the 1950s that large numbers of married women have begun to enter into wage labour in the centres of large-scale industry (with the notable exception of the two world wars) – a fact which Braverman does recognize elsewhere in *Labor and Monopoly Capital*.

In addition, Braverman conflates several different questions when he asserts that women produce the same use values within capitalist commodity production as they produced within the domestic economy. There are in Britain examples of women being employed in industries to produce use values which they had previously produced within the domestic economy (for example, in the textiles industry and in food and drink production). There are instances of women losing their hold on the production of particular use values as production became organized on a capitalistic basis (as in the brewing industry). There are also instances in which women drawn into production as wage labourers are engaged in the production of completely new use values (for example, in electrical engineering in the inter-war years). Clearly, it is not possible to generalize about whether women are producing the same use values within capitalist production as they produced within the domestic economy – this is a question for concrete historical analysis. It is important not to confuse the question of whether women produce the same use values in domestic and capitalist production with the issue of the form of labour process which is employed and the organization of the sexual division of labour within it. As well as investigating what use values are produced, we need to know whether the sexual division of labour changes under the impact of large-scale industry. Evidence suggests that this is also historically variable; the form of sexual division of labour changed in Lancashire textiles production, for example, but not within the Leicestershire hosiery industry, according to Nancy Osterud (1977). Finally, we need to investigate the form of patriarchal social relations which develop with the emergence of large-scale industry and with the appropriation of control over the labour process by industrial capital in place of the male head of household. That is, we need to understand the differential impact of transformations in the form of control over the labour process on the sexual division of labour and on the experiences of female and male workers.

Braverman's analysis of the capitalist form of family is problematic. He states:

> Apart from its biological function, the family has served as a key institution of *social life, production* and *consumption*. Of these three, capitalism leaves only the last, and that in attenuated form, since even as a consuming unit the family tends to break up into component parts that carry on consumption separately. The function of the family as a co-operative enterprise pursuing the joint production of a way of life is brought to an end, and with this its other functions are progressively weakened. [Braverman, 1974, p. 277]

Thus, in Braverman's view, the only role of the family in capitalist society, apart from that of biological reproduction, is an attenuated role in consumption. However, the family in capitalist society remains crucially involved in social life, production and consumption, although the relationship between these is different from the one that obtains in the case of the pre-industrial family. Braverman is mistaken in presuming that it is possible to separate social life, production and consumption in this way and fails to recognize that the transformation of aspects of the family's role under the impact of the development of the capitalist mode of production does not entail their obliteration. For instance, the family is no longer a unit in which all use values are produced. It has a multi-faceted relationship to production, however, in that (a) some use values are still produced within the domestic economy; (b) labour power is reproduced both generationally and on a daily basis within the family; (c) one aspect of the reproduction of labour power involves consumption, as Weinbaum and Bridges (1976) point out; (d) the family is one source of the industrial reserve army of labour. My objections to Braverman's account of the family can be summarized in the following terms. Despite the fact that Braverman's account of the effects of industrialization on the family is a 'pessimistic' account, it shares a number of characteristics with more 'optimistic' structural-functionalist sociological accounts of industrialization and the family (for example, Smelser, 1959). Braverman's notion of the family is ahistorical and idealized – indeed, in so far as the capitalist form of family departs from Braverman's idealized conception, he uses this to condemn capitalism morally (for its destruction of the family and the

'community'). Braverman's view that the family is virtually destroyed within capitalism and that its functions have gradually been
taken over by ever-extending areas of capitalist commodity production underestimates the point which feminists have consistently
argued, namely, that the family within capitalism is a central agency
of the oppression of women. It also fails to take into account the ways
in which the capitalist form of family is related to the total
organization of the capitalist mode of production within the spheres
of both production and reproduction.

Braverman's isolated account of the family within his chapter on
'The Universal Market' has its counterpart in his analysis of the
sexual division of labour in the labour process. For Braverman's
accounts of deskilling, the industrial reserve army of labour and the
class structure isolate the labour process from the institutions with
which it is crucially connected within capitalist society, the state and
the family. In the following sections I shall attempt to show that
Braverman is not able satisfactorily to account for the sexual division
of labour because he loses sight of the vital, historically changing
relationship between the family and production.

Skill and deskilling

The basic thrust of Braverman's arguments about the organization of
the labour process under monopoly capitalism is to emphasize the
extensive process of deskilling, or the degradation of labour, which
has accompanied the development of monopoly capitalism. This
involves the substitution of detail labour for complex labour, the
diminution of the labourer's control over the labour process and
increasing levels of alienation at work. It occurs at various levels of
the production process, and Braverman contributes an account of
deskilling in a number of occupations. Thus, for example, traditional
occupations like engineering have become transformed into mass
occupations and have begun to exhibit the characteristics of other
mass occupations – rationalization and the development of the
division of labour, the simplification of tasks, the application of
mechanization, a downward drift in relative wage levels and some
unionization. This is also true, Braverman argues, of the newer
'middle-class' occupations – technical and scientific work, the lower
ranking supervisory and management occupations and professional
occupations in marketing, finance and administration, as well as in
schools and hospitals. Some of Braverman's most interesting

discussions of the changing occupational structure concern the new 'working-class' occupations, like clerical work, service occupations and retail trade occupations. These have been increasingly standardized, rationalized and degraded, according to Braverman, but to a lesser extent than occupations in large-scale industry.

Braverman argues that the structure of the working class has been transformed by the changes in the labour process under monopoly capitalism. First, there has been a relative diminution in the proportion of manual labourers employed in manufacturing industry and a relative growth in the proportion employed in service occupations. This shift has had implications for the sexual division of labour in production, since operatives in manufacturing industry are generally male, while clerical and service workers are overwhelmingly female. Indeed, Braverman suggests that the typical form of division of labour in the working-class family is one in which the man is employed as an operative and the woman as a clerical worker. Second, there has been an increase in the proportion of workers who do not own the means of production and therefore have to sell their labour power – labourers who are employed under the direct domination of capital, as formerly 'middle-class' occupations have become increasingly subject to the separation of conception and execution and the process of deskilling.

There are several problems with Braverman's conception of skill and his conceptualization of the process of deskilling, however, which have implications for his analysis of the sexual division of labour. Braverman's notion of skill derives from a conception of the male artisan/mechanic, who is regarded as the 'original' kind of skilled labourer, whose skills have been wrenched away from him by the subordination of labour to capital and the separation of conception and execution. In this respect Braverman's idealized conception of the skilled worker parallels his romanticization of the pre-industrial family. This conception of the skilled artisan/mechanic embodies a number of different aspects of skill, however, and it is not clear to which of these Braverman is referring. First, the concept of skill can refer to complex competencies which are developed within a particular set of social relations of production and are objective competencies (in general terms, skilled labour can be objectively defined as labour which combines conception and execution and involves the possession of particular techniques); second, the concept of skill can refer to control over the labour process; and third, the concept of skill can refer to conventional definitions of occupational status. These different conceptions of skill are not necessarily coterminous with one another, although they are frequently conflated within the literature and may well coexist in particular concrete instances. There are, for instance, forms of labour which involve complex competencies and control over the labour process, such as cooking, which are not conventionally defined as skilled (unless performed by chefs within capitalist commodity production). And there are forms of labour which are conventionally defined as skilled but do not involve both conception and execution and lack complex competencies, yet because of trade union control or custom and practice have become (or have remained) socially defined as skilled. This is true in Britain of sections of the engineering industry, where some groups of workers perform labour which is conventionally defined as skilled but which might more accurately be defined as semi-skilled if an objective definition of skill were provided; in the print industry, where machine minders are called machine managers and perform labour which is defined as skilled but is objectively semi-skilled; and in welding, which is defined as a skilled occupation in Britain but is considered to be semi-skilled in many other capitalist societies.

Unfortunately, in failing to differentiate between the different aspects of skill and to clarify which aspects he is dealing with, Braverman's account tends to oversimplify the problem of defining the concept of skill. It is extremely important to clarify what is meant by skill, since the adoption of different criteria of skill has different theoretical and political implications. For example, the analysis of objective differences in complex competencies enables one to provide an account of the ways in which developments in the labour process provide a *real* basis for sectional struggles or for overcoming sectional struggles, while an analysis which is couched in terms of a conventional conception of skilled status tends to emphasize capital's attempts to divide and rule the working class and thereby to become conspiratorial in form, without analysing the ways in which objective changes in the labour process give rise to changing forms of skilled, semi-skilled and unskilled labour. It is also important to clarify what is meant by skill if one is interested in the reasons why particular categories of labour (for example, female labour, black labour, migrant labour) have generally been excluded from skilled occupations. Unfortunately, the critical arguments offered by Baxandall, Ewen and Gordon (1976), which emphasize the housewife's decline of 'craftswomanship', and by Davies and Brodhead (1975), who suggest that Braverman is analysing the breakdown of the 'crafts-manship of daily life', do not adequately clarify the problems which are involved in talking about craft and skill and the application of these concepts to the position of women.[3] To state that the housewife's labour, like wage labour, has been degraded and deskilled ignores one of the most important features of domestic labour, that it is not subject to direct capitalist control as wage labour is. It also ignores the fact that the work of women wage labourers has rarely been defined as skilled because women have not been very successful at following any of the routes to the acquisition of skill – education, training and apprenticeship in the case of objective skill, and successful collective bargaining in the case of convention-ally defined skill.

It is an oversimplification to analyse the changes in the labour process solely as a tendency towards deskilling, and the degradation of labour. It is important to recognize that as capital has introduced new forms of machinery in order to simplify tasks and thereby to increase the rate of extraction of surplus value, it has also created new skills. Samuel (1977b) shows how the development of large-scale industry in the nineteenth century gave rise to new skilled occupations. The development of monopoly capitalism with its new institutional apparatuses – the development of departments con-cerned with planning, finance, marketing, personnel management and so on – gave rise to a whole gamut of new managerial and technical and supervisory occupations. Furthermore, the electronic revolution described by Mandel (1978) as providing the technologi-cal breakthrough through which late capitalism developed has given rise to new occupations such as computer programming and systems analysis. Thus the history of capitalist production must be seen as the history of the destruction and the recomposition of skills. Further-more, the development of the collective labourer is an important concomitant of the development of large-scale industry.[4] This suggests that while individual tasks may be subject to the process of the simplification of labour and to further the subordination to capital's control of the labour process, the collective labourer (as the collective organization of labour brought together by capital within the capitalist labour process) may have increased workers' control over the labour process. The question of workers' resistance to, and control over, the labour process brings the question of trade union organization and other forms of shop floor organization immediately into the foreground of analysis.

I shall conclude this section by outlining some of the ways in which I think deskilling arguments might be useful for analysing the employment of women as wage labourers. First, there are instances in which women have been introduced into production as unskilled and semi-skilled labour, replacing forms of skilled labour. The classic example of this process occurred during the First World War, when individual capitals employed female labour in the engineering and munitions industries both because there was a shortage of male labour and as a means of breaking entrenched forms of worker organization. The engineering industry was already undergoing a rapid process of objective deskilling, and the Amalgamated Society of Engineers was struggling to maintain conventional skilled status for its members, despite the loss of complex competencies and control over the labour process which was occurring. It would be wrong to assert that all forms of 'dilution' involve the substitution of female labour for male labour or that the introduction of women into production is always as 'dilutees'. It is important, however, to investigate those conditions in which women have been introduced into production in the process of deskilling and the implications of capital's attempts to introduce female labour into production in this way for the ensuing forms of class struggle. Where women have been introduced into production as 'dilutees' in the process of deskilling, this move has accompanied the formation of a simplified labour process and the creation of the collective labourer in which women have a subordinate function. Women have also been introduced into production as new commodities have been produced or as ones previously produced within the domestic economy have been produced under capitalist control for the first time. It is not appropriate to see the employment of women under these conditions as simply part of the process of deskilling. Deskilling which occurs in one industry may have extensive implications for the form of labour process which develops subsequently in other industries, either on a national or on an international scale. For example, the deskilling of the labour process which occurred in engineering and munitions production during the First World War affected the form of labour process which capital developed in the light engineering industry in the inter-war years, in which women were extensively employed.

The introduction of female labour as an agency of deskilling is linked to another question, the 'feminization' of certain occupations – that is, the shift in certain occupations from being predominantly male to being predominantly or exclusively female. Consideration of 'feminization' leads us to examine not only shifts in capital's demand for different forms of labour but also ideological assumptions about 'women's work' which have accompanied shifts in the sexual composition of the labour force, and which have become part of the general assumptions which govern the future definition of jobs as 'men's jobs' or 'women's jobs' and the future location of women within the workforce. When discussing 'feminization', however, it is important to investigate the extent to which it is the same occupation which is being 'feminized', or whether the process of deskilling results in the creation of a new occupation or function within the collective labour process. Thus when we speak of the occupation of the clerk being 'feminized', so that it changed a masculine occupation in the nineteenth century to a female occupation within the twentieth century, we are not really describing the same occupation; the labour process within which clerical work exists has been extensively transformed since the nineteenth century.

The industrial reserve army of labour

Braverman follows Marx in arguing that capital accumulation requires an industrial reserve army which can be brought into employment as wage labour when required and repelled when no longer required by the exigencies of capital accumulation. The crucial determinant of changes in the industrial reserve army, for Braverman, is the mechanization and automation of industry, which requires a decreasing labour force. Thus, Braverman (1974, p. 383) argues: 'Those industries and labor processes subjected to mechanization release masses of labor for exploitation in other, generally less mechanized, areas of capital accumulation.' Conversely, in those industries in which mechanization and automation have not developed on any significant scale, there is an increasing demand for labour. This in turn creates the tendency for capital to invest in methods of organization of the labour process which utilize low-wage labour. Braverman thus ties fluctuations in the demand for labour to his analysis of the expanding and declining sectors of the economy. Manufacturing industries and occupations have been declining in the period of monopoly capitalism, according to Braverman, while service industries and occupations (especially service work, sales and other forms of marketing and clerical work) have been increasing.

The functions of the industrial reserve army, according to Braverman, are that it provides on the one hand, a flexible and disposable working population which is sensitive to the requirements of capital and, on the other hand, cheap wage labour for the new service industries and occupations. In periods of rapid accumulation, such as the period since the Second World War, the relative surplus population, which Braverman regards as the 'natural' product of capital accumulation, has been augmented by other sources of labour. The United States, like Britain, has drawn upon an international pool of labour from the developing world and, increasingly, upon female labour. This Braverman considers to be the major source of labour power in the post-war period. Braverman identifies the sources of labour by reference to Marx's notions of the floating, stagnant and latent forms of the industrial reserve army. Women drawn into wage labour are taken to represent an enlargement of the floating and stagnant sections of the industrial reserve army.

Braverman argues that in the post-war period it is male workers who have been expelled from employment as the manufacturing industries have declined and female workers who have been attracted into employment with the emergence of the tertiary sector and service occupations. There has thus developed a tendency, according to Braverman, towards the equalization of participation rates for male and female workers, which is created on the one hand, by the decline in manufacturing industry and the expansion of the service sectors of the economy and, on the other, by the increasing difficulty of surviving economically on one wage within a family, which has led more women to seek employment outside of the home. Braverman sees this tendency as leading to the breakdown of family and community life.

The theory of the industrial reserve army in the first volume of *Capital*, on which Braverman relies in *Labor and Monopoly Capital*, is a problematic theory. Part of the difficulty with attempts to use Marx's theory in analysing specific changes in the composition of the labour force concerns the relationship between what is essentially an abstract law of accumulation and the concrete realities of the supply and demand for labour within the history of the capitalist mode of production. A further problem concerns the fact that the whole concept of the industrial reserve army is imprecisely specified in Marx's theory. Unfortunately, Braverman's particular application of Marx's theory does not satisfactorily clarify the conceptual problems involved in its use. Braverman is most interested in how the composition of the industrial reserve army has changed as a result of the development of monopoly capitalism and in very long-term shifts in the structure of employment and unemployment, which he analyses in terms of the changing composition of the industrial reserve army. His notion of the industrial reserve army is so general, however, that it does not satisfactorily explain the phenomena which it is invoked to explain.

In particular, Braverman is not able to explain why women have been drawn into wage labour in the service industries and occupations in preference to men. His analysis suggests the importance of two factors: first, that there are masses of women awaiting employment, functioning as an industrial reserve army; second, that women tend to enter low-wage occupations. However, Braverman is not able to explain why married women became an active component of the industrial reserve army at a particular historical period (the 1950s) by reference to his broad account of shifts in the industrial reserve army. He is also not able to explain why women enter low-wage occupations. Women's low wages themselves need explaining. As I have argued elsewhere (Beechey, 1977), the specific position of women as part of the industrial reserve army can be explained in terms of (a) their labour power being paid for at a price below its value; (b) their labour power having a lower value; and (c) the existence of the family, and of women's dependency within the family, and the ideological assumptions which surround this, which enter into the determination of the value of female labour power.

In my view it is useful to understand certain aspects of women's employment in terms of the concept of the industrial reserve army of labour, and especially instances in which women are introduced into employment for specific periods and then expelled from employment. The two world wars are the clearest examples of women constituting an industrial reserve army in this way. Other examples can be found in the use of female labour as casual or seasonal workers who have been introduced into wage labour in response to changes in production, due either to seasonal variations in the production cycle or to cyclical processes of growth and recession. In these instances, in which women are brought into employment for 'short, sharp shifts' (in the words of one Coventry personnel manager) and dispensed with in response to seasonal fluctuations or fluctuations in the business cycle, they can usefully be seen as comprising part of an industrial reserve army which is activated in certain periods. It is not particularly useful to describe the long-term shifts in the structure of the working class which Braverman elaborates in *Labor and Monopoly Capital* in terms of the concept of the industrial reserve army, however. The introduction of female labour on a fairly long-term or permanent basis into particular branches of industry can more usefully be seen in terms of capital's attempts to employ forms of labour power which have a lower value and in terms of the process of deskilling. If one delimits the use of the concept in this way, the objections of critics like Milkman (1976), Gardiner (1975–6), and Baudouin, Collin and Guillerm (1978), who argue that the use of the concept of the industrial reserve army mistakenly suggests that women's work is not central within the production process but is marginal to it, can be met. These critics are correct to point to the centrality of female labour, at least in some branches of production. This does not mean, however, that women never comprise part of the industrial reserve army of labour, or that the concept is not useful, but rather that the concept should be much more precisely and empirically delimited than it is within *Labor and Monopoly Capital.*

There is a further important consideration which must be raised in discussing the introduction of female wage labour into production, whether as 'dilutees' or as part of the industrial reserve army of labour. Where women have furnished capital with forms of labour power which have a different value from that of male labour power, their distinctive position within production has to be understood by reference to the family and the role of women within it. For women have been introduced into production from the family; when they work as wage labourers they invariably also work as domestic labourers, and when they are expelled from production, they are frequently forced to retreat into the family. This has the advantage to individual capitals that their labour force is flexible and can easily be made redundant, and to capital in general that women can be dispensed with from production with little cost to the state, frequently without rights to redundancy benefits and often obscured from unemployment statistics. In restricting his discussion of the family to one chapter on 'The universal market', Braverman does not discuss the role of the family in supplying female labour to capital. Even though in his chapter on 'The universal market' Braverman is clearly aware that women are drawn out of the family into commodity production, this does not inform his discussion of deskilling and the industrial reserve army of labour.

To put this another way, in Braverman's development of his theory of monopoly capitalism the family and the labour process are defined independently of one another. Thus when he discusses women in the labour process he makes no reference to the family, and when he discusses the family this is isolated from his discussion of the labour process. Tony Elger in Chapter 2 has criticized Braverman's conception of the labour process and has argued that *Labor and Monopoly Capital* divorces the labour process from the organization of capitalist production as a whole and from the laws of motion which govern it and, in particular, that Braverman does not explore the relationship between valorization and the process of deskilling. The arguments of this paper would suggest that Braverman's discussion of the family and of the position of women within the labour process represents another side of the same coin: the conceptual isolation of the family from the labour process and of both the family and the labour process from an analysis of the capitalist mode of production as a whole, and the tendency towards valorization which governs it. Thus the relationships between the reproduction of labour power which takes place within the family and the organization of capitalist production and between consumption and production are unexplored within *Labor and Monopoly Capital*, with the result that Braverman is unable to explain the specificity of female wage labour within monopoly capitalism. The underlying theme of my critique has therefore been to suggest that *Labor and Monopoly Capital* does not provide a satisfactory conceptual framework for analysing those questions with which we ought to be most preoccupied: the questions of the changing forms of sexual division of labour and patriarchal social relations which exist within the capitalist mode of production.

On class

I wish to conclude this paper by discussing tentatively one of the problems with which Braverman begins *Labor and Monopoly Capital*, the definition of class and, in particular, the constitution of the working class. Although Braverman does not explicitly enter into contemporary Marxist debates about class, restricting himself instead to some extremely pertinent criticisms of bourgeois sociological conceptions of class, it is clear that *Labor and Monopoly Capital* is a major contribution to contemporary arguments about the structure of the working class under monopoly capitalism. Braverman locates his analysis of class within his account of the production process and defines the working class broadly as all those who lack ownership of the means of production. He argues that the changing structure of production under monopoly capitalism has had far-reaching consequences for the structure of the working class, since more and more sectors of the population have become property-less and are engaged in wage labour, and have in turn become increasingly proletarianized as a consequence of the separation of conception and execution and the process of deskilling.

In order to pose some questions which I think Braverman's analysis of class raises, I shall briefly counterpose this approach to structuralist analyses of class, which constitute the main framework within which contemporary arguments about class have taken place, in order to highlight some of the problems which these different approaches to class analysis throw up. Take, for example, Poulantzas (1975, 1977). He argues that the working class is defined as those who perform productive labour – those who produce surplus value directly – and states that all other labourers who lack ownership of the means of production but are not productive, or are only indirectly productive, cannot be considered to be part of the working class but comprise the new *petit bourgeoisie*.

Braverman's account of the class structure has the advantage of seeing class in processual terms, as a social relationship; of analysi¯g the class structure as being in a state of constant transformation as the process of capital accumulation proceeds; and of providing a broad conception of the working class. His analysis can be criticized, however, for focusing solely upon the labour process and for failing to analyse the relationship between the labour process and the organization of monopoly capitalism in its totality; for being overly economistic; for failing to analyse class consciousness; for having an undifferentiated conception of the working class; and (despite his extensive consideration of sexual divisions) for being unable to explain why women occupy a specific, subordinate position within the class structure.

Despite his discussion of political and ideological levels of analysis, Poulantzas's account of the working class under monopoly capitalism (like Braverman's) can be criticized for focusing almost exclusively on the labour process. It can also be criticized for having a mistaken conception of productive labour, which refers only to the production of material commodities (Hirst, 1977); for having an exceptionally narrow conception of the working class; for failing to consider the fact that many women work in occupations which have become increasingly proletarianized (West, 1978). The structuralist approach more generally can be criticized for being overly abstract and concerned mainly with definitional problems of class; for exaggerating the distinction between separate levels of the mode of production (the economic, the political, the ideological) and for exploring the relationships between these different levels in very formalistic terms[5]; and for failing to analyse class as a form of social relationship[6] which is constituted in the process of history and, in particular, in the process of class struggle.

In the face of these problems which arise from some of the most important Marxist texts that deal with the analysis of class, I wish to suggest, by way of a conclusion, that we need both a conception of class as a historically constituted social relationship and a conceptual framework which enables us to explore concretely the forms which the relationship between labour in its various forms (wage labour, domestic labour) and capital assume in different historical conditions. This framework should enable us to analyse the relationship between particular forms of labour process and the other social institutions through which social classes are constituted (for example, the family, the various state apparatuses). As far as the analysis of women is concerned, an approach which (a) considers the different forms of labour process and different forms of labour and (b) explores the relationship between the labour process and the other social institutions within a particular mode of production would enable us to bring the sexual division of labour into a central position in the analysis of class.[7]

Finally, since one of the purposes of providing a class analysis is to contribute to discussions of, for example, political forms, political parties, the women's movement, I think that it is important to recognize that it is not possible to 'read off' an account of the appropriate forms of political organization from an analysis of the class structure, as both Poulantzas (1977) and Hunt (1977) attempt to do in debating Eurocommunist strategies.[8] The relationship between the class structure and the forms of political organization is a changing, organic relationship, in which political forms are rooted in an analysis of class and class-consciousness but in turn contribute to the process of constituting classes as effective forms of political organization.

4 Taylorism, responsible autonomy and management strategy

Stephen Wood and John Kelly

As we saw in Chapter 1, one consequence of Braverman's methodological omission of class struggle is a marked tendency to portray capitalist management as virtually omniscient. The implementation of management strategy is therefore taken to be unproblematic. Again, by equating Taylorism with capitalist management in its essence, Braverman is able to depict post-Taylorist developments as either complementary or irrelevant; anti-Taylorist strategies are inconceivable.

By contrast, Friedman (1977a, b) and R. Edwards (1979) have attempted to argue for the existence and importance of such alternatives. Friedman in particular has argued that it is precisely because of resistance to direct control that in certain situations managements have adopted less restrictive systems, involving the concession of 'responsible autonomy'. While Edwards lays equal stress on the need for managements to adapt to worker resistance, his argument rests as much on the reasons for the extensive non-implementation of Taylorism as on the problems created by its utilization. It was resisted by workers but was also not popular with managers and was not adopted in any general fashion. Those managements who adopted it did so in a piecemeal way; in short it was a failed experiment.

Despite this, Edwards concludes that managements did learn from and adopt some of the underlying ideas of Taylorism, such as the need to wrest control of production knowledge from workers or to define jobs in terms of output and to link this with pay, and these features were taken up and have endured. Any conclusion about the implementation and efficacy of Taylorism depends in part on how broadly it is defined at the outset. The broader one's definition of Taylorism, the more one sees it as all pervasive, as Braverman appears to regard it, while a narrower definition suggests a lesser degree of influence (cf. Palmer, 1975). But there is equally the danger that in reacting to Braverman's over-reliance on Taylorism we fall into the trap of minimizing its importance. In this chapter we shall attempt to show that one way in which these problems may be circumvented is through a recognition of the limits and constraints of Taylorism. This involves more than simply emphasizing worker or managerial resistance to Taylorism: it also requires a reconsideration of the nature of Taylorism in order to clarify its limitations. This chapter will thus fall into three sections. The first deals with Braverman's treatment of Taylorism; the second outlines certain important but neglected features of Taylorism; and the third concludes by discussing the question of alternatives to Taylorism.

Braverman: Taylorism as the quintessence of capitalist management

According to Braverman, *all* labour processes require some degree of co-ordination, in so far as they are based on division of labour. In modes of production based on social classes there also arises the necessity for control, a need which is far more thorough and more comprehensive under capitalism because of its dynamic character, evidenced by the constant drive to accumulate. Capitalism is also distinguished, however, by formally free labour – workers may dispose of their own labour power as they wish – and this, according to Braverman, further imparts to capitalist production an unusually antagonistic character.

These features of capitalism resulted, in Braverman's view, in constant attempts throughout the nineteenth century to develop a specifically capitalist mode of management that would exercise control over the labour process. Braverman sees the domestic, sub-contracting and putting-out systems as imperfect approximations to Taylorism, 'the specifically capitalist mode of management'. Detailed control over the labour process at the turn of the century was exercised, in Taylor's (and Braverman's) view, not by management but by skilled workers, who could and did thereby obstruct capitalist innovation and rationalization.

Deskilling originated historically in the management drive against such skilled workers, but the tendency is found throughout all sectors of the economy and continues well beyond the alleged decline of traditional craft work. This is because deskilling allows increased capitalist control over production, since opposed centres of knowledge are destroyed and the labour process is fragmented. It also permits, on the Babbage (1971) principle, a considerable cheapening of labour and an increased rate of exploitation.

For Braverman, Taylorism and its assumptions 'reflect nothing more than the outlook of the capitalist with regard to the conditions of production' (1974, p. 86), because it articulates the need to control labour, provides means (in the form of time-and-motion study and other techniques) for dispossessing workers of their knowledge of production and thereby provides management with the basis on which to *control* the labour process. Braverman describes Taylorism in the more abstract terms of three principles: the rendering of the labour process independent of craft, tradition or workers' knowledge, and their replacement with experiments (or science); the separation of conception from execution; and the use of the managerial monopoly over knowledge to control the labour process in detail. Post-Taylorist developments in management are seen as complementary to Taylorism ('human relations'), dismissed as inconsequential (for example, job redesign) or ignored (for example, productivity bargaining). Since management under capitalism is taken to have reached its purest expression in Taylorism, no further development of an anti-Taylorism character is possible. Braverman regards the human relations movement simply as a means for adjusting workers to the deleterious consequences of Taylorism.

The key to Braverman's assessment of Taylorism and its significance lies in his structuralist conception of capitalism as a law-governed system whose laws inevitably work themselves out without contradiction (Elger and Schwartz, 1980; Burawoy, 1978). For neither the capitalist mode of production itself nor the practices derived (analytically) from it, are treated as potentially contradictory. There is no notion of capitalist development itself issuing in pre-socialist forms, such as rudimentary planning, the growing interdependence of enterprises and the increasing democratization of work. Braverman's concept of control is also far from adequate, even in his own terms. His inflation of the control or autonomy exercised by pre-Taylorian craftsmen has been commented upon elsewhere (see Chapter 2) but there is another difficulty, which is that he works implicitly with a zero-sum concept of control and its bases, particularly knowledge. Thus if management investigates, and acquires, knowledge of a production process, the workers are supposed either to lose this knowledge or to be incapable of regaining it, however partially. In other words, Braverman conflates acquisition of knowledge with monopoly of knowledge and examines control historically in terms of a simple shift from worker to employer control (see also Burawoy, 1978). He cannot, then recognize different modes of managerial control, post-Taylor, and as we have said must treat Taylorism as the highest form of management under capitalism and as incapable of being transcended.

Against Braverman's conception of a working class dominated by the laws of capitalism and its consequences has been counterposed worker resistance and struggle. This has been seen by many writers as a methodological corrective, but has also been used (Friedman 1977a) as the ground from which to explain the limits of management control as well as major changes in the means and relations of production. Yet the 'class struggle' critique of Braverman also remains within the Taylorist problematic of control. It does so by assigning great theoretical and empirical significance to the potential for working-class organization and struggle to evade full capitalist control of the labour process and thereby to thwart capitalist objectives. This tendency to inflate control to the point at which it becomes the central problem of capitalist management is at variance with most analyses of capitalism, including that of Marx, which emphasize the pursuit of profit as the directing aim of capitalist management.

But this is not all, because even in Marxist terms surplus value has not only to be *produced* but also to be *realized*. Control of the labour process by capital, the maximum rate of extraction of surplus value (consistent with continued accumulation and labour supply) and the realization of surplus value were analysed by Marx as integral but separate moments in capitalist production. This means that it is possible for contradictions to arise between any of these moments. Labour exploitation may be relatively high but control weak, as may be the case with skilled craft workers; or realization of surplus value may be constrained by structural or other limits to its production, such as output regulation.

The development of Taylor's scientific management

While Braverman is correct to emphasize the significance of the labour process (Elger, 1979), and of Taylorism within that process, it should also be recognized that management in general does not revolve simply around labour. Taylorism is very much more complex than Braverman suggests, and although it has always centred on labour productivity, there was a growing emphasis throughout Taylor's work on the technical preconditions for raising it, such as adequate materials flow and machine maintenance, and implicitly on the problems of implementing his proposals in the face of worker suspicion or hostility. The initial and central concern was 'task management' – that is, the determination of possible levels of performance (given improved methods and so on) and the search for ways of securing these levels as effectively as possible. Hence Taylor emphasized the importance of financial incentives and the pay-performance link and later came to stress the importance of assigned work quotas for individual workers.

As Braverman notes, Taylor's system arose from his observations of output regulation by workers, a practice that was adopted as a defence against rate cutting and a possible loss of jobs as a result of an increase in productivity. For its part, management was compelled to resort to rate cutting to increase its exploitation of labour, because it lacked the detailed knowledge of production required to raise productivity. It was this knowledge which Taylor set out to acquire through time-and-motion study, though he soon came to realize that if labour productivity was to be raised, then simultaneous improvements had to be effected in machine maintenance, materials and tools supply, work flow and detailed supervision (F. W. Taylor, 1919).[1]

Taylor's conception of control, however, occupies an ambivalent position within his work, a fact obscured by Braverman's abstract and monolithic account of a 'Taylorism' that was free of contradiction and that underwent no development.[2] In *A Piece Rate System*, Taylor's second published work, there was very little emphasis on control. At that stage Taylor still worked within a classical economics conception of the employment relationship as an economic exchange. Time-and-motion study would be accepted because workers would realize that with increased productivity would come increased wages. His own experiences at Midvale and Bethlehem Steel eventually convinced him that economic interest was insufficient to promote change, and that it was necessary to use the knowledge gathered through the 'scientific' investigation of production to control the labour process. Thus in 1906 Taylor could write of the slide rule used to codify and apply knowledge of machining:

The gain from these slide rules is far greater than that of all the other improvements combined, because it accomplishes the original object, for which in 1880 the experiments were started; i.e. that of taking the control of the machine-shop out of the hands of the many workmen, and placing it completely in the hands of the management thus superseding 'rule of thumb' by scientific control. [Taylor, 1906, p. 252]

This much quoted statement is also much misunderstood, by Braverman and others. In short, they argue that if management does in fact acquire such knowledge of production, then workers either lose it or are unable to regain it. Yet knowledge is not a commodity that can be 'lost' in this manner, and Braverman has conflated the acquisition of knowledge with its monopoly (Burawoy, 1978). Even after time-and-motion study craft workers continue to possess their knowledge – they 'simply' lose the advantage of management ignorance. On this basis craft workers have continued to resist deskilling and have retained important positions in many branches of production (see Brown, 1977).

It is possible that Taylor himself recognized this problem, even if only dimly, because by 1912, in his Testimony to the House Committee, he was stressing heavily the necessity for a 'mental revolution' among workers and managers. In view of the American Federation of Labour's campaign against Taylorism (which culminated in the House Committee hearing) and the strike in the previous-year at the Watertown Arsenal against time-and-motion study (Aitken, 1960; Nadworny, 1955), it is tempting to dismiss the 'mental revolution' as a public relations exercise designed to allay public hostility and suspicion. A more plausible interpretation, in the light of Taylor's experiences and the hostility of both employers and unions, was that Taylor was beginning to articulate the pre-conditions for the implementation of his techniques.[3] It was the same issue which led his associates, Cooke and Valentine, to the very different conclusion that Taylorism could only be implemented with trade-union co-operation in a framework of 'industrial democracy' (Haber, 1964, ch. 3; Nadworny, 1955, ch. 5).

Implicit in these observations is a distinction between techniques – time-and-motion study, control of workflow, stores inventories – and the strategy required for their implementation. For Taylor the introduction of scientific management did not require union co-operation and would in time render unions superfluous. It was to be introduced by a paternalistic but autocratic management which was itself subject to Taylorist principles. Managers would therefore demonstrate that their decisions were subject to the same discipline as the workers, namely, the authority of science, but in practice Taylor protested in 1912 that 'nine-tenths' of the problems of introducing his system could be laid at management's door. A key component of the strategy was individualism. Workers were to be paid by their individual performance; grievances and suggestions were to be received only from individuals; and the labour process, as far as possible, was to be composed of individualized work roles (Kelly, 1982). As the embodiment of collectivism, unions occupied no place in Taylor's world.

The techniques/strategy distinction[4] is absent from Braverman because he assumes its implementation to be unproblematic. In fact, Taylorist techniques have been implemented within a number of quite different strategic frameworks. In the Japanese context Taylor's emphasis on managerial control of workers and of work processes harmonized well with the paternalistic structures of large industrial organizations and with their drive to modernize Japan and to attack the arbitrary role of owners (Nakase, 1979; Okuda, 1972). Taylor's works were quickly translated into Japanese and sold in enormous quantities, and the Japanese branch of the Taylor Society was one of the first to be formed. It was the larger Japanese organizations, including government bodies and foreign companies inside Japan, that pioneered Taylorism. This strategy coexisted throughout the 1920s both with welfare strategies which constituted the foundation of the life-long employment security system and with collective bargaining and joint consultation with trade unions. Taylorism as such began to decline during the Depression, when workers started to resist it more strongly and it began to be located within nationalist discourse as a foreign ideology alien to Japanese culture.

In Britain, by contrast, the existence of strong union organization in the major branches of production limited the spread of time-and-motion study. Where piece rates were introduced on the basis of such study, as in the car industry, they were often the subject of bargaining and regulated by mutuality clauses (limiting unilateral management changes) rather than by 'science' (Friedman, 1977b; Brown, 1977).

There was also a very intense debate on the nature of Taylorism and its applicability to a socialist mode of production in the early Soviet Union. Lenin's 1914 moral critique of Taylorism's oppression and exploitation of the workers (Lenin, 1965a) and its contrast with the economic anarchy outside the enterprise was replaced with a quite different view in 1918. Writing during the Civil War, at a time of serious economic dislocation, Lenin stressed the importance of using the 'scientific' components of Taylorism, such as time-and-motion study and planned work flow, as opposed to its 'bourgeois' ideological elements, principally intensification of labour. Having said this, Lenin introduced a critical ambiguity into his view by asserting that the overall intensity of labour in Russia was low by international standards and would have to be raised (Lenin, 1965b). The ensuing debate in the USSR centred on the question of labour intensification, with one group (the Council on Scientific Management) arguing it was unnecessary and counter-productive, while the eventually successful Gastev and his supporters argued for the introduction of piecework and method study and increased labour intensity (Bailes, 1977; Traub, 1978). Taylorism also found favour in Fascist Italy, where it was often introduced in a very authoritarian manner and, instead of raising wages and reducing working hours, was used to achieve precisely the reverse (by contrast with the Soviet Union, where wages did increase in some sectors under piecework (Carr, 1966; Rollier, 1979). What perhaps unites these otherwise distinct applications of Taylorism is, as Maier (1970) suggests, a radical, technocratic opposition to liberal capitalism. Equally, the insistence in Taylorism on the non-zero-sum basis of conflict, of the possibility of raising wages and profits simultaneously, appealed to the national, anti-class views of Fascism and the unitarist ideology of some American employers in the 1920s.

For many writers evidence of the diffusion of Taylorism emerges from its equation with enhanced division of labour. Braverman, as well as Littler (1978), argues that 'Taylorism' entails a 'dynamic of deskilling' because of its insistence on the division between conception and execution and its implicit acceptance of the Babbage principle. In 1835 Babbage wrote:

the manufacturer, by dividing the work to be executed into different processes, each requiring different degrees of skill and of force, can purchase exactly that precise quantity of both which is necessary for each process. . . .' [Babbage, 1971, pp. 175–6]

While it is undoubtedly the case that Taylorist techniques were used to further the detail division of labour, it is also true that the phenomenon was not peculiar to Taylorism and predated it by a considerable period. Division of labour was subordinated in Taylor's work to his overriding objectives: securing control over the labour process and raising the productivity of labour (Haber, 1964; Kelly, 1982).

Distinguishing management strategies

Given the importance of the context in which Taylorism is implemented and of avoiding the conflation of scientific management
with specific techniques, it is necessary to develop modes of
discussing strategies which are not rooted in Taylorism. The most
recent attempt at such discussion is that of Friedman (1977a, 1977b,
1978).

His attempt to delineate different managerial strategies is an
important corrective to Braverman's view that one can isolate an
invariant and essentially capitalist managerial practice, namely,
Taylorism. Equally, Friedman implicitly rejects the arguments of a
number of French sociologists that contemporary efforts to 'humanize' or reorganize work through the devolution of autonomy and by
other methods are merely new forms of Taylorism (see, for example,
Montmollin, 1974).

Although as we shall see there is some ambiguity in Friedman's
conceptualization, he seems to identify two types of strategy
according to their mode of control: direct control and responsible
autonomy. In the first (of which Taylorism is the clearest expression)
management exercises its control directly, by means of the specification of work methods, close supervision and coercion. The second
type entails the concession of elements of control, or 'responsible
autonomy', to workers so that they can exercise discretion over the
immediate process of production. In another formulation he argues
that the direct control strategy seeks to control or suppress the
variability inherent in labour power, whereas the responsible
autonomy strategy seeks to exploit it and to harness it to capitalist
objectives.

These two types of strategy relate to a series of specific determinants, namely, the phase of development of capitalism, the competitive conditions of the industry, the production position of groups of
workers (whether central or peripheral) and the central or peripheral
position of particular industries. Direct control is thought to be more
effective with peripheral workers and peripheral industries and in
less developed areas of capitalism.

Despite its intuitive appeal, there are a number of difficulties with
this conception. First, the components of both strategies are not
clearly identified. Responsible autonomy is variously described as
consisting of worker discretion and commitment to capitalist objectives (a job-redesign type of practice); as counselling, improvements
in social relations, the stimulation of intergroup competition,

suggestion schemes and participation (a classical 'human relations' type of exercise); and as the concession of improved material benefits – high wages and incentives, job security, good fringe benefits and working conditions (Friedman, 1977a, p. 97; 1977b, pp. 48–52). These practices may coincide empirically, but there are many cases where they do not, and it is thus important to be clear about the components of the posited strategy and to avoid defining strategies, or even tactics, in terms of techniques.

Equally, direct control is variously described as Taylorism (separation of conception and execution, centralization of conception and close supervision and pay incentives), and as an effort to limit the variable effects of labour power. The criticial ambiguity in both conceptions (since they are related by exclusion) centres on the role of pay and pay incentives, described by Friedman as attempts both to control and to harness labour power variability (1977a, pp. 79, 93, 97; 1977b, p. 49). Friedman's attempt to resolve this issue by distinguishing money piecework (where work methods remain unspecified and payment is by the piece) from time piecework (where methods are specified and payment is by time saved) seems unsatisfactory. For many contemporary pay systems fall between these two extremes, combining method specification and piece payment, and both systems reflect the attempt to control output through the pay system, rather than by the manipulation of other non-financial rewards (1977a, p. 219).

Secondly, on the narrower conception of responsible autonomy (as argued especially in 1977b) which resembles forms of job redesign, Friedman is empirically incorrect to trace their origins to worker resistance or struggle, unless one wants to extend these latter terms to cover labour turnover and absenteeism. Third, Friedman tends to accept at face value the theories of 'responsible autonomy' as defined in the terms of their originators and disseminators rather than subjecting them to independent and critical analysis. Thus when management theorists describe concessions of autonomy to work groups and posit a dichotomy between their practices and Taylorism (or 'direct control') Friedman accepts their arguments. He therefore fails to consider the possibility that autonomy, or control, may not be a zero-sum concept, and that management control over production may increase simultaneously with worker control over its more immediate aspects (Brighton Labour Process Group, 1977; Pignon and Querzola, 1976).

More seriously, Friedman fails to analyse the connections between responsible autonomy and direct control and to consider that certain forms of the former actually function because of classic Taylorist mechanisms and may conform to Taylorist principles. There is also a strong tendency in Friedman, as in Braverman, to treat management under capitalism principally as a control function, in which the recalcitrance of labour – class struggle – is elevated to paramount status. Yet for Marx the two principal defining features of the capitalist mode of production were that labour existed as a commodity and that the major objective of social production was the production and realization of surplus value. Although formally acknowledging these features, Friedman draws the conventional (but crude) distinction between the co-ordinating (or technical) and the authoritative functions of management: the latter is specific to capitalism while the former is 'part of any complicated economic process' (1977a, p. 77). What is missing from either of these functions is the production of profit in its various modes, an activity that has been reduced to the ahistorical category of 'co-ordination'. Capitalism therefore ends up being characterized in effect specifically by control over labour and its various modes.

A further consequence of Friedman's argument is that managerial activity tends to be abstracted from tactical or strategic frameworks, incorporating finance, sales, marketing, and to be conceptualized at the level of task management, or control over directly productive activity. He assigns considerable significance to the 'product cycle' under capitalism, in which sales of a new product rise at first only slowly, accelerate and then fall off, and links this with changes in managerial strategy towards 'responsible autonomy'. Yet this useful link is not carried through into an analysis of differences *within* managements.

Finally, one can question the justification for writing of management strategy, rather than say, tactics or practices. The first concept has connotations of comprehensiveness, coherence, long-term perspectives and consciousness. Do we really want to attribute these characteristics uniformly to capitalist management, or would the latter concepts (tactics, practices) be more appropriate?

Taken overall, then, Friedman's work may provide a valuable starting-point, but his central dichotomy as formulated seems unable to support the weight that one could reasonably expect it to bear. A more elaborated conception of managerial practices must recognize shifts in principal managerial objectives. Equally, such a conception must recognize both the connections between practices and the different forms which a single practice – such as Taylorism – may assume under different conditions.

What is important here is Friedman's insistence on the theoretical significance of analysing management practices in relation to class struggle. He argues that worker-initiated schemes of shop-floor control are more likely to reflect workers' own interests than those originating with management, and while this may be true in some cases for example, Fiat as compared with Volvo, there is a further level of analysis which complicates the picture. In their transition from conception to implementation, managerial schemes are invariably modified (to differing degrees) by workers' own counter-initiatives, and it would be necessary to appreciate such modifications in any analysis of managerial practices and their consequences (Goodrich, 1975; Wood and Kelly, 1978). We must also take into account some of the contradictions generated by Taylorism and the detail division of labour under the changing circumstances of the post-war economic boom (cf. Burawoy, 1978; Elger, 1979).

Limits and developments of Taylorism and detail division of labour

During the post-Second World War economic boom both Taylorism and detail division of labour encountered problems, stemming in part from worker resistance but much more from structural contradictions (see Pichierri, 1978). To appreciate these contradictions, we must abandon Braverman's implicit treatment of manufacturing industry as a homogeneous sector and distinguish, for example, along the lines of Woodward (1958) mass production, batch production and continuous process industry (see also Heckscher, 1980).

The Ford moving assembly line, pioneered in the Highland Park vehicle works in 1914, was used solely for the mass production of the Model T Ford. Likewise, its extension into other car industries and into the manufacture of consumer goods such as electrical appliances was based on long production runs of a small range of products. Throughout the 1950s manufacturers of domestic appliances and of other mass-produced items expanded their product ranges in line with growing domestic and world markets (Corley, 1966). This process, however, increasingly came into conflict with the structure and limits of the assembly line. Realization of surplus value dictated that an ever-growing range of commodities be produced to meet diverse consumer 'demands'. Production of surplus value dictated that product range should be kept small to ensure long production runs and thereby to minimize production time lost because of product, parts and tools change-over (for examples, see Gowler, 1970; Kelly, 1982).

The major strategy used to resolve this contradiction was product obsolescence: this allowed old lines to be deleted from the product range (see Baran and Sweezy, 1968, ch. 5; Mandel, 1978, ch. 7). Manufacturers also attempted to reorganize distribution, either by stipulating a minimum batch size for wholesalers' orders or by allocating small orders into a 'queue' until there were sufficient orders for a single product to justify a production run. Other manufacturers tried (though unsuccessfully) to reach agreements on production swapping, whereby each of two companies would produce only one type of appliance in a particular factory and obtain other appliances through barter (Corley, 1966).

But a small number of firms reorganized production rather than distribution, either by shortening assembly lines or by abolishing them altogether. Instead of changing a long flowline every day or two in response to market fluctuations, firms could specialize in each of a number of shorter lines or single work situations, on the same product and thus reduce the frequency of product change-over. This trend was represented within management theory as an 'enrichment' of jobs – which, of course, it was, although its origins had less to do with under-utilized and bored workers than with overstretched production systems.

This reversal of detail division of labour did not signify the abandonment of Taylorism. On the contrary, such transformations of assembly lines frequently led to an individualization of work roles, to the replacement of group by individual incentives and to greater management control arising out of increased worker visibility (Kelly, 1982; Coriat, 1980). These new work roles were invariably determined by Taylorist techniques – time-and-motion study – within a Taylorist strategy of individualization. At the same time, many of these instances involved simultaneous increases in both worker's control over immediate aspects of production and management control, through the greater ease of accountability of individualized work roles. If we operate with a zero-sum concept of control, as is implicit in Braverman, this feature of mass-production systems cannot be grasped.

The limits to Taylorism are revealed in a different industrial sector, that of continuous process production. Precise specification of individual work roles depends for its efficacy on a relatively predictable input of work. Where there is considerable and unpredictable variability in production, either because of variations in the raw materials, (for example, in coal mining, textiles, certain chemicals) or because of variations in the production process itself (for example, in certain branches of metal manufacture and processing), the application of Taylorist techniques generates a series of 'problems' for capital. Workloads are likely to vary significantly between individuals, and with an interdependent production process some individuals or groups are likely to be underutilized while others are kept very busy. Sudden upsurges of work are likely to strain the production system or will generate higher labour costs if a reserve pool of utility workers is employed for such emergencies (Kelly, 1977).

The significance of sociotechnical systems theory, in this context, is that it articulated this contradiction between detail division of labour and the means of production, that is, between control over the labour process and the production of surplus value, and recommended the creation of autonomous groups. Each group is assigned a series of tasks and is responsible for their distribution within the group. The results of such initiatives have been to iron out work-load inequalities through flexibility of labour and, therefore, to raise the average intensity of labour, under the influence of group pay incentive schemes. Clearly, there are instances where shortened assembly lines and 'autonomous' groups have been inaugurated in response to trade-union initiatives, as Friedman has noted. Though the examples of Fiat and Volvo involve an industrial sector which is generally highly organized throughout the world, the majority of examples of the reorganization of mass-production systems have occurred not in vehicle manufacture but in electrical engineering, a sector characterized (in the UK) by lower union density, weaker union organization and a higher proportion of women employees.

The extent to which reversals of Taylorism or of detail division of labour are responses to structural contradictions and/or class struggle is a purely empirical question and cannot be determined *a priori* on the basis of a desire to upgrade the elements of class struggle or of contradiction, so obviously neglected in Braverman.

Conclusions

Our discussion of Braverman and Friedman and our analysis of Taylorism and its limitations and contradictions clearly raise a wide range of substantive issues in the analysis of management and organization. Yet a number of key conceptual and methodological distinctions can be identified as necessary components of any analysis that aims to transcend some of the oversimplified views we have discussed.

The first point is that one cannot infer the successful implementation of a management strategy merely from its existence. In other words, the determinants of successful strategy formation are unlikely to coincide exactly with the conditions required for implementation. Taylor himself recognized the problems of implementation, even if he was unable to theorize about them effectively and could produce only the concept of a 'mental revolution' whose social determinants were not articulated.

Several writers have observed carefully the ways in which the implementation of a strategy or practice become the object of class struggle, and the best example here is that of incentive or piecework payment systems. By the more or less systematic modification of work methods and the regulation of output, workers have often been able to thwart the objectives of managerial initiatives (Roy, 1952, 1954; Lupton, 1963; Friedman, 1977a), and it has also been observed that Taylorism was implemented in the 1920s only in a piecemeal fashion (Edwards, 1979; Palmer, 1975). Once implementation is seen as problematic and uncertain, we can avoid the kind of error made by Bosquet (1972) in his assessment of increased worker participation in management decision-making. Bosquet argued that the concession of a degree of autonomy to workers would engender a desire for even greater influence and thereby precipitate an unstable and (to management) threatening process that could even call into question management's control of production. The argument is based on the premise that managerial initiatives are successfully implemented in the forms discussed by management theorists, which overlooks the problems of implementation, not to mention the ideological character of some management theory.[5]

The second conclusion we can draw is that it is dangerous to privilege one particular area of management concern as the overriding problem in need of solution. Braverman's (1974) insistence that the problem of management can be reduced to the problem of control is true in the sense that control can never be complete and predictable. But the significance of control over labour and the labour process has to be understood in the context of management's having a series of objectives (and hence potential problems) linked with the full cycle of capitalist production. Labour supply, job performance and surplus value extraction, product sale and product markets all can and do present problems for managements. The heads of several large British corporations such as British Steel or BL are currently less concerned with control over the labour process and surplus value production than with declining markets because of the world recession (see also Mandel, 1978).

The significance of a 'labour problem' is also likely to vary over time and to be associated with the capital–labour ratio of the company or firm, and we noted that detail division of labour had thrown up different kinds of problems in mass-production, flowline industries as compared with continuous-process production (see also Heckscher, 1980; Woodward, 1958). We cannot therefore assign priority to a single factor in management strategy, whether it be labour, technology or markets, but must determine such problems empirically.

Third, the notion of 'management strategy' is itself open to question on two counts. Management, except in very small firms or at departmental level in larger firms, is unlikely to function as a homogeneous entity, united in the pursuit of a single objective. Specialization of function has also generated specialization or differentiation of interests (Crozier, 1964). Equally, the notion of strategy cannot be taken at face value, with its connotations of conscious and clearsighted formulation of means and ends. In other words, the degree to which management holds and operates a strategy has also to be determined empirically (Thurley and Wood, 1982).

Both the differentiation of management and the variations between firms suggest, as we argued before, that alternative strategies are certainly available. Taylorism, for instance, may have been appropriate under conditions of an abundant labour supply, expanding markets and weak union organization but may reach the limits of its effectiveness in different circumstances.

Overall, the thrust of this paper has been to argue for a more careful and more detailed study of management strategy, coupled with a sensitivity to the complexities of employing organizations, which together will enable us to transcend simplistic formulations and generalizations (Wood, 1980).

5 Skilled manual workers in the labour process, 1856–1964[1]

Roger Penn

This chapter will analyse the position of skilled manual workers in the labour process. It will be demonstrated that the collective control that workers managed to secure through trade unions enabled those workers to preserve both their skilled status and their wage differentials. Such control took the form of mechanisms of social exclusion, by which both management and other workers were exluded from the utilization and operation of machinery. These mechanisms were established in factories prior to automation, so that skilled status was maintained despite changes in the labour process. Where work groups were unable to establish control through social exclusion before the introduction of factory automation, no secure base existed from which to resist changes in the labour process and to establish skilled status. This was compounded by the fact that many of the work groups brought into already automated factories were composed of women.

By locating the preservation of skilled status within a historical analysis which takes account of specific factors facing workers organizing in local labour markets, it is possible to question some of the conclusions reached by Braverman (1974). This chapter will begin with an examination of the historical development of skills in engineering and cotton as a basis for assessing the adequacy of Braverman's mode of explanation as well as his substantive claims about deskilling. I shall draw particularly on research on the engineering and textile industries in Rochdale in Lancashire.

The engineering industry

Exclusive controls, 1800–80

The engineering industry expanded dramatically with the onset of the industrial revolution. The construction of the machinery and steam engines used to propel other sectors into the factory era of industrial capitalism provided the basis for the development of expertise in engineering. In the period before 1820 most of the machines constructed were one-off jobs, made by itinerant millwrights who were both highly skilled and very scarce. The millwrights possessed their own tools and moved from mill to mill to build the machinery. Entry into the occupation was limited by means of apprenticeship, and the artisan had to develop a wide range of skills in order to be able to handle the different requirements of each new job. After about 1820 the first major transformation of the work force began with the expansion of the industry into large factories. The basis for this move was the massive increase in demand for steam engines, which could be produced in large numbers, and more efficiently, by standardized work processes. For the millwrights this represented an attack on their status as skilled craftsmen, but in fact, despite the development of factory production which incorporated new machinery like Maudlay's improved lathe, the new factories required a work force of engineers with considerable skills.

Although the transition to factory production merely involved a change in the skills required by engineering workers, it was, nevertheless, a significant shift in social and industrial relations, since most of the tools required for production became fixed-plant machinery. Indeed, the history of the subsequent hundred years revolved around the successive attempts of the employers and management to develop machinery and to sub divide tasks in order to eradicate any need for skilled craftsmen.

The main aim of the Amalgamated Society of Engineers (ASE) upon its inception in 1851 was to destroy the over-supply of labour, since this threatened their relative economic and social position within the manual labour force. Four policies were adopted to achieve a reduction in excess labour which took the form of opposition to systematic overtime, to more than one apprentice to four journeymen, to non-apprenticed ('illegal') men and to piece work. These policies led to a national lock-out in January 1852 and eventually, after a lengthy struggle, to the complete defeat of the ASE. Nevertheless, despite the 1852 defeat the ASE continued to fight locally to limit the number of craftsmen by means of apprentice restrictions and to oppose the employment of 'illegal' men.

By the beginning of the 1880s engineering craftsmen had achieved the transition from handicraft production to the production of machinery by means of machines. This transformation of the labour process had not eliminated industrial skills, but it changed their content. The ASE was essentially a craft union, sectional and exclusive. Indeed, exclusion took two distinct forms: the exclusion of non-skilled labour from membership and from the performance of work regarded as proper only for the engineers, and also the exclusion of other craft unions, notably those of the boilermakers and shipwrights, by means of demarcation rules. However, the society had suffered a serious defeat in 1852, followed by the failure of the Sunderland apprentice battle in 1883, and had managed to organize less than 10 per cent of the labour force in the industry. The precarious balance between exclusion and the strength of the society was to a large extent obscured in the golden years of the 1860s and early 1870s, when Britain was 'the workshop of the world'. In the subsequent half-century after 1873 the pressures of foreign competition and technological revolution revealed the weaknesses of the ASE and prompted dramatic changes in the social relations of engineering workers.

Exclusive controls, 1880–97

The period after 1880 witnessed considerable and perhaps fundamental change in the British engineering industry. Growth continued, both of production (especially exports of machinery) and of employment. Furthermore, the range of products developed swiftly. In the 1850s most engineering production was concentrated in three areas: textile machinery, locomotives and steam engines. The 1890s saw the continuing manufacture of these products but also the addition of new commodities like armaments, agricultural machinery, cycles and, as a direct result of the 'second industrial revolution', electrical engineering. This growth was accompanied by increasing foreign competition, particularly from Germany and the USA, which stimulated concentration in the industry, itself facilitated by the Limited Liability Acts of 1856 and 1862.

However, the most crucial results of foreign competition were increasing concentration and larger firms and the adoption of new technologies and, in particular, new tools. New machines were introduced to supersede the centre lathe. These machines, the capstan and turret lathe, vertical borer, radial drill and universal milling machine, were far more specialized than earlier machinery and incorporated in their mechanisms far more skill than hitherto. The productive emphasis was on the interchangeability of parts rather than perfect accuracy. In addition, new metals like high-speed steel and new hand instruments like verniers and protractors made for standardized production. In this context of the increased rationalization of production there was a sharp movement towards payment by piece work and bonus systems, which reached their apogee in Taylorism, the 'perfect' embodiment of the principles of mass production. The crucial result of all these processes, as far as workshop relations in the engineering industry were concerned, was the growth in the proportion of semi-skilled machine operators. Clearly, this was a far more serious threat than the four major issues of the mid-century: systematic overtime, piece work, apprentices and 'illegal' men. Semi-skilled machinists ('handymen') could be seen as an example of the latter, but in fact they were a threat to the entire position of skilled men in engineering, since their existence constituted a denial of any rationale for widespread social exclusion and suggested a potentially new form of the division of manual labour within the industry, involving the wholesale removal of skilled men from routine production.

In the 1890s the conflict between the ASE's attempts to control the establishment of the new machinery and the 'power to manage' claimed by the engineering employers reached flash-point. The period as a whole was one of increasing labour militancy. The ASE itself was reorganized in 1892, and the number of permanent officials was increased. More significantly, the union organization became far less centred on London. In addition, new occupations became eligible for membership, notably electrical engineers, roll-turners and machine men. The new strength given by such reorganization to the union districts quickly led to renewed and bitter hostilities between the ASE and the employers. In 1895 the Clyde employers intervened to support their Belfast counterparts in their dispute with their local ASE district by locking out the Glasgow men. This was followed by 1896 by the formation of the Federation of Engineering Employers' Associations, prompted mainly by the armaments producers, especially Armstrong's of Newcastle. Early in 1897 the men founded an Eight Hours Committee for engineering workers, which provided the pretext for a test of strength between the rejuvenated ASE and the newly formed Employers' Federation.

The ostensible cause of the 1897 lock-out was a conflict over the eight-hour day, which the employers were unwilling to concede. They claimed that the new machines required longer, not shorter, hours to cover the overhead capital costs of their installation. To the union this claim appeared somewhat specious in the face of profits like Armstrong's, which were £358,000 net in 1896. However, the main aim of the employers was to 'smash the union'; this was made explicit by Siemen, president of the (newly formed) London branch of the Federation, who stated publicly that the goal of the lock-out was 'to get rid of trade unionism altogether'. The employers fought for thirty weeks, with the aid of the Free Labour Association's blacklegs, and forced on the ASE a virtually unconditional capitulation. Jefferys (1946) states that 'the longer purses of the employers had won', though this view has been challenged by R. O. Clarke (1957), who claims that 'the reasons for the defeat were not primarily financial.' While one cannot deny the success of the employers in their propaganda battle in the press and in their efforts to sway wider influential opinion – Alfred Marshall wrote in 1925 'I want these people to be beaten at all costs' (cited in Clarke, 1957, p. 134) – Jefferys appears to have got the emphasis right: a major factor in the defeat was finance. The cost of the lock-out rose to almost £30,000 a week, and this exposed the fragility of the union's funds, which stood at £134,000 by the end of the struggle. Nevertheless, money alone does not explain the defeat. A crucial weakness was the failure of the ASE to secure the co-operation of the other sectional unions in the engineering industry, notably the Boiler-makers. However, the underlying reason for the conflict can be seen from the Terms of Settlement imposed by the employers, which required the ASE to drop all its claims over the exclusive control of the new machinery.

However, despite co-operation between the Executive of the ASE and the Engineering Employers' Federation at a national level, the ASE membership as a whole did not accept the radical change in power embodied in the 1898 Terms of Settlement. At first, isolated workshop tactics, involving a general refusal by craftsmen either to train 'handymen' or to rectify ('follow') a handyman's 'bodged' job, were the engineers' response. Subsequently, the district committees on the Clyde and the Tyne defied the National Executive of the ASE and forced increasing delegation of power to the district and the local shop stewards. This bifurcated structure of the Engineering Union, always present in embryo since the foundation of the ASE, was to become crucial after 1914. By 1914 there was considerable variation nationally in the success achieved by these local actions. Jefferys (1946, p. 129) provides evidence that 46 per cent of fitters and 37 per cent of turners were on piece rates – an indication of declining craft control nationally. But in Rochdale only 15 per cent of fitters were on payment-by-result systems by 1914, as a result of the local strength of the ASE in the tight labour market for engineering workers within the town.

The First World War swiftly transformed the situation. It was a war fought with the aid of military hardware that required the total mobilization of the British engineering industry. Many skilled engineering craftsmen volunteered for military service, and their numbers were decimated in the disastrous campaigns of the early war. This loss of manpower exacerbated the labour shortages resulting from expanded production, particularly of munitions. In this context the traditional issues once more came to the fore: new entrants, piece work and the manning of machinery. The state demanded the sacrifice of all customs and practices that inhibited maximum output, thereby attacking at a stroke all the mechanisms of exclusive manning that preceding generations of skilled engineering workers had built up to defend their position in the labour process. The national officers of the ASE made a voluntary declaration in March 1915 that lifted shop restrictions. However, this proved insufficient in practice, mainly because the rank and file objected to its abuse by the employers, but also because of the progressive divorce of the union leadership from the rank and file in the pre-war era, symbolized by the growing influence of syndicalist views among the workforce. As a result of the failure of munitions production to match government expectations, the National Advisory Committee on Output was set up on 17 March 1915. This was promptly followed by the 'Treasury Agreement' of 25 March 1915 between government, employers and unions. Under this agreement the unions gave up the right to strike, agreed to relax all customs which restricted the output of munitions and permitted 'dilution' on government work.

As food prices rose sharply and rents rocketed, profits increased dramatically. These factors precipitated the first general struggle by engineering workers on the Clyde. Traditional grievances also increased. The 'dilutees', generally women working on machinery previously the prerogative of ASE men, were paid on piece rates and, as a consequence of extensive overtime, they were often earning as much as, if not more than, the skilled craftsmen, paid at an hourly rate. The Report of the Committee on Labour Embargoes in 1918 stated the problem clearly: 'A striking difference exists in many cases between the earnings of certain sections of skilled timeworkers and those men and women employed on systems of payment by results who entered their occupations since the beginning of the war as dilutees.'

In June 1917 the National Administrative Council of Shop Stewards was formed and was closely involved in the continued militancy in the industry throughout the last eighteen months of the war and beyond. Hinton (1973) has subjected the 'ambiguities' of the British Shop Stewards Movement to caustic analysis, demonstrating convincingly the inner tensions of the movement. The rationale behind the engineering craftsmens' hostility to the 'managerial prerogative' was the exclusion of management from control over the labour process in order to preserve craft privileges such as wage differentials and autonomy in the sphere of production. This also involved the exclusion of non-skilled, non-members of the ASE from the same processes, since they represented the instrument whereby management could eliminate such privileges. This stance involved a rejection of the fullest rationality of the capitalist mode of production, and in this hostility to the capitalist employers the mass of craftsmen were at one with their revolutionary syndicalist leadership. However, their approach could scarcely be regarded as the epitome of egalitarian socialism, for they had no great interest in the 'dilutees'. Indeed, the rank and file shared this indifference with the ASE leadership, which spent the war period evolving a *modus vivendi* with the general unions in the engineering industry, whereby the latter were cajoled into acceptance of the restoration of a pre-1914 *status quo*.

The onset of the Depression in late 1920 coincided with a 6d per hour wage claim by the newly formed Amalgamated Engineering Union (AEU). The Employers' Federation, after some delay, during which the signs of the severity of the slump became more and more apparent, responded with the demand for a major cut in wages in order to restore international competitiveness. This was reluctantly conceded. Despite the new organizational strength of the AEU, it was in a weak position, since there was growing unemployment among its members and the Federation itself had increased its own membership to over 2000 affiliated firms.

However, the real issue of contention between the employers and the unions centred on the perennial problem of managerial functions. With about 25 per cent of its membership unemployed and faced with the drain of funds throughout 1921 in unemployment benefits, the AEU was in no state to resist the employers' ensuing lock-out. After three months of struggle the membership capitulated, and the following principle was accepted: 'The employers have the right to manage their establishments'. At the end of the conflict the AEU, which held resources of £3.25 million at its inception in July 1920, was left with only £35,572 in the general fund and had been forced to suspend all its benefits apart from sickness and superannuation.

This was an enormous defeat for the AEU. Indeed, the 1922 defeat prompted a series of structural changes in the AEU that appeared to change it from a craft union to an industrial union catering for all grades of engineering workers, including the non-skilled. The first step was taken in October 1922, when sheet-metal workers, pipe fitters, motor mechanics and pipe benders were allowed entry to the union. However, the major step was taken in 1926, when the union was opened to all ranks of male engineering workers.

The development of superficial industrial unionism ran parallel to the progressive collapse of the privileged position of skilled engineering workers. By 1938 the erosion of apprenticeship had advanced considerably, and a union inquiry of that year discovered that only 16 per cent of firms engaged apprentices. The relative decline of skilled men (mainly fitters and turners) can be seen in Table 1. The importance of these figures is that they demonstrate the complexity of the interrelationships between technology and skill. For the rate of increase of semi-skilled operatives was higher between 1921 and 1926 (a period of depressed demand and low investment) than between 1914 and 1921 (a period of expanding demand and massive investment). Clearly, the tendency towards the eradication of skilled engineering manual workers was prompted more by the balance of power in industrial conflict within engineering than by any simple technological determinism.

Table 1 *The proportion of skilled, semi-skilled and unskilled workers in firms belonging to the Engineering Employers' Federation*

Year	Skilled (%)	Semi-skilled (%)	Unskilled (%)
1914	60	20	20
1921	50	30	20
1926	40	45	15
1933	32	57	11

Source: Jefferys (1946, p. 207).

If the national picture for skilled engineering craftsmen was bleak, the position in Rochdale was considerably better. 51 per cent of engineering workers were skilled in 1964, a proportion little different from the 57 per cent of 1935. These ratios are significantly higher than the Engineering Employers' Federation national averages reported by Jefferys above. Far from there being evidence in Rochdale of a secular deskilling of engineering workers, there is a remarkable constancy in the skilled–non-skilled proportion. It might be added that this uneven pattern has persisted into the post-war period in a manner that suggests that the deskilling pundits have misunderstood empirical trends in skilled engineering work in the twentieth century. One piece of evidence for this is that there are still a large number of such workers in Britain. The Donovan Commission (the Royal Commission on Trade Unions and Employers' Associations, 1968) reported that in engineering and electrical goods manufacture nearly 580,000 skilled men were employed in 1966. In December 1972 there were 290,580 section 1 (apprentice-served) members of the Amalgamated Union of Engineering Workers (AUEW) out of a total of 1,146,087. In addition, the upsurge of wage militancy in the Leyland toolroom and among skilled maintenance engineers at Heathrow Airport in the spring of 1977 reminds us that skilled engineering workers are still very salient.

Certain structural features of the engineering industry help to explain the continued strength of skilled manual workers. On the union side, there is a structural bifurcation within the AUEW itself, whereby national minimum rates are negotiated by the national union leadership and the Engineering Employers' Federation. As a result of competition with the Transport and General Workers' Union (TGWU) and the General and Municipal Workers' Union (GMWU) for the organization of the non-skilled, the AUEW negotiates national minimum rates for all grades of work. It is these rates that led Knowles and Robertson (1951) and Turner (1952) to argue that a progressive collapse of differentials was occurring within the post-war engineering industry. Unfortunately, as Hart and MacKay (1975) have shown, the proportion of engineering earnings made up by the national minimum rate has declined progressively since 1918. A larger and larger proportion of engineering earnings during the period between 1918 and 1964 was made up of special piece and bonus rates, all of which were determined by either local officials or, more often, shop stewards. Herein lies the rub. Local union negotiators are drawn overwhelmingly from the ranks of apprentice-trained, skilled engineering workers. It would appear, therefore, that just as after the 1852 and 1897 lock-outs a national defeat for the union was retrieved through local action against local employers, the 1922 defeat again promoted such action. The seriousness of the defeat was indicated by the growth of non-skilled work in engineering, yet the skilled men in Rochdale, through local action, succeeded in regaining considerable ground after the early 1920s and in maintaining their relative position throughout the period between 1930 and 1964.

What, then, of management? Why has it tolerated such a situation? Why has it not deskilled the entire labour force? It is possible to distinguish two kinds of labour process during the period since the 1890s: type A, deskilled, involves lathes set up for specific purposes and operated by non-skilled machinists, a process that might incorporate such mechanisms as an American tool-post or a turret swivel to facilitate mass production; type B, skilled, involves the constant changing of the lathe to perform a series of different tasks by skilled craftsmen. However, given that the machines are identical, it is possible to envisage type A production being done with type B forms of manning. How might this occur? It would appear that the relative power of the contending parties in the local labour market has been crucial. Management in Rochdale requires skilled engineering workers for various tasks in the enterprise, mainly of a maintenance or a 'setting-up' kind. The AUEW in places like Rochdale controls the supply of such men and can therefore insist upon the monopolization by its members of certain tasks and certain kinds of machinery. Management in places like Rochdale is in competition for such labour and cannot say 'Take it or leave it' to local officials or shop stewards. As Jones argues in Chapter 10, other variables, like size of firm, extent of market and degree of the division of labour, are relevant as well. Nonetheless, type B forms of manning have existed in Rochdale where type A production methods could, technically, be used. Disruption by skilled craftsmen, particularly in a tight labour market, constitutes a serious potential cost for employers. Furthermore, as Blackburn and Mann (1979) have demonstrated in their analysis of the labour market for non-skilled workers in Peterborough, employers value reliability and responsibility above all the other characteristics of their labour force and are not always interested in the cheapest possible source of labour. Given these structural features, it is not surprising, first, that employers are prepared to accept a degree of skilled work on processes that could technically be performed by non-skilled men or, second, that the local nature of such bargaining procedures means that the character of skilled work varies from locality to locality. We may hypothesize that the greater the salience of engineering employment in a local labour market and the greater the competition between firms within that market, the higher will be the proportion of skilled engineering workers.

Exclusive controls in the cotton industry

Turning to the cotton industry – as equally important as engineering in industrial centres such as Rochdale, as well as in economic and social history literature – we will concentrate on those occupations in which questions of skill have arisen and attempts at exclusive controls have been made.

The loom overlookers (maintenance men for weaving looms)

The most interesting aspect of the exclusive mechanisms used by overlookers involves the election of new members. The Association of Powerloom Overlookers vote in their Districts on whether to accept into their trade workers nominated by the management. If there is a positive vote, then the individual concerned may enter the union by paying an entrance fee and thereby becomes eligible for training as an overlooker. However, this is not an adequate means for retaining skill, since there are also 'primary' controls over machine maintenance tasks, as is revealed in the 'horizontal' demarcation rules against members of the AUEW and the 'vertical' rules preventing weavers from maintaining their looms. This example points to a more general principle. The maintenance of skill depends upon control over tasks associated with specific processes of production. Particularistic criteria of entry, such as family connections in docking or religious denomination in both the Belfast shipbuilding industry and the Glasgow metal industries, may be termed 'secondary' rules and cannot support skill on their own. In the case of docking there were no primary controls, and consequently it was never a skilled occupation, whereas both shipbuilding and metal working are suffused with 'primary' controls, and skills have been maintained.

*The gaining of skill: the case of the strippers-and-grinders**

The rise to skill by the stripper-and-grinder is the major exception to the fundamental stability of social categories within the working class discussed above. The history of this rise to skill can only be sketched here, since much of the evidence is lacking; indeed, my account relies heavily on Turner's (1962) definitive study of the cotton trade unions. The strippers-and-grinders underwent a serious decline in skill during the period of the transition to factory production and up until the 1870s. Their occupational functions were progressively differentiated from those of their early position as mechanics and supervisors in the cardroom by the elimination of their supervisory roles and the subdivision of their machine-tending functions. As Turner (1962, p. 165) puts it, 'by the 1850s their position differed little from that of general labourers . . . in the mid-'70s their wages were actually falling when those of every other class of cotton operatives were still moving up'. Entry to the occupation was entirely 'free' and the employers kept their position depressed by the use of a permanent surplus of cardroom labourers.

However, by the 1920s the position had changed dramatically. By 1903 they had secured agreements that stipulated the proportion of men to machines, and by 1914 they had erected an 'apprenticeship' barrier around the job. As a corollary to these increasing restrictions, the wage rates paid to strippers-and-grinders rose between the 1880s and the post-1945 era, with the result that they eventually reached parity with the group traditionally most highly paid, the mule-spinners. How was this parity achieved? Again, we must rely on Turner's brief explanation:

But following the successful initiation of the Cardroom Amalgamation, the strippers-and-grinders set about a determined attempt to elevate them-selves. One of the Amalgamation's first acts was to press for (and secure) a preferential wage increase on their behalf; its Second Annual Report noted that '. . . their status and position as skilled artisans has during the year made gigantic strides towards the ideal that increasing numbers think it should be.' And to that aim both the unions and the operatives concerned worked persistently. The two then separate occupations of stripper and grinder were gradually merged from the 1880s on. Their members exploited every minor technical change in carding to increase their responsibility: while according to the Amalgamation's present General Secretary, strippers-and-grinders in

*Strippers-and-grinders strip the carding machines' drums and file and maintain their teeth.

his own original district had taken, in the 1920s, to setting their own machines despite managerial prohibition. [ibid., p. 164]

Clearly, the essential strategy behind the strippers-and-grinders' rise to skill was the limitation of the employers' and managements' control over the manning of machinery. In particular, the strippers-and-grinders' tactics in the work place were strongly supported by their virtual monopolization of union offices within the Cardroom Association.

The mule-spinners

The mule-spinners' exclusive controls involved detailed manning arrangements, control over the maintenance of the mule by the spinner and over subcontracting. The spinner, or 'minder', contracted a price for a piece of work and then paid himself and his two assistants, the 'big' and the 'little' piecers, out of the price contracted in the proportions of 60:40:26.

There has been considerable confusion over the nature of divisions within the working class associated with subcontracting. Stone (1974), in her analysis of the US steel industry, has shown how the employers broke the control of the skilled steel workers over large areas of the labour process at the turn of the century. She contrasts the results of this employers' offensive with an idealized version of the traditional set of labour relations in the industry, writing in terms of the steel employers' attempt to 'break down the basis for unity amongst the steel workers' (p. 20). Yet her own evidence on wage differentials between the skilled subcontractor and his subordinate helpers of between one-sixth and one-half contradicts the allegation of a unified work force. Similarly, Howard's (1973) analysis of the contract system in the iron industry in the third quarter of the nineteenth century fails to emphasize this system as the basis for a structural division within the manual workers in the industry. Yet his evidence on a five-month strike points to the manifestation of this division: 'Two clergymen who intervened were threatened with assassination, but the main anger was directed against non-unionists, particularly the underhands who were being used to break the strike' (p. 420). The implication is clear, as in the cotton-spinning industry, that the unskilled assistants of the skilled subcontractors act as a permanent threat to skill, since in reality many are as technically competent as their skilled superiors.

The incorporation of the piecers into the Spinners' Union had the effect of reinforcing the exclusive mechanisms associated with subcontracting and manning restrictions that have been mentioned. Overall, these mechanisms involved a double exclusion of managerial agents of capital – first, from direct control over the labour process and, secondly, from direct wage negotiations with the piecers themselves. The concentration of artisans in factories achieved the separation of workers from the means of production but did not guarantee strong entrepreneurial control over the labour process. The structures or patterns of rules that were used by the spinners' organizations to establish their control over the labour process were successfully transferred from pre-mechanized to mechanized conditions of production.

Alternative models of the development of capitalist production

These accounts of the social organization of skills as an outcome of the interplay between the power and organization of management and workers not only challenge Braverman's account of deskilling but also imply a critique of his general account of capitalist development; furthermore, they suggest an alternative framework for understanding that development. These implications of the case studies of engineering and cotton are best spelled out by contrasting Braverman's model of the development of the capitalist labour process and deskilling with that alternative.

Braverman's model implies three stages in the development of industrial capitalism and identifies three correlated types of labour process.

1   *Competitive pre-industrial*
    The labour process under this stage can be labelled artisan production. The skills involved are derived from long apprenticeships. There is no separation of mental and manual functions in the work process or of the direct producers from the means of production. There is a large degree of self-employment, and consequently most Journeymen hope to become Masters. Conflict between Masters and Journeymen is sporadic and limited to wages and wage-related issues, such as the overall number of journeymen and apprentices. Examples of such artisans would be masons, shoemakers and millwrights.

2   *Competitive industrial*
    The labour process here can be termed craftsman production.

There is a separation of the direct producers from the means of production but an incomplete separation of conception and execution. Hence, mechanized skills remain. Conflict between craftsmen and employers is endemic and centres on craft controls over machinery. Examples of such craftsmen would be turners and printers.

3   *Oligopolistic industrial*
The labour process can now be termed deskilled. Manual work has become completely routinized as a result of the total separation of conception and execution promoted by 'scientific management'. Examples of such deskilled work would be assembly-line workers and machinists.

The general argument in this developmental scheme is that increased technological development produces decreased skill in a unilinear fashion. Clearly, such a viewpoint is a form of technological determinism, and consequently it is highly misleading, since it leaves out of the model the crucial factor mediating the relationships between technological development and skill in the labour process, namely, organized resistance by occupational groupings within the manual working class. Indeed, it was the differences in forms of worker organization and worker resistance during the transition to highly mechanized factory production in Rochdale that largely determined whether or not specific groups of workers were skilled in Rochdale in the 1850s. This is illustrated by Figure 1. The main difference between the two routes shown in the figure is that in the case of the 'skilled' route factory production preceded automation,[2] whereas in the case of the 'non-skilled' route the two occurred simultaneously. The vital difference between mule-spinners and engineers on the one hand and weavers and cardroom workers on the other is determined by the insertion of the former groups (spinners and engineers) into factories prior to automation. What this meant effectively was that both spinners and engineers were able to maintain the structural supports of their skills through organized resistance to managerial attempts to restructure work processes during the period of automation. The entry of skilled engineers and skilled spinners into factories facilitated the development of collective forms of resistance to managerial strategies that attempted to break these structural supports. This is the significance of the continuous arrows depicted in the 'skilled' route. The workers who

Figure 1 *Skill and the labour process during the period of industrialization in Rochdale*

	'Skilled' route	'Non-skilled' route
Form of transition to industrial capitalism	1 Artisan production 2 Factory production 3 Automatic production in factories (with existing labour)	1 Artisan production 2 Domestic production 3 Automatic factory production (with new labour force)
Examples	Engineers Mule-spinners	Weavers Cardroom workers

were utilized for automatic factory production in spinning and engineering were those who were already working in the factories. The exclusive structures that were developed during the transition to automatic factory production in spinning and in engineering involved strong elements of the previous modes of collective organization.

The 'non-skilled' route involved a radical disjunction between the work force of the former factory and that of the automated factory. The domestic production of the weavers could produce no effective collective resistance and no organized craft unionism because of the individualistic, petty-bourgeois structure of domestic handloom weaving. The work forces that entered the automated weaving sheds and cardrooms were not the pre-existing artisans but a new workforce (predominantly female) with no antecedent craft forms of resistance. Furthermore, the high degree of automation of the new factory looms made the establishment of exclusive controls extremely difficult.

What, then, were these craft forms of resistance? What were the structural supports of craft skill in the labour process that were successfully transmitted to the new mechanized factory environments? My argument has been that they centred on mechanisms of *social exclusion*. More precisely, skilled manual workers in factory milieux are defined by their high degree of social control over the utilization and operation of machinery. These exclusive controls involve a double exclusion, both of management from direct or complete control over the labour process and of other workers who represent a potential threat to such controls. Furthermore, the battles over skill in British industry since the mid-nineteenth century have focused on conflicts between capitalist employers and organized skilled labour over these exclusive arrangements concerned with the manning of machinery.

Conclusions

Essentially, what appears to have been involved in the cases of the engineering and cotton industries are attempts by certain sections of the manual working class to increase their market power as sellers of labour within the framework of the capitalist system of production. What is at stake is an attempt to restrict the power of capital and its management within the work place, to modify certain aspects of the fundamentally asymmetrical relationship of power involved in capitalist production, yet the effort secures such alterations by controls over other manual workers. These involve indirect controls over the supply of labour and direct controls over other workers in production itself.

Apprenticeship and subcontracting are not, in themselves, constitutive of skill. What both have in common is that 'secondary' exclusive mechanisms are used for the 'primary' purpose of restricting managerial controls over the manning of machinery. Clearly, management rarely encounters an industrial *tabula rasa* when it attempts to alter methods of producing. It confronts the organizations of labour, and historically, in the case of skilled manual work, it comes up against the strategies of exclusion focused on manning arrangements that have been erected to maintain and, on occasion, even to create skill. Skill is to be seen as a function of strategies of social exclusion in the work place which succeed in controlling the manning of machinery. However, it is not being suggested that skill is simply an arbitrary social definition. This is because successful exclusion is a function of the relative power of capital and labour. A complex of factors has been involved in the successful exclusion tactics of skilled manual workers, which can be analysed only in terms of the relative strengths of local skilled manual labour and capitalist employers. Organization by skilled manual labour around the mechanisms of exclusion is clearly necessary, and in this respect sectional organization in factories prior to widespread mechanization was certainly of crucial historical significance in the initial maintenance of exclusive practices.

However, what has been central to, and crucial for, the success of these sectional organizations of skilled manual workers in their struggles to preserve their exclusive controls over work processes is their strong organization and (from the perspective of bargaining) the relatively weak structure of local capitalist employers – in other words, the nature of the local labour market. In Rochdale there has always been a relatively tight labour market for engineering workers during the period under review. This is due in part both to the large number of engineering firms in the town and to the proximity of other industrial centres like Oldham and Bury, which have had the effect of promoting keen competition among engineering employers for certain types of engineering labour, especially those skilled workers able to maintain and 'set up' the various machines. The tightness of the local labour market has facilitated high levels of unionization among engineering workers. It is the conjunction of certain scarce skills and strong union organization that has enabled skilled workers to extend the boundaries of exclusion and, in particular, to extend the degree of control over the manning of machinery.

Management or design engineers face contradictory forces in their identification of skilled and non-skilled tasks. First, there is the tendency for management to rationalize work practices in order to extend its control over production and enhance predictability. Second, there is the opposite tendency for organized labour to extend the scope of skilled work. The empirical outcome in any specific case is determined by the interplay of these two forces. In Rochdale the strength of the AUEW and the need for skilled engineering workers to fulfil certain tasks has led to a situation in which skilled craftsmen control the performance of tasks undertaken by the non-skilled in other engineering centres.

In the cotton industry the same factors appear to have determined the boundaries of skill. For both skilled spinners and strippers-and-grinders used their powerful trade union organizations to confront management in a competitive labour market. The multiplicity of cotton firms and the 100 per cent trade-union organization of such skilled occupational groups as mule-spinners, overlookers, tape-sizers and strippers-and-grinders meant that much the same forces were at work as in engineering.

Braverman's model of the relationships between technological change, class structure and skill cannot be supported by evidence from Rochdale. Changes in the content of jobs do not necessarily produce isomorphic effects on the class structure. The deskilling of mule-spinners derived more from the collapse of the cotton industry in the 1950s than from the workshop tactics of capitalist employers. In engineering the battle for skill has been a prominent and persistent feature of workshop relations.

The exclusive practices discussed above have long characterized the British class structure. Far from being merely a post-1945 aspect of class relations, such practices have existed since the mid nineteenth century and even before. The real significance of skill within the manual working class cannot be grasped from aggregate data; we must examine the local labour markets and local industrial relations structures where most of the battles over skill are fought. There is clearly a need for more research into such areas, but if it is to be adequate, it must examine the real bases of skill in the work place.

It should be clear now that deskilling involves not technical change *per se* but social changes, whereby management gains control over the manning of machinery. This 'prerogative' is in no way guaranteed by capitalist ownership rights. Technology does not simply mean machinery around which there is a given 'logic' of working or paratechnical relations; it involves negotiated structures of producing. Technology, as opposed to 'technicality', is dependent upon the conflict between agents of capital and representatives of sections of workers.

Here lies the contemporary relevance of this paper. Recent industrial conflicts on the railways (ASLEF) in Fleet Street (the NGA), in construction (the Laggers) and in the engineering industry reveal the persistence of the battle for skill. Management attempts to impose its prerogative, while the organizations of skilled manual workers continue to struggle for the continuation of the exclusive structural supports of their skill itself. Far from having a deskilled, homogeneous working class, Britain possesses a sectionalized working class, among which the battle for skill remains an endemic feature of social relations.

6 Skill and the survival of apprenticeship

Charles More

The main purpose of this paper is to highlight the ambiguity of the term 'skill' and to see how far historical evidence can help in the restoration of an unequivocal usage for the term, at least in the context of late nineteenth-century Britain. The conclusions of this discussion will then be related to the problem of deskilling.

The ambiguity arises because skill can be conceived of either as a necessary input to the efficient production of goods or as a social artefact which comes into being through the artificial delimitation of certain work as skilled, the purpose of this delimitation being the reservation of certain kinds of work for those who have also acquired the label 'skilled', thus ensuring for them high wages, better chances of employment or some other advantage.

Before considering either the ambiguity of skill or the problem of deskilling, I should briefly mention that whether or not it is accepted that skill is needed for efficient production, there is a lesser ambiguity in the term which should be resolved first. Does skill mean the ability to perform complex manual operations, the knowledge of materials and tools, or some combination of these attributes? While it is true that skill is often used to mean merely the former ability, it is fair to say that most people would accept that a skilled worker (as opposed to a semi-skilled worker) should possess both attributes. Braverman quotes approvingly the following description of skilled work, a description which would seem generally acceptable:

skill covers his [the skilled worker's] ability to imagine how things would appear in final form if such and such tools and materials were used . . . he can estimate accurately both aesthetic appeal and functional utility, organize his tools, his power and his materials in a way which accomplishes his task and gains him livelihood and recognition . . . [Braverman, 1974, p. 444 note; see also Seymour, 1967, pp: 159–60]

The problem we are faced with is how far workers in modern industry who are recognized as skilled, through the serving of an apprenticeship or some other accepted route to skill such as seniority, actually need their skill, and indeed how far they have acquired it. For it may be possible for workers to erect controls which prevent a proper assessment of the work they do and which thus make it possible that the workers neither need skill nor even possess it.

The belief that workers do not need to be skilled (or, in other words, that skill has been socially constructed) has been most influentially stated by H. A. Turner (1962). Turner is concerned primarily, with devices for delimiting skill, such as seniority rules in the cotton industry, by which mule-spinners became artificially delimited from the next grade, the big piecers, who in fact did much the same work; but he extends his analysis to apprenticeship: 'The sharp demarcation between skilled and unskilled workers in, say, the building and engineering industries is largely a product of the traditional apprenticeship system, by reference to which those who may perform "skilled" tasks are distinguished from those who may not' (Turner, 1962, p. 111). Turner does not consider, however, that such workers actually lack skill. On the contrary, he points out that employers will be concerned to ensure that workers who are paid skilled wages do possess some genuine skill, and that the time spent in apprenticeship, in spite of its basic rationale as a method of 'socially constructing' skill, is a period during which genuine skill can be acquired. Turner's theory does allow for the existence of workers skilled in the way that Braverman described, therefore, but it is of fundamental importance to realize that, in Turner's view, modern factory production does not actually require such workers, although if they exist, they are put to use (Turner, 1962, p. 111).

The reason why apprenticeship in particular has persisted as a method of delimiting skill is attributed by Turner to historical factors, and it is on these that I wish to concentrate. Turner argues that apprenticeship was the normal method of training for many handicraft occupations before the industrial revolution and was maintained by employers because, apart from any other advantages, it restricted entry to their own ranks. In some trades, such as printing, which were still conducted by handicraft methods even after the onset of the industrial revolution, these constraints still existed, and 'apprenticeship . . . suffered no direct attack by employers, and survived naturally'. But in large-scale industry the apprenticeship system became 'an obstacle to the spread (and hence cheapening) of skills'; employers became hostile to it, and the 'journeymen were driven to assume the burden of its enforcement alone. . . .' Turner sees the actual mechanism by which this enforcement was made effective as hinging on the salience of woodworking crafts (such as millwrighting and patternmaking), to the early engineering industry: through these crafts, for which apprenticeship was the norm, the latter institution was introduced to the engineering industry, where it continued to flourish (Turner, 1962, p. 195).

Although there has not been much study of what apprenticeship in pre-factory handicraft trades really involved, Turner's account of it seems perfectly reasonable. What we are interested in is the mechanism by which apprenticeship became transferred to large-scale industry, notably engineering, although it flourished in some other industries, such as shipbuilding. If it is to be accepted that apprenticeship was enforced against the wishes of employers, then certain implications which Turner does not explore must also be accepted. I will now consider what these implications are.

It will be helpful first to outline the mechanism by which apprenticeship acts, or might act, as a method for socially constructing skill. Its success in this role depends upon the maintenance of certain workshop practices, which employers, in their ideal world, will not accept. Therefore it must be assumed that these practices are enforced unilaterally by the journeymen (that is, the workers who had already served their apprenticeship). These practices will involve, first, the definition and limitation of the types of work which non-apprenticed workers are allowed to perform; otherwise employers will always prefer to employ such workers, who earn less than journeymen. (It is true that Turner argues that employers will attempt to make the latter earn their higher wages by creating work for them which does require genuine skill, but this only comes about as a result of the social construction of skill; originally, it must be assumed, the work could have been divided up among less skilled workers.) The second implication of Turner's argument is that once some work has been defined as skilled, then the journeymen must make sure that not too many workers are available to do it. If there is a large surplus of eligible workers, then the pressure on wage rates would be such as to render the maintenance of a skilled differential very difficult. Journeymen have, therefore, to enforce the limitation of apprentice numbers so that the number of new journeymen is never excessive.

We now have to consider how journeymen enforce these workshop practices – or, to be accurate, how they enforced them in the nineteenth century, the period when, according to Turner, employers in large-scale industry actively attempted to do away with apprenticeship. The fundamental point to be remembered here is that in Turner's model the workshop practices concerned – the reservation of certain work for journeymen only and the limitation of apprentices – are inefficient. Employers might mitigate the inefficiency by utilizing the journeymen's real skills as effectively as possible, but the fact remains that it must be more expensive to employ 'skilled' workers, paid at higher rates, than to make use of those with less skill.

This analysis makes it clear that journeymen, according to the logic of Turner's argument, would have to impose on employers practices that are, in economic terms, inefficient. But in a market in which some employers are able to purchase their factors of production at the lowest price, the employers who are not able to do so will eventually be driven out of business. Turner's argument implies, therefore, that no (or very few) nineteenth-century employers were able to purchase labour at the lowest price available. The journeymen must have controlled all or most of the supply of labour and hence were able to dictate their own terms in connection with its price. To put the argument in a less theoretical way: in a relatively free market some employers would have been able to employ less skilled men and therefore would have enjoyed a competitive advantage over those forced to employ skilled men at higher wage rates, thus driving the latter out of business. Therefore we must assume that journeymen were able to prevent the great majority of employers from doing this, presumably because most workers belonged to unions and/or because sanctions like blacking could be made effective and could bring employers into line.

The evidence related to union power, the density of union membership and union tactics suggests that for the nineteenth century this analysis is not supportable. Unions were not strong enough to enforce inefficient working practices on the great majority of employers. In 1861, for instance, an estimate of union density among north-eastern engineering workers put it at between 12 per cent and 42 per cent depending upon the trade; nationally, a reliable estimate puts the absolute maximum of unionized skilled engineering workers at 50 per cent at the same date (J. F. Clarke, 1966, p. 66; Jefferys and Jefferys, 1947, p. 30). Furthermore, we have to remember that in Turner's model employers were technically able to use less skilled labour – and, indeed, would find it more efficient to do so. Yet unionization among unskilled workers was notoriously weak until the second decade of the twentieth century, suggesting that if employers had really been free from technical constraints on the use of less skilled workers, there would have been nothing to stop the much more extensive use of the latter than was in fact implemented.

A variety of sources make it clear that the proportion of skilled workers in apprentice-taking industries remained very high. The Engineering Employers' Federation issued figures suggesting that before the First World War some 60 per cent of workers were rated and paid as skilled (Jefferys, 1946, p. 207). My own calculations, based on the 1906 wage census, suggest about 50 per cent (More, 1980, p. 186, Table 9.1). In construction work it has been suggested that the 50 per cent of the labour force who were skilled in the inter-war period constituted a lower proportion than before the First World War (Richardson and Aldcroft, 1968, p. 120 and note 2).

Union tactics also suggest that unions were not – and did not feel themselves to be – in a position to construct skill on a large scale. A common strike tactic in the nineteenth century was the 'strike in detail', the removal of unionized workers from an employer against whom the union had a grievance (Clegg, Fox and Thompson, 1964, pp. 8–9). Far from suggesting that skill was socially constructed, the use of this method suggests the opposite: such tactics could only have been effective if the workers did exercise genuine skill which it was not easy for the employer to replace. Unions used this 'strike in detail' tactic for several reasons, one of which was to minimize public awareness of the union's role; another, almost certainly, was their realization that large-scale action against employers was rarely effective because of union weakness. Although there were occasions when such large-scale action seems to have met with partial success, as in the well-known dispute over the manning of machines at Oldham in 1852, which ended with a compromise giving journeymen the right to work on certain machines in the future, there were other disputes for which this was not the case (Fraser, 1974, p. 100). The iron founders' attempt to impose apprenticeship limitation met with failure in the mid-century, as did a two-year long engineers' strike in Sunderland, over the same issue, in the 1880s (Fyrth and Collins, 1959, pp. 59–60; Jefferys, 1946, pp. 102–3).

If we accept that unions were not strong enough to enforce apprenticeship unilaterally, then we have to explain its persistence by looking at other factors. This is not to deny that unions, in certain trades at least, wished to retain apprenticeship and to make it effective: the fact that they were willing to strike over the issue demonstrates this. It is merely to note that this is not by itself a satisfactory explanation of why apprenticeship survived. To explain its survival we need to look at two other points: the attitudes of employers towards apprenticeship and the technological reasons why apprenticeship remained a valid method of training.

It is not hard to explain why employers wished to take on apprentices. Since apprentice wages were low (starting in the 1900s at around 5 shillings per week and rising in the last year of apprenticeship, with variations according to region and occupation, to around 15 shillings), employers could in theory make a substantial profit out of apprentices by using them as unskilled labour. Boys usually began their apprenticeships at the age of 14 or 15 and remained apprentices for between five and seven years, so for the last two years or so they could do adult work. Since even an unskilled adult male earned 20 shillings per week or thereabouts, the employers' profit from apprentice labour was potentially considerable.

While employers may have wanted to make a profit by thus exploiting apprentices it would hardly have suited the apprentice himself. For at the end of his time, having forgone the higher wages he might have earned elsewhere, he would be turned out on to the labour market without a worthwhile skill. It is likely that as long as there was any choice in the work available, the scope for employers to exploit apprentices in this way was limited. When employers tried to retain apprenticeship in deskilled occupations, such as pottery and hosiery in the 1840s, there is evidence that apprentices broke their contracts and went where they could earn a wage which fully reflected their value to the employer (Royal Commission on the Employment of Children, 1843, pp. 219, 1156). And although breaking an apprenticeship agreement was technically illegal, it seems that the legal sanctions against doing so were rarely enforced (Board of Trade, 1915, p. 55).

We must accept, therefore, that where apprenticeship survived it can only have done so because the apprentice learned something of value, so that at the end of his time he would be worth the higher wages which he would receive as a journeyman. Consequently, the employer was obliged to teach the apprentice. How could the provision of a reasonable training be reconciled with the making of a profit (or with not making a loss) out of employing apprentices?

In the eighteenth century and earlier it had been common for employers to take a sum of money called a premium at the beginning of the apprenticeship; with this they could cover the cost of providing training. But by the late nineteenth century this practice was unusual among ordinary trade apprentices, and the only apprentices who paid large premiums were those who expected to receive a much wider training than was usual, embracing managerial and commercial aspects of the work (Jackson, 1909, pp. 1078–82).

In spite of the decline of premiums, the apparently incompatible aims of making a profit out of, and providing a training for, apprentices could still be reconciled. The key to this reconciliation is the fact that the usual apprenticeship period of between five and seven years was longer than was required to make a boy reasonably competent at his trade. This is not to suggest that trades were easy to learn: usually an apprentice would spend the first six months or so as an errand boy, experience which had some value as he would become acquainted with the different types of work, the names of tools and other practical information; after that, at least in engineering and woodworking, he would spend two or three years learning the work. At first he would work with a journeyman, doing the simpler jobs, practising the more complex and just watching; later he might work by himself under the supervision of the foreman. For the last two years or so he was reasonably independent and could do work of considerable value to his employer, although it should be added that the finer points of some trades might take many years to master fully (More, 1980, pp. 139–42). The process was summed up by J. M. Allen, managing director of the large engineering firm of Hawthorn Leslie:

In any of the many trades embraced in the term 'Engineering', the first two years of apprenticeship are of little value to any but the apprentice himself. . . . By the end of the third year he is becoming of some value to his employer, and it is during the fourth and fifth years that the benefit of his help is felt and some return obtained for the earlier years of apprenticeship. [Board of Trade, 1915, p. 130]

The fact that after three years or so of training an apprentice was worth more than the value of the wages he actually received would suggest that apprentices might have been tempted to leave in search of better wages elsewhere – as we have seen, they did so in certain industries in the mid-century. There were two constraints on their doing this, apart from the law, which does not seem to have played much of a part. On the one hand, employers were reluctant to take on apprentices who had served part of their time elsewhere; in some areas employers' associations had district agreements not to do this (More, 1980, p. 77). A more compelling constraint, however, was that if apprentices did not serve their full time they would not receive their 'lines', the document issued at the end of an apprenticeship which was the guarantee to future employers that the apprentice was fully skilled. Apprentice failure rates, therefore, seem to have been fairly low, a fact that was important to employers if apprenticeship was to be profitable from their point of view (Board of Trade, 1915, p. 55).

The reasons why employers were willing to take apprentices cannot alone explain the continuation of apprenticeship on such a large scale in industries like engineering. (It is a fair guess that at any one time in the 1900s there were about 90,000 apprentices in this industry alone; see More, 1980, ch. 5, app. 1). If apprenticeship had merely been one of a number of alternative methods of training for skilled work of equal merit, then it is unlikely that it could have survived, for other methods of training generally offered higher wages to young employees and therefore would have been more attractive to them. It is true that even in trades in which apprenticeship was the dominant method of training, such as the skilled engineering trades, there were workers who learned simply by picking the work up gradually (More, 1980, pp. 113–14). But such workers were in a minority, and the reason is clear when we look at the content of the work.

The pre-First World War engineering industry in Britain was marked by the heterogeneity of its products (Saul, 1967; Ministry of Munitions, 1922, vol. 4, part 4, p. 74). This heterogeneity had two implications which are relevant here. First, it was expensive and uneconomic for manufacturers to invest in large numbers of special-purpose machines which could only be used for certain lines of production, and thus it was necessary for their workers to master a number of techniques on general-purpose machines. Second, the use of general-purpose machines without special jigs meant that the amount of manual skill needed was very considerable although possibly less than had been needed in the 1880s (Rowe, 1928, pp. 90–2; Rolt, 1971, p. 87). The number of techniques that an apprentice turner was expected to master is illustrated by the following list (taken from Board of Trade, 1915, p. 127):

1 Drawing office and machine tool store
2 Small slotting machine, helps at marking-off table
3 Small planing machine
4 Larger planing machine
5 Lathe for turning shop tools
6 Lathe for turning belts, pillars, hand wheels, etc.
7 Small centre lathe
8 Larger centre lathe
9 Chuck lathe   } In all these turning
10 Larger chuck lathe   a number of different objects
11 Screw-cutting lathe

It should be noted that while the evidence presented above relates to the engineering industry, similar arguments could be advanced in relation to a high proportion of occupations in the building industry (More, 1980, pp. 138–40, 157–8; Stinchcombe, 1959).

The acquisition of knowledge of a variety of different techniques and of considerable manual skill in each of these techniques was therefore a necessity for the apprentice. To acquire manual skill demands practice, and it is very difficult, in the early stages, to turn out saleable work as well. Thus an apprentice in his first few years was, as we have already noted, a cost to his employer, who had to devise some mechanism for recouping this cost; apprenticeship provided this mechanism by ensuring that the trainee continued in service after he became skilled in order to repay his employer. We can contrast this method of training with that for other types of skilled work, as in process industries like steel-, tinplate-, and paper-making, where the emphasis was on knowledge (for example, of temperatures and the composition of the raw materials) and not primarily on manual skills. A trainee could gradually acquire this knowledge while at the same time performing other useful work and hence could earn higher wages than an apprentice. It is worth noting in this context that in paper-making, where apprenticeship had been strictly maintained by one of the strongest of the early unions, it broke down almost completely once the machine process was introduced (Coleman, 1958, ch. 10; More, 1980, p. 116). If unions had been the dominant force behind the retention of apprenticeship, then it is hard to see why they failed to retain it in this industry. But if instead we see the logic of the productive process as the key to the survival of apprenticeship, then it is clear why in paper-making, where it was no longer appropriate, it faded away.

Apprenticeship survived because it served the interests of employers and of skilled workers and because of the technological rationality of the industries in which it remained important. To employers the taking on of apprentices yielded a profit – or at least it did not involve them in a loss – but it was not so easy to make a profit on apprentices that over-production was encouraged, because the employer had to provide a genuine training; to journeymen apprenticeship remained a convenient method of delimiting skill. The thrust of my argument, however, is that workers' interests, and such action as was taken in support of these interests, were the weakest forces making for the retention of apprenticeship rather than, as Turner would have it, the strongest, although an exception to this will be mentioned below. Finally, apprenticeship survived because it was the most efficient form of training for industries like engineering and woodworking, which still demanded all-round manual skill.

In certain circumstances worker influence could be a major factor in delimiting skill. This happened most frequently where the productive process involved team-work rather than individual work. Very often in these circumstances several members of the team might exercise some skill, but only one or two would receive skilled wages. The social construction of skill in these cases was at the expense not so much of employers as of other members of the team.

More often than not skill in such teams would be delimited not by apprenticeship but by some other method, such as seniority. Thus in the case of mule-spinners in the cotton industry there were usually three workers in each team: a 'little' piecer (a boy earning a low wage), a 'big' piecer (a youth or young man earning a very modest wage) and a skilled spinner (earning a high wage); promotion occurred when there was a vacancy in a higher grade. As far as real skill was concerned, the relatively limited skill that was required, compared with engineering, was possessed more or less equally by the 'big' piecers and the spinners, and the latter gained their high wages at the expense of the former.

In rare cases, however, apprenticeship did serve to delimit skill in this artificial way. In shipbuilding, for instance, apprenticeship was the normal method of recruitment for skilled work, including trades like riveting, which were not in reality highly skilled (the latter taking only about six months to learn). Again, this was team work, a team usually consisting of two riveters, a 'holder-up' (who was a less well-paid tradesman) and a 'rivet boy' (who was sometimes, in spite of his name, a low-paid adult worker). The riveters could and did earn high wages, at the expense of the other members of the team. In these circumstances it was not necessarily in the employers' interests to do away with apprenticeship, as long as they could be sure that no other employers were undercutting them by employing non-apprenticed riveters at lower rates of pay. And here it was the effectiveness of the riveters' union – the extremely powerful Boiler-makers and Iron Shipbuilders – that was almost certainly a major factor in the retention of apprenticeship. It should be added that, as has already been suggested, the shipbuilding trades were atypical, and that the probable reason for their atypicality, the strength of the Boilermakers' Union, has never been properly investigated (More, 1980, pp. 161–3).

A number of conclusions can be drawn from the evidence presented so far which are salient to any discussion of skill. The first and most important is that, at least in this period, skill should be regarded primarily as a product of the technological rationality of industrial production and not as 'socially constructed'. Whether or not this holds true of other periods is another question, although it is worth quoting Dunlop (1964) in his review of Turner's *Trade Union Growth, Structure and Policy*: 'Technology and the economics of factor combination fundamentally determine job classification.' Of course, Dunlop admits that 'the rules of apprenticeship and the shop may affect the duties of an occupation to some extent,' and it was noted earlier in this paper how team work in particular gives opportunities for the 'construction' of skill (Dunlop, 1964, p. 89). The fact that many firms, and in some cases departments of firms (such as maintenance departments), may to some extent be sheltered from market forces should also be taken into account. But such sheltered positions – the product, perhaps, of favourable factor supplies or, in the case of individual departments, the internal politics of the firms themselves – cannot last for ever. One of the hallmarks of apprenticeship in engineering and woodworking in Britain is that it has lasted for a very long time.

If technology does have the power to be the most potent force for dictating skill requirements in industry, there are certain implications which are pertinent to the deskilling controversy. Before discussing these, it should be noted that both Marx and Braverman also seem to have a technological orientation towards skill. Marx stresses that the development of machine processes of production, which he calls 'machinofacture', leads to an 'equalization or levelling down of the work which the assistants of the machinery have to perform', and he also notes the emergence, again for technical reasons, of a small class of highly trained maintenance and scientific workers (Marx, 1976, p. 448). Braverman's failure to recognize the potential of workers to 'construct' skill is commented on in several chapters in this book, notably Chapter 5, although it is true that Braverman modifies Marx's determinism by stressing management's ideological attachment to deskilling through Taylorism (see Chapter 1).

The question we have to answer is why a Marxist model of technological change involves deskilling, whereas our picture of the development of engineering does not, or at least does not to the same extent or in the same way (see also More, 1980, ch. 9). It could be argued that this is because engineering remained for a long time in a semi-handicraft state, needing a considerable amount of manual skill, which could best be acquired by apprenticeship. As the amount of manual skill that was needed declined, so did the rationale for apprenticeship, leaving its existence in the post-First World War period to be explained by a 'social construction' model of skill, as it is explained by Penn in Chapter 5 (although he accepts that strategic position in the production process and hence, by implication, technology have a part to play).

I would suggest however, that although the amount of manual skill needed in engineering has declined, the decline becoming particularly noticeable in the late nineteenth century, this has not necessarily made apprenticeship a technologically obsolete method of training, retained only as a result of tradition, trade-union pressure or some other 'social' factor. The findings of a careful study of skill in the engineering industry undertaken in the 1920s found that as manual skill declined, the amount of technical knowledge needed tended to increase (Rowe, 1928, pp. 97–102). Furthermore, this knowledge was not the sort of craft knowledge which workers could pick up as they went along but was knowledge which could only be taught formally or semi-formally. It seems reasonable to suggest that apprenticeship has retained an economic rationale as a period during which adolescents can spend time not on productive work but on the training necessary to make them productive in the future, 'paying' for this training by foregoing the higher earnings they might obtain elsewhere.

If this is the case and if engineering work retains a considerable and genuine skill content, then it would appear that the prediction that deskilling would occur as industries changed from manufacture (that is, production with hand tools) to 'machinofacture' has not come to pass and that Braverman considerably exaggerates the actual changes that have occurred. In an early example of mass production, the cotton industry, skill was indeed limited, and in so far as it existed it did so partly through its artificial delimitation by groups like the spinners; but many industries did not and do not use mass-production techniques because they are inappropriate. In the engineering industry, for instance, the bulk of the work before the First World War involved one-off or small-batch production, and even after the war only sections of the industry, such as motor vehicle manufacture went over to mass production. In small-batch production the variety of the work makes it much less susceptible to routinization and deskilling. It may be suggested, therefore, that predictions about necessary tendencies towards deskilling are invalid, partly because of social factors (see Chapters 5 and 10) but also because technological developments do not universally contain within themselves deskilling tendencies.

We can summarize our arguments as follows. The strength of apprenticeship in the nineteenth century can be explained, for the most part, by the continued demand for apprentice-trained workers; and this demand arose because of the nature of technology in the industries concerned rather than as a result of pressure from trades unions or other groups. The implications of this are that altering demands for skill, at least in the nineteenth-century arose primarily through the agency of technological change. This need not, of course, necessarily be the case in all periods, and the increased power of trades unions in the twentieth century, together with the withdrawal of more and more sections of industry from the unfettered constraints of the market, must increase the possibility that some 'social construction' of skill will take place.

Finally, it should be noted that there is no real evidence of widespread deskilling in the nineteenth century. It might tentatively be suggested that this was because the level of skill is (broadly speaking) inversely related to the number of units of goods produced and that the persistence of one-off or batch production therefore led to a continuing demand for skilled workers in many industries.

7 Deskilling and changing structures of control[1]

Craig Littler

Braverman's concept of deskilling has four dimensions: first, the process whereby the shop-floor worker loses the right to design and plan work (that is, the divorce of planning from working); second, the fragmentation of work into meaningless segments; third, the redistribution of tasks among unskilled and semi-skilled labour, associated with labour cheapening; fourth, the transformation of work organization from the craft system to modern, Taylorized forms of labour control. All these processes are linked; however, in this chapter I will focus primarily on the fourth and will examine the structures of shop-floor control in late nineteenth-century British industry and the slow transition to a semi-bureaucratized labour process.

One point should be clarified. Throughout this chapter the first three processes identified above will be termed deskilling processes, while the fourth will be conceptualized as a transformation in the structure of control.

This chapter will focus particularly on a critique of Braverman's idealized conception of the traditional craft worker. He postulates a simple transition from craft control to Taylorite forms of work organization, which makes no allowance for an uneven pattern of rationalization and mechanization (Littler, 1978). I shall argue that a simple model of craft deskilling is untenable and that an empirical investigation of the institutionalization of Taylorism in Britain leads to a different and more complex picture.

In effect, Braverman offers a convergence theory. He perceives an inevitable, immanent tendency within capitalism. This mechanistic view ignores the differences between capitals and societies. From our point of view, we need to remember that Braverman is talking largely about the USA; his arguments cannot be transposed directly to Britain. I shall argue that the context of industrial change and the periodization of change were different in the two countries.

Nineteenth-century workshop relations

There are two contradictory models of nineteenth-century workshop relations which are widespread. First, there is the 'Old Wilfred Workmaster' view. This assumes direct, personal relationships between an owner-manager and all the workers, associated with an authoritarian, centralized form of control (amidst numerous examples of this view are Kynaston-Reeves and Woodward, 1970, pp. 53–4; Litterer, 1961, pp. 469–70; and R. Edwards, 1979, pp. 25–7). This model of simple, direct control, with its overtones of the heroic entrepreneur, is historically misleading because it was applicable only to a minority of firms. This type of control we will term 'entrepreneurial control'.

Second, in total or partial contradiction to the 'Old Wilfred Workmaster' conception is the assumption of widespread craft control. It is this second model of relationships that permeates Braverman's work. It is the transfer of job knowledge from the crafts and its monopolization by management that Braverman sees as the essence of Taylorism and modern capitalism. The assumption of craft control ignores considerable differences between industries and indeed, between craft and non-craft workers in the workshop. In this and the next section I will suggest a more adequate means of conceptualizing nineteenth-century structures of control over task performance, which highlights some of these differences.

There was no general theory of organization during the industrial revolution. There was a surprising lack of management theory, especially in relation to labour and labour control (Pollard, 1968, pp. 296–301; see also Hobsbawm, 1964, p. 352; Payne, 1974, pp. 32–3; Bendix, 1974, pp. 202–3). This was partly because of the widespread avoidance of direct employer/employee relationships. As Hobsbawm (1964, p. 297) points out: 'Capitalism in its early stages expands and to some extent operates, not so much by directly subordinating large bodies of workers to employers, but by subcontracting exploitation and management.' Thus the immediate employer of many workers was not the large capitalist but an intermediate, internal subcontractor who had a contractual relationship with the overarching employer and in turn was an employer of labour himself. The employer provided the fixed capital, supplied the raw material and much of the working capital and controlled the sale of the finished product. The contractor hired and fired, supervised the work process and received a lump sum from the employer for completed work. The contractor's income consisted of the difference between the wages he paid to his employees or gang (plus the cost of any working capital he might provide) and the payments from the employer. (Schloss, 1898, pp. 180–1; Gospel, 1982; cf. Buttrick, 1952, pp. 205–6).

Typically, the role of the contractor involved control over the following:

Personnel functions

(a) hiring and firing
(b) discipline and supervision
(c) wage payment and the determination of other terms and conditions
(d) training

Production functions

(e) task allocation
(f) work methods
(g) production planning (in so far as there was any planning, this was usually the responsibility of the contractor).

In addition, the contractor was sometimes responsible for his own financial control and much of his own purchasing. This enabled the capitalist to shift part of the risk of operating onto the contractors: the capital risks were spread, as well as the managerial problems. In practice, the extent of the autonomy of the internal contractor varied between industries and over time, so that no one concept can capture adequately all the transitional and hybrid situations that arose.[2]

Apart from the variation in autonomy, the institution of internal contract varied along a skill dimension. The basis of the contracted work group could vary from a skill or craft to unskilled gang work. Related to this skill basis is the size of the work group. As Pollard points out, most industries varied between 'having a small number of subcontractors, as in mining, or large numbers of skilled workers as subcontractors each employing only a few child or unskilled assistants' (Pollard, 1968, p. 59; also Hobsbawm, 1964, pp. 299–300).

In general, there were three main types of internal contract, which can be distinguished in terms of traditional patterns of relationship.

1   Familial relations and familial control. For example, in cotton-

spinning the skilled spinners were put in charge of machines on the understanding that they paid and recruited their own child assistants and that the employer did not deal with the assistants at all. Initially, the children employed were the spinner's own family, and this reproduced the conditions of domestic labour (Smelser, 1959). It is important to note that the children and helpers were not necessarily learning the trade.

2   The master craftsman role and craft control. A good example of craft control is provided by the nineteenth-century ironworks. The ironmaster paid and recruited his own men and determined hours of work, discipline and even the organization of production. Moreover, whenever an ironmaster moved to another ironworks, he took all his workers with him (Pollard, 1968, p. 201). The primary commitment was to the master and not to any wider organization or social group. Similarly, in shipbuilding the shipwrights employed their own gangs, and apprentices were bound to the craftsmen, not the yard owners (Pollard and Robertson, 1979, p. 164).

3   Team work in a gang with a gang boss. This form of work organization is exemplified by the docks and the well-known butty system in the coal mines. (For the docks, see Smith and Nash, 1889. For the butty system, see A. J. Taylor, 1960; Goffee, 1977; and Storm-Clark, 1977). The gang bosses tended to assimilate their position to that of craftsmen, but it is a mistake to see these work-group relationships in terms of craft control: the reality was different. The position of the 'ganger' was more vulnerable and was often based as much on extraneous factors, such as his personal relationship with his employer, as on intrinsic, skill-based factors.[3]

The bases of authority were different in the three cases, but all three relationships were founded on legitimated dependence and subordination, and these sets of relationships were institutionalized in nineteenth-century British industry within the mechanism of internal contact.

How widespread were internal contract systems in the nineteenth century? It seems difficult to exaggerate the extent of some forms of contracting. Pollard (1968) concludes that internal contract was prevalent throughout the entire range of industries, and Hobsbawm (1964) echoes this view. The system was particularly well entrenched in textiles, mining, ironworks and shipbuilding.

As with any other social institution, we need to understand the reinforcing advantages of internal contract for capitalists. These were fivefold. First, it was a flexible mechanism that enabled the work system to meet 'sharp fluctuations in demand without having to carry a permanent burden of overhead expenditure' entailed by a large office staff (Hobsbawm, 1964, p. 298). Second, not only did it spread capital risks, but it enabled capital risks to be determined in the first place: the employer was saved from numerous complex cost calculations. Thus systems of internal contract acted as a substitute for accounting. Third, internal contract provided financial incentives and a path of upward mobility for key groups of workers. Fourth, it bypassed the awkward fact that many employers lacked technical skills and technical knowledge. Finally, it was the agency of effort stabilization and task allocation. In general, internal contract systems and decentralized modes of control provided an historical solution to the contradictions between the increasing size of firms and simple entrepreneurial control (cf. R. Edwards, 1979, p. 34).

What are the implications of the widespread existence of systems of internal contract in nineteenth-century British industry for processes of deskilling? The major point is that internal contract acted as a means of job control, a structural support for craft and non-craft skill. In so far as the subcontractor controlled hiring and firing, he could use this power to maintain exclusiveness and to control access to jobs (Hobsbawm, 1964, p. 299). Similarly, his control over task allocation and his power to make decisions affecting production increased his strategic position on the shop floor.

Moreover, many subcontracted work groups maintained either a skill hierarchy or a hierarchy based on length of attachment to the 'ganger'. For example, in the flint glass industry the basic work team was called a 'chair'. It consisted of a 'gaffer', a 'servitor', a 'footworker' and a boy or 'taker-in'. Early in the nineteenth-century the 'chair' was a subcontracted work group, and the 'gaffer' enjoyed virtually unlimited power over the underhands. Control of hierarchies such as these enabled subcontractors to restrict the work activity and status of underhands, learners and apprentices. It must always be remembered that underhands could be as technically skilled as the 'gaffer', and this constituted a running threat to skill status and the contractor's position. Many of the early British trade unions were primarily associations of internal contractors, and they often used the union to develop a set of rules regulating the work done by helpers and underhands (Warburton, 1939, p. 35; Fox, 1955, pp. 62–9; Clegg, Fox and Thompson, 1964, p. 15; Goffee, 1977, p. 46; cf. Ashworth, 1915; p. 36).

The skilled contractors were also frequently concerned to limit the collective power of the unskilled and semi-skilled and often tried to prevent or minimize strikes of the underhands, especially if they meant loss of earnings. It was in this vein that the ASE refused to support a rash of unskilled and semi-skilled engineering disputes in the 1880s (Burgess, 1975, p. 51). As for the contractor himself, the contract system allowed him, especially if he was a craftsman, to retain and maintain a high degree of independence in the work process, an independence which has traditionally been valued in British industry (see, for example, Hinton, 1973, pp. 96–7).

It should not be thought that internal contract functioned merely as a mechanism of skill maintenance and craft autonomy; on the contrary, it could be used as a mechanism of deskilling. For example, Fox, in discussing the nineteenth-century metal trades in Birmingham tells us:

Each subcontractor/workshop owner was paid by the employer on straight piece-prices, and made his own arrangements with his employees . . . concerning their wages. The vital difference was that while he was paid on piece-prices, he paid his team on fixed day-wages. The more economically and efficiently he organized production, the larger his profit. He usually sought this through elaborate subdivision of labour, each member of the team being kept for the most part on one or two simple skills which could be fairly easily acquired. Being under the maximum incentive to get his labour cheap, he often employed boys and youths. . . . At the age of 16 or thereabouts their rising cost in wages would prompt the subcontractor to discharge them and seek younger and cheaper labour. [Fox, 1955, pp. 59–60]

In general, subcontractors and piece-masters could be encouraged to hire cheap semi-skilled labour in place of skilled labour, especially in the latter years of the nineteenth century. Thus the contract system, like Taylorism later, could function as an agency of deskilling and dilution (Schloss, 1898, p. 221; Burgess, 1975, pp. 20–1).

Finally, we should note that the internal contractor was an intermediate shop-floor figure who was both an employer and employee within the capitalist enterprise. Thus the contractors complicated the confrontation between capital and labour (see Fox, 1955, p. 61).

In attempting to understand the modes of control in nineteenth-century workshops we should not throw the total burden of explanation on to internal contract systems. Nineteenth-century British industry presents a varied and complex picture. In particular, the scope of internal contract was limited by two factors. First, it was unusual for a nineteenth-century British firm to place all its operations under forms of internal contract. Typically, a proportion of the labour force would be directly employed. Indeed, some of the early nineteenth-century factory labour was coerced by various means, most notably the pauper apprentices, though these would rarely amount to as much as a third of the labour force (Pollard, 1968, pp. 194, 203). Second, the contract system did not extend to all industries. As we shall see below, some new industries and some service organizations represented alternative models of direct employment and control. Nevertheless, these industries employed a small proportion of the labour force. And even within the areas of direct employment the foreman would normally be granted absolute and arbitrary powers to hire and fire and to set pay rates, for example. Thus traditional foreman/worker relations were still modelled on the capitalist/worker power relationship (cf. Nelson, 1975, pp. 34–48; R. Edwards, 1979, p. 33).

To summarize this section: nineteenth-century British industry presented a spectrum of modes of control consisting of, first, entrepreneurial control (that is simple, direct control); second, internal contract systems (these included familial control, craft control and the gang-boss system); third, traditional foremanship (often modelled on entrepreneurial control). The advantages of the above typology is that it enables us to move away from both simplistic ideas of craft control and confused ideas of the labour aristocracy.[4]

Classification of British industries in relation to modes of control

Many of the current arguments over craft control and deskilling would be clarified if we had an adequate sociological classification of industries. While it is not comprehensive, I attempt such a classification below.

A primary distinction is that between those organizations based on direct employment and control and those based on indirect employment and control, that is, on systems of internal contract. Within the indirect category there are three main threads. The principle of classification here relates to the three types of traditional relationships described in the previous section. Finally, it is worth noting the outwork trades as a separate group, largely distinct from the internal contract industries.[5] The structurally based classification of nineteenth-century work organizations, together with some indications of structural trends through the century, are set out in Table 2. The classification outlined in the table should make it clear that systems of internal contract did not cover the entire spectrum of industries and organizations in the nineteenth century. Specifically, the subject of internal contract excludes categories A1, A2 and C. Moreover, the extent of craft forms of internal contract was even more limited.

The overview of employment systems in Table 2 has two important implications for the issue of deskilling. First, we need to consider at least two forms of deskilling or fragmentation, namely, deskilling from a craft base and fragmentation from a non-craft base. It is easy to forget non-craft deskilling and to confine one's attention to the more dramatic processes of craft deskilling. This brings us to the second implication. The salience of non-craft fragmentation will vary with the employment context. Thus in A1, A2, B3 and C industries it could be argued that it was the employment relationship rather than the division of labour that stratified the labour force. It is clear that for many workers in these industries it was the question of casualization and employment security that was uppermost. For example, in the nineteenth-century docks the entire non-specialist labour force was affected by the reality or fear of casualism. The practice of casual hiring created two broad groups: the permanent men, who were on a regular weekly wage, and the 'casuals', who were hired by the hour at the dock gates. Among the casuals was another group, the 'preferable men', who were preferred by the subcontractor or the foreman at the call-stand. At some docks the 'preferable' system had become institutionalized, and 'preferable men' held tickets which entitled them to work; hence the name 'ticket men' (Smith and Nash, 1889, pp. 20–1). However, the dockers were only a particularly dramatic and well-publicized example of casualism; as the Webbs pointed out, there was a long and extensive tradition of casualism in British industry (Webb and Webb, 1909, pp. 186–8).

Thus, the second major point raised by the overview of employment systems is that transformations in the labour process in non-craft employment contexts could be masked by issues of employment security, and if, for example, technological changes did not effect employment, they would fail to achieve collective salience.

Table 2   *Classification of nineteenth-century work organizations*

A Direct employment and control*	1 *Process, pre-planned industries* Some new industries, usually of a quasi-chemical nature, began on a relatively large scale and involved considerable pre-planning of the production process (e.g. brewing, distilling, sugar-refining and soap-boiling). All these industries involved heavy work, employed a low proportion of boys and women and few skilled men and tended to be more centralized, with direct employment and little internal contract. 2 *Monopolistic service organizations* The Post Office, the railways and the police are examples. Usually these organizations were in a monopoly or quasi-monopoly position.

B Indirect employment and control	1 *Industries founded with a domestic background*
	Examples are textiles and some final-goods industries. These employed an increasing proportion of female labour throughout the nineteenth century. This had the effect of pushing the skilled men on to a higher plateau of status and control. For example, the status of the male cotton-spinner increased during the middle years of the century, which meant that the kinship of the contracted work group drained away, and there was a faster shift to direct modes of control than in some other groups of industries.
	2 *Industries founded on a craft basis†*
	  (a) traditional assembly industries, such as shipbuilding, coachbuilding and the construction industry
	  (b) metalworking industries and non-traditional assembly industries
	  (c) others, such as the glass industry and the potteries
	3 *Gang-work industries*
	The extractive industries and the docks, for example. In these industries systems of internal contract proved the most resilient.

Table 2 *Classification of nineteenth-century work organizations*

C External subcontract	*The 'sweated' trades*
	These were largely the consumer-goods indus-tries, such as clothing, boots and shoes and toys.

* For all the industries in this category the direction of change during the nineteenth century was towards the bureaucratization of the structure of control, followed by the bureaucratization of the employment relationship. (For the basis of this distinction, see Littler, 1978.)

† All these groups employed a high proportion of skilled men and were founded on an internal contracted craft basis. There were two contrary trends in these industries during the nineteenth century. On the one hand, the craft element was drained away from the contractual work group, leaving an ugly husk of piece-mastership and exploitation. On the other hand, there was a gradual compression of the scope of contract and power was pulled up the hierarchy, leaving the residue of 'one man and his mate'.

The slow decline of traditional modes of control

The classification of industries in the previous section should sensitize us to the fact that the trends and timing of bureaucratization and Taylorization may be different in different industries and provides a framework for specifying these differences.

I have dealt elsewhere (Littler, 1980) with the vexed question of the survival of internal contract systems and have concluded that the available historical evidence is not sufficient to permit us to be definite about different industries and precise practices. However, it is fairly clear that by the 1870s and 1880s internal contract in some form was still widespread in a large number of British industries in categories B1, B2 and B3. In general, forms of contract survived longest in categories B2(a) and B3 and still operate today in the building industry, despite the agitation against the 'lump' (see Schloss, 1898, ch. 14, 15; Dobb, 1963, pp. 266–7; Hobsbawm, 1964, pp. 299–300; Pollard, 1968, pp. 18 and 53; Bendix, 1974, p. 57; Samuel, 1977a, pp. 33–4, 73–5; Pollard and Robertson, 1979, pp. 164–5).

If we recognize the widespread importance of internal contract systems through most of the nineteenth cenutry, this leads us on to ask questions about their demise. There is not space here to discuss the demise, and the mechanisms of the demise, of internal contract and other traditional modes of control in detail, especially as there are significant variations between industries. However, simplifying and generalizing, the pattern of events was as follows: the Great Depression in the last quarter of the nineteenth century shifted the economic setting of the wage–effort bargain beyond the normal trade downturn. This altered economic setting combined with a stronger labour movement to change the logic of the employer's position. As a result, employers sought to reduce labour costs via a more intensive use of labour. But the initial processes of effort intensification were attempted within the existing structures of control, namely, systems of internal contract. The effects of this, in turn, were twofold: first, it created extensive opposition to 'sweating' among the work groups, trade unions and the public. Second, it led to the deterioration of social relationships between contractors and workers. 'Sweater' and subcontractor became interchangeable terms, and both were terms of opprobrium. Few hands were raised to protect the 'slave-driving subcontractor' because new ideas, new methods and new technology influenced many employers to reach down for more control over the shop floor. Thus subcontractors were squeezed from both ends.

However, this squeeze was long and protracted, and it was not until the First World War that the transition process was largely complete. Thus Cole tells us in 1928:

In most of the coalfields the butty system has disappeared; the worst forms of the contract system have been driven out from the iron and steel industry; the power of the subcontractor at the docks is largely gone. In fact the pure 'contract' system, under which the engagement and dismissal of the vast majority of the workers employed, and the rate and amount of their remuneration, were in the hands of a few intermediaries between the firm and the workers employed in its works, has almost ceased to exist in any organized trade. [Cole, 1928, p. 33]

And this view of the final decline of contract systems was endorsed by Goodrich (1975, p. 120) in his careful survey of the industrial scene after the First World War.

The decay of traditional modes of control merged with the intensified problems of co-ordinating the new division of labour which were emerging in some metal working factories in the 1890s. In the American context Edwards argues, these twin processes led to a 'crisis of control' (R. Edwards, 1979, pp. 52–7). This is probably too strong a characterization of the British shop floor in the 1890–1914 period because the concentration of capital and the transformation of the labour process was extremely uneven, as we shall see in the next section.

Development of new structures of control

Workshop reorganizations, 1890–1914

The late Victorians could not clearly understand how an industrial organization which was not permeated by the profit motive could function. They could not clearly see beyond petty capitalism towards a concept of bureaucratic control. The result was experimentation and employer hesitancy (Littler, 1980, pp. 165–6). Yet despite the hesitancies and ideological fog of the late Victorians, from the late 1880s to the First World War workshop reorganizations did occur in a number of firms. However, it is important to stress that the reorganizations during this period affected only a small percentage of firms, primarily metal working ones which were in the vanguard of industrial change. The majority of firms remained unaffected, as the tensions and struggles of the First World War and the inter-war years amply demonstrate. And even in the firms that were affected the current of change represented only the first stirrings of systematic management.

Given, then, that we are talking about a small minority of firms, what was the nature of these reorganizations? The workshop reorganizations entailed several elements from a sociological point of view. There is space here to consider only two essential aspects: (a) the creation of a new supervisory role system; and (b) the implications of the new payment systems. I will then consider the effects of the new structures of control in relation to deskilling.

The first aspect of the workshop reorganizations was the slow stumbling, emergence of a new supervisory role system. By the 1890s and the early 1900s the internal contractor and piece-master had given way to the directly employed foreman in many industries. However, this process was no simple, single change. I have tried to make clear in earlier sections that it is necessary to think in terms of different forms of internal contract, and what these structural differences imply is that there were patterns of change from systems of contract to traditional foremanship. These patterns are complex and confusing, but in short either the contractor became more fully integrated into the wider organizational frame as a directly employed foreman, or he relapsed into the work group itself as a semi-supervisor (a chargehand, chargeman, leading hand or ganger), answerable to a directly employed foreman, or he became a 'submerged' work-group leader. Alfred Williams, in his classic study of a Swindon locomotive works, describes an example of the second process, by which the piece-master becomes a despised chargeman, his previous exploitations now restricted to a few privileges – primarily the right to a 10 per cent bonus from the surplus earned by his gang (A. Williams, 1915, pp. 282–3).

Despite the spread of the directly employed foreman in the 1890s and 1900s, no drastically altered set of role conceptions emerged, largely because of the absence of a systematic management movement (see Littler, 1981). In many respects the traditional foreman performed the same functions as the larger contractors. Thus in the closing period of the First World War one employer assessed the role of the foreman in this way:

In most works . . . the whole industrial life of a workman is in the hands of his foreman. The foreman chooses him from among the applicants at the works gate; often he settles what wages he shall get; no advance of wage or promotion is possible except on his initiative; he often sets the piece-price and has the power to cut it when he wishes; and . . . he almost always has unrestricted power of discharge. [*Athenaeum*, 1917]

Thus the traditional foreman was the undisputed master of his own shop and, like the internal contractor before him, he hired and fired, set wages, planned and allocated work. However, there were fundamental differences between the contractor and the traditional foreman: the foreman did not employ his own labour; his wage or salary was his main source of income; and he did not have the same petty capitalist interest in costs and profits (Gospel, 1982).

The traditional foreman's power started to be modified almost as soon as it had emerged from the decay of internal contract. The period 1890–1914 was one during which the foreman's area of discretion was whittled down by the employers and indeed changed rapidly on some shop floors. There were a number of aspects to these changes. First, there was the subdivision of the foreman's role. Feed and speed inspectors, quality-control inspectors, rate-fixers all started to appear on the shop floor in the early 1900s, and all represented some incursion into the foreman's autonomous empire. Perhaps the most crucial erosion of the foreman's autonomy was in relation to hiring and firing. Whereas recruitment had been at the personal choice and whim of the foreman, it was gradually replaced by a more formal system of examination and selection via a central office or 'Employment Department'. (A. Williams, 1915, pp. 274–7; Gospel, 1982; cf. R. Edwards, 1979, p. 104). In general, the new structures of control, which were the first steps towards systematic management, meant the insertion of a stratum of white-collar workers and technicians between the employer and the shop floor, diminishing the role and status of the old subcontractor and the traditional foreman (Cole, 1928, pp. 72–3; Hobsbawm, 1964, p. 297).

The second essential aspect of the workshop reorganizations was the development of new payment systems, especially the premium bonus system (PBS). But PBSs did not operate in isolation. It is necessary to look at what the payment systems entailed on the shop floor and in the factory.

The development of complex payment systems meant that most large works had to create large wages departments, and all workers received 'payment through the office'. This is more significant than it sounds to modern ears because it represented the work organization's acceptance of responsibility for wage payments to all the workers. This was new. Before this the company would pay lump sums to the internal contractor or piece-master, who would often pay his men in the local pub – and he paid them what he pleased. Many men were robbed blind.

Apart from the creation of a central wages office, the new payment systems entailed the continual shop-floor recording of job times. This introduced rate-fixers on to the shop floor, often attached to a central rate-fixing department. Not only did rate-fixing bypass the traditional foreman and harass the skilled worker, but it had a more fundamental significance as well. Previously the contractor or traditional foreman would have been the only superior to have known the measure of his men. Usually a skilled man himself, he had been through the trade and knew what constituted a day's work. He could be as much the upholder of customary effort norms as the craftsman himself (for example, see A. Williams, 1915, p. 99). In general there was a congruence of superior and subordinate skills. But PBSs brought with them the measuring and recording of job times. This meant that knowledge of effort levels and of work performance was lifted out of the work group or shop and made accessible to a wider range of superiors. In sum, the beginnings of task measurement increased the observability of work behaviour. The establishment of time standards for jobs, while providing the details necessary for premium bonus schemes, also acted as the basis of a new structure of control.

Some of the more far sighted workers in the 1900s were aware of what was happening:

A riveter: '. . . the employers could now gauge the capacity of their workmen with absolute accuracy, and if a workman took the full estimated time to do his work, the firm soon wanted to know the reason why'.

A brass finisher: 'One feature of the system was that each man's individual ability could be ascertained and those who were not quite up to the maximum standards of efficiency were weeded out.'

A fitter at Chatham Dockyard: 'As a general rule, the men liked the extra money but abhorred the system, which was a lever in the hands of the Government by which they could whip one man with another, and by creating rivalry between one man and another squeeze the utmost out of their employees. He would be only too glad if the Government would revert to time rates and conditions; although now they had an accurate knowledge of a man's capacity, he was afraid that if this did occur the authorities would expect the men to do a day's work on a premium bonus standard. . . .' [TUC, 1910, pp. 31, 34, 62]

However, though pre-1914 bonus systems saw the start of job measurement, the move in this direction should not be exaggerated. There was no systematic time or method study in Britain before the First World War, as far as I can discover. All the observers at that time agree that the fixing of basic job times in Britain under PBSs was ad hoc and haphazard in much the same way as piece-prices had always been fixed (TUC, 1910, *passim*; Cole, 1928; Watson, 1935, p. 92; Stearns, 1975, p. 216). Moreover PBSs were not based on Taylorite elemental time studes and job analysis. In many ways the systems were still based on the foreman's judgement and the skilled worker's knowledge. Essentially, PBSs accepted past performance as the basis for effort norms. Thus PBSs represented the beginnings of a shift to formal standards of effort, but only the beginnings.

What were the effects of the workshop reorganizations and the emergent new structures of control in relation to deskilling? First, the relationship between the worker and the supervisor changed. Many skilled men experienced a loss of supervisory functions and a more marked subordination to the employer and to capitalist rationality. But there was no simple transfer of power to the foreman: on the contrary, as I have suggested, there was a steady erosion of the foreman's previous autonomy and power and their transfer to a new stratum of technical staff. Indeed, the division of the foreman's role reduced the bargaining capacity of that role. The value of a single-role supervisory system, from the worker's viewpoint, is that the locus of decision-making is visible and known – one can hope to persuade and influence 'old Fred'. A multi-role supervisory system introduces a qualitative difference – the decision-making becomes stretched between the feed and speed inspectors, the rate-fixers and the foreman. And in so doing it becomes socially intangible. This withering of personal bargaining and influence relationships was a powerful stimulus to the development of shop stewards and workshop committees in the 1900s.

Second, with this loss of supervisory control went decreased job control and work autonomy. Many workers experienced a loss of control over the methods of working: 'Speed and feed tables replaced the experienced judgement of the craftsman' (Hinton, 1973, p. 98). An essential aspect of craft skill is a high degree of control over the quality of the finished product. However, the emergent system of control, especially the PBS, encouraged a more or less systematic carelessness. The worker was not supposed to produce a good job, only a fast one. The control system breeds in the operative an obsessive concern for throughput and nothing else (see TUC, 1910, pp. 61, 68–9, 73–4).

In general, many skilled engineering workers in the 1900s experienced a new sense of vulnerability, which was heightened (as far as one can determine) by increased casualization and by a daily experience of the new systems of control. No longer could workmen who knew their trade sufficiently well wrap themselves in an opaque cloak of skill and expertise; the beginnings of task measurement penetrated such traditional practices (TUC, 1910, 18–20, 22, 23, 52–4, 73).

The engineering worker's sense of vulnerability must also have been increased by the mode of deskilling which was common in the 1890s and 1900s. I have already distinguished between craft deskilling and non-craft fragmentation, but it is also necessary to recognize a distinction between direct, confrontational deskilling and indirect forms of deskilling based on inter-industry changes (for example, the shift from small woodworking firms using skilled joiners to equally small plastics companies using women, immigrants and no skilled men). Though there was the growth and expansion of some new industries in the 1890–1914 period, deskilling frequently took a much more direct form during this period. The situation at Elswick Ordnance Works, Newcastle, was not uncommon. There 100 fitters were dismissed 'in order that labourers and handy men might be fully employed' and many of them were subsequently re-engaged as *labourers* (TUC, 1910, p. 37; see also Watson, 1935, pp. 12–13).

Despite the tendencies towards systematic management and bureaucratic control in the 1890–1914 period, it is important to reiterate that the workshop reorganizations only affected a small percentage of engineering and metalworking companies. In general, techniques of labour control remained traditional. Thus change was slow and hesitant. Top management failed to move quickly to restructure shop-floor control completely because new ideas and new managerial practices had not congealed into an integrated theory of management in Britain. Consequently, British employers did not have the social resources to create effective alternatives to traditional foremanship even if they had wanted to. As a result, many internal contractors made the transition to directly employed foreman but retained much of their previous autonomy. This was very different from the case of the United States, where the ideology and practice of Taylorism provided the means of factory co-ordination. In contrast there was literally no shop-floor development of Taylorism in Britain before 1914.

If we accept that 1880–1914 was the period of the decay of internal contract systems and other traditional modes of control, that it was a time of organizational experimentation and of employer hesitancy, often in the face of supervisory resistance, then the question arises of when Taylorism was institutionalized in British industry. When were bureaucratic forms of control imposed on the shop floors of British factories? This question takes us on to an analysis of the inter-war period.

The inter-war period

The pressures of the First World War and the American involvement in the war led to a flow of ideas concerning Taylorism and scientific management across the Atlantic. Various technical missions sent to the USA returned with practical experience of, and occasionally enthusiasm for, Taylorism (Devinat, 1927, p. 28). After the war Taylorism became embedded within broader perceptions of America as a model of industrial productivity and economic prosperity. Such visions of progress and prosperity acted as cultural conduits by means of which ideas of Taylorism seeped into the European consciousness. However, according to Maier, there was a pattern of receptivity to these ideas, and both Germany and Italy proved more receptive than Britain (Maier, 1970, p. 37). It was not until the late 1920s and early 1930s that the problems of the British economy and employers' desperate attempts to lower costs created broad and continued interest in Taylorism.

A little-known figure who was important in the international spread of 'scientific management' and crucial to the diffusion of Taylorian workshop practices in Britain was Charles E. Bedaux. Bedaux's system spread first in the USA and Canada, but by the 1930s there were nineteen offices around the world and schemes had been installed in at least twenty-six different countries (Laloux, 1951, p. 11). Bedaux clearly enjoyed remarkable international success. His system swept American and European industry and created a fortune for its founder. Despite at least two American imitators, Haynes 'Manit' and Dyer, no other managerial control system had such a widespread success (see AFL, 1935, p. 936; Nadworny, 1955, p. 179).

After a slow start in the late 1920s the Bedaux system spread rapidly during the 1930s in Britain. Some of the firms involved were in the new and expanding industries – food-processing, light engineering, motor components (though not motor vehicles) and chemicals. However, this is not the entire story. Bedaux was also applied to more traditional industries, such as iron and steel, textiles and hosiery. By 1939 approximately 250 firms had used Bedaux techniques, including ICI, Lucas, Joseph Lyons and Wolsey. Moreover many of these firms were industry leaders and acted as guides to other firms in the same industries. As a result, Bedaux became the most commonly used system of managerial control in British industry. Even when the popularity of Bedaux declined many of the firms which discarded the Bedaux system itself went on to adopt other forms of 'rationalized' management. Thus Bedaux, the man and his techniques, opened up the way to the spread of neo-Taylorite systems. Certainly, the history of 'scientific management' in Britain in the inter-war period is largely the history of Bedaux (see Livingstone, 1969, p. 49).

There is not space here to analyse the Bedaux system in detail. In general, the system is not well understood, partly because of its complexity. Given this fact, I will attempt briefly to relate the system to Taylorism and will make three essential points about it.

According to Layton, 'Bedaux claimed to have solved the problem which had eluded Taylor, namely that of discovering the precise, scientific relationship between work and fatigue' (Layton, 1974, p. 382). Taylor's position had been open to attack, and indeed was

attacked in Britain and the USA, because he never could effectively ground in science his notions of a 'proper task'. Taylor wrote
almost nothing on fatigue and rest periods, and when ques-
tioned about over-work, as at the Hearings of the House of Representatives, he could only fall back on personal experience, assertion and cliché (see, for example, F. W. Taylor, 1947). What
Bedaux did was to attempt to combine the emerging studies of
fatigue and Taylorism. 'In place of the arbitrary allowances utilized
by Taylor, Bedaux claimed to be able to determine the exact
proportions of work and rest needed for any task' (Layton, 1974, p.
382). Thus Bedaux's ideas had an appeal because they covered one
of the embarrassing areas of nakedness manifested by Taylor. Once
employers had the capacity to determine the exact nature of 'strain',
and thus the exact allowance for relaxation, they were in a position to
arrive at a universal measure for all work. Within the Bedaux system
the universal measurement was the Bedaux Unit or the 'B'. This was
defined as follows: 'A 'B' is a fraction of a minute of work plus a
fraction of a minute of rest, always aggregating unity, but varying in
proportions according to the nature of strain' (Morrow, 1922, p.
243). It is the 'B' that is the really ingenious notion in the whole
system. By incorporating the rest allowance in the unit of effort,
Bedaux at a stroke jumped over the minefield of comparability of
work in a pseudo-scientific blur.

This unit of labour measurement made it possible to make
comparisons of the relative efficiency of workers, departments and
factories, even though the types of work were substantially different
(TUC, 1933, p. 6; AFL, 1935, p. 940; J. H. Richardson, 1954, p. 79;
Layton, 1974, p. 382). This feature was a major selling point stressed
by the Bedaux consultants. If it is possible to reduce all work to a
common basis, to encapture all work activity – the worker at the
milling machine, the lathe operator, the assembly worker, the
female packer and the supervisor's supervising – within a single
measuring grid, then all barriers to 'observability' have been broken.
It is possible for the first time to set up a monitoring and control
system which provides the works manager with a comprehensive
picture of all work activity throughout the plant. This was what the
Bedaux system offered. Theoretically at least,

Taylor's system was expensive and slow to install, requiring at least three
years for a given plant. It involved painstaking and protracted investigation
of every aspect of the productive process. It met resistance because it also

involved a major restructuring of management and restriction on the authority of traditional management. [Layton, 1974, p. 383]

Bedaux, on the other hand, offered a system which appeared to be quick and easy to install and which could be clipped onto the existing, traditional management structure.

According to Braverman, Taylorism was the rabid destroyer of the craft system. Given that there was very little development of Taylorism on British shop floors in the first two decades of this century, then the periodization of the institutionalization of Taylorism is pushed forward to the inter-war years. Was there any evidence that Bedaux, as the inheritor of Taylorian principles, confronted craft workers during these years?

If we look at the distribution of firms which implemented the Bedaux system, nearly half of the companies were in three industries: food, drink and tobacco; chemical and allied industries; and textiles (Littler, 1981). None of the industries had been established on a craft basis (see Table 2); on the contrary, they all depended largely on unskilled and semi-skilled labour. The Bedaux Archives show that job analysis and job fragmentation did occur in these industries during the process of Bedaux systematization, but such processes cannot be subsumed under a model of craft deskilling. Even within a traditional metalworking firm (Richard, Johnson and Nephew) with all the signs of craft deskilling, the transition to non-craft working had largely occurred before Taylor's disciples set foot on the factory floor. Taylorism 'rationalized' the new industrial system that was evolving and developed an organizational model which was applied to factories where the craft system had already declined or was in a state of decline.[6] We must, however, also consider the pattern of opposition to the Bedaux system. For as Wood underlines in Chapter 1, it is the interplay of employer structures of control, forms of resistance and employer counter-pressures that primarily shapes the labour process.

It is clear from the Bedaux Archives and other source material that there was considerable worker opposition to the rationalizations of Bedaux. As the system penetrated British firms, it met with a good deal of rank-and-file hostility and unrest. The primary cause of this was the fear of unemployment. This was a period when national unemployment rose above 20 per cent, while in certain communities in Wales and the north-east it reached as high as 70 per cent. The last walk through the factory gates was a walk into real, and probably sustained, poverty. Fears of unemployment and poverty were mingled with fears of deskilling and resentment at being 'spied upon' (see Jenkins, 1974, p. 6). Moreover, the workers 'felt that in the name of science they were having unlimited speed-up and rate-cutting imposed upon them without negotiations, and they could neither calculate nor control their own earnings' (Branson and Heinemann, 1973, p. 96).

Real though the worker opposition to the Bedaux system was, it should not be overemphasized. Most of the strikes were like the one at Amalgamated Carburettors in February 1932. This involved 250–300 female workers but only lasted from Tuesday to Thursday, and the result was not the withdrawal of Bedaux but only some vague employer guarantees about wage rates and unemployment (Bedaux Archives, 1926–39; Brown, 1977, p. 241). The important point is that the slump and the stench of unemployment both stiffened worker opposition and undermined working-class bargaining power. The outcome was that worker opposition proved ineffective in its attempts to prevent the diffusion of Taylorism. Moreover, the extent of worker opposition was often influenced by the relative acceptance of Taylorism by the trade union officials of the 1930s. It is only necessary to compare the outright and wholesale condemnation of PBSs by the TUC committee in 1910 with the relative acceptance of the Bedaux system in the 1933 TUC report (TUC, 1933, p. 16) to realize that the official trade union movement had shifted from opposition to centralized management systems to collaboration and compromise. However, beyond the ambivalent position of the trade union movement, there were other sources of resistance to centralized, bureaucratic control.

One of the earliest British companies seriously to introduce job analysis and systematic time study, essential ingredients of Taylorism, was W. and T. Avery in Birmingham in 1921. Though its introduction seems to have aroused little concerted resistance from the workers, the interesting point is that it aroused considerable opposition from the foremen. The foremen insisted on controlling the scheme and the time-study practitioners, so that instead of a central time-study office, each department had a time-study man under the foreman. Even sixteen years later an observer comments: 'chargehands are in effect running the shop as a collection of almost independent small factories . . . each man making what he thinks is required, or what happens to be an easy job for any machine' (Bedaux Archives, Film 22, 1937). Clearly, the supervisors in this factory were insisting on retaining their traditional shop-floor control. This proved to be a common pattern in the inter-war period and the Bedaux consultants consistently found foremen and supervisors a major source of resistance to managerial centralization and control.

The basis of supervisory resistance is related to the dynamics of bureaucracy. The natural tendency in all bureaucratic systems of organization is for the bargaining power of the supervisor to dwindle. Circles of autonomy are compressed, and freedom for manoeuvre is reduced (Crozier, 1964, p. 194). Lupton reaches the same conclusion:

There is little wonder that there is much common ground between shop stewards and front-line supervision in many industries on the point that work-study men are 'a pain in the neck'. It is much easier for them to reach agreement, say about piece-work prices, where there is plenty of vagueness and room for manoeuvre than it is when there is someone around with sheets full of synthetic times to 'blind you with science'. [Lupton, 1957, p. 17]

In Britain, then, the transition to bureaucratic forms of employment and control was carried through slowly in most industries, and though eventually able to override most collective opposition, it failed to integrate oppositional groups. Partly this was because the institutionalization of Taylorism occurred in Britain without ideological reinforcement. Once it is realized that the crucial period for Taylorism in Britain was the inter-war period, the ideological context becomes clearer. As Maier points out:

the conditions of the Depression necessarily undermined all Americanist industrial utopias. Economic contraction destroyed the postulates for class collaboration and discredited the managers of the system. At least until the Second World War and its aftermath America's model of industrial productivity lost its catalytic inspiration . . . the supreme confidence in technology and production, in engineering as social redemption, perished with the other dreams of the twenties. [Maier, 1970, p. 61]

Against this background, the employers would have been utterly unable to engage the workers and foremen on British shop floors ideologically, even if they had tried.

Conclusions

In relation to the deskilling hypothesis a number of points emerge from an examination of the changing structures of control in British industry.

First, a simple model of craft deskilling is not tenable. In order to make some historical sense of the changes in the labour process, it is necessary to distinguish between job fragmentation from a craft base and from a non-craft base. In addition, we can distinguish between different modes of deskilling: confrontational and non-confrontational. These two dimensions enable us to locate the significance of Bedaux in the inter-war period (see Table 3). In general the processes of craft deskilling have occurred within a non-confrontational framework of occupational redistribution in terms of the growth of new industries, new geographical locations, the emergence of new firms and the development of new production processes (see Chapter 8).

Second, Braverman totally ignores the pattern of resistance to the processes that he describes. But beyond the more obvious point of trade-union and work-group opposition is the fact that *foremen and even managers could constitute a significant source of resistance, not necessarily to deskilling as such but to the associated changes in the structure of control.* This pattern of resistance is more common than is generally realized, and changes in the labour process need to be reinterpreted in terms of this fact.[7]

Third, there is the question of motivation. It should not be assumed that rationalization processes are aimed exclusively at the workers. Top management was frequently as much concerned with the attitudes, motivation and power position of the foreman. Senior management wanted to encase the foreman/worker relation in rules, not simply to exercise greater control over the manual operatives. As Gouldner points out:

Table 3   *Craft deskilling and the significance of Bedaux between the wars*

Existing labour process	Mode of deskilling	
	Confrontational	*Non-confrontational*
Craft base	British engineering in the 1890s	Shift from wood-working production process to plastic-based production processes
Non-craft base	Bedaux in the 1930s	Relocation of the textile industry in the Far East, Hong Kong, etc.

bureaucratic rules flourish, other things being equal, when the senior officers of a group are impressed with the recalcitrance of those to whom they have delegated a measure of command . . . bureaucratic patterns are particularly useful to the degree that distrust and suspicion concerning role performance has become diffuse and directed to members of the 'in-group', as well as those on the outside. [Gouldner, 1954, p. 168]

This problem, that of 'the enemy within', was not new, of course. The widespread distrust of agents or managers at the end of the eighteenth century led many contemporaries to argue that industrial capitalism was sociologically impossible! What was new was the solution to the miasma of distrust. In the early nineteenth century the typical solution was an organizational form based on the principle of co-ordinated self-interest, namely systems of subcontract, the whole framework permeated by the profit motive. In the early decades of the twentieth century the solution, or the attempted solution, was the elaboration of bureaucratic rules – the development of a watertight code of internal laws, with successive levels for the monitoring of subordinate activity.

Fourth, a comparison between the development of work organization in Britain and the USA points to the conclusion that there are different forms of Taylorism and that Taylorism can be institutionalized under different conditions. To begin with, Taylorism and the efficiency movement occurred in the USA during an expansionary economic period. In Britain the neo-Taylorism of Bedaux coincided with the worst depression of the twentieth century. This affected the pattern of resistance. Next, American shop-floor rationalizations were underpinned by the ideology of the systematic management movement and Taylorism. By the 1930s in Britain rationalization was a weak glimmer flickering in the consciousness of a few. Furthermore in the USA supervisors became more fully integrated into the system. In Britain they continued as a sceptical group, corrosive of shop-floor bureaucratization.[8]

Finally, in examining the changing structures of control in British industry and the imposition of bureaucratic control it is vital to recognize that there were periodic waves of rationalization affecting different core industries. The first wave, which occurred between 1890–1914, primarily affected engineering and metalworking firms and was not influenced by Taylorism. The second wave, which occurred in the 1920s and 1930s, affected primarily the food, drink and tobacco, chemical and textile industries. As we have seen, this wave of change *was* influenced by Taylorite ideas.

8 Beyond deskilling: skill, craft and class[1]

David Lee

In this contribution my intention is to place the arguments surrounding Braverman's controversial book in a broader context, namely, the long-standing debate about the evolution of class structure in the advanced industrial societies. From this perspective his work loses a certain amount – by no means all – of its uniqueness. In fact, it shares with a number of analyses the attempt to offer a theory of how the changing organization of industrial production impinges upon average skill levels in the work force. On this basis generalizations are made about the future development of the class structure. I want to show that such a simple relation between skill and class structure is unlikely.

The tendency to assume a simple linkage between the technical content of skill and the manner in which class structure as a whole will evolve is to be found at its most basic in the now dated technological theories of writers like Kerr *et al.* (1964), Galbraith (1969) and, in large measure, D. Bell (1973). By assuming that average skill requirements in industry are being progressively upgraded, such work attempted to establish an inevitable embourgeoisement or professionalization of the social hierarchy. Though he was a leading critic of such prognostications Braverman's own model is hardly more sophisticated. The technicist view involves the simple relation:

$$\text{technical change} \rightarrow \text{rising skill levels} \rightarrow \begin{array}{l}\text{changes in} \\ \text{class structure} \\ \text{(professionalization, etc.)}\end{array}$$

Braverman merely substitutes for this a straightforward equivalence between, on the one hand, the supposed outcome of the exploitation of the worker in the work place (that is, deskilling) and, on the other, the proletarianization of the working class. In diagrammatic form his view may be represented thus:

exploitation ⟶   falling skill levels ⟶   changes in
(realization of   class structure
surplus value in   (proletarianization)
the labour process)

    Criticism of these theories (Braverman's in particular) has brought to light the simplification which occurs in both positions, namely a failure to consider the institutional 'filters' which complicate the relationship between production methods, skill levels and class.

    Two distinct types of criticism may be discerned. The first stresses that worker resistance can and does prevent the development of any straightforward relationship between employers' production methods and the rate of disappearance of given skills from the work-force structure. Yet although writers sympathetic to Braverman's overall position recognize this as a major weakness in his account of deskilling, they still accept his objectives. A Marxist analysis, they say, must show how proletarianization of the working class is bound up with valorization, that is, the realization of surplus value within the labour process. Once the fact of worker resistance is admitted, however, it becomes very difficult to offer any theory at all about the resultant job mix in the work place or the skill input into the class structure. What the capitalist now has to contend with is the fact that both jobs and workers attract certain social labels which affect the rate which he must pay for labour, as the diagram below shows (broken lines indicate indeterminate relationship):

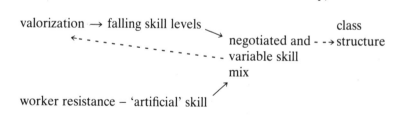

The real degree of technical skill, dexterity or knowledge used by the worker at any given time, therefore, may be less relevant to valorization than the extent to which he has or has not been accepted as skilled within the politics of the work place. The most recent Marxist analyses admit that valorization is affected by 'specific exigencies', among them the degree to which workers can organize effective resistance to the extraction of surplus value (Elger, 1979; Friedman, 1977a). In doing so, they do little more than confront and reformulate an old problem: is it possible to distinguish the technical from the political/social input into skill and, further, to say which in the last instance determines either the fate of a particular group of workers or the evolution of the class structure of capitalism?

A second source of criticism is the failure of both the Braverman school and its predecessors to recognize the difference in levels of analysis required in moving from statements about skill requirements within individual firms and processes to statements about class structure as a whole. As Rubery (1978) observes of Braverman, for example, many hypotheses about the direction of change in the labour process can be considered only after a detailed examination of the changing nature of the external structure of industrial activity and demand for grades of labour has been carried out. This is not simply a matter of controlling 'extraneous factors' before getting down to the real business of relating changes in skill requirements to the evolution of class structure. The notion of class itself calls for an awareness of the situation of particular groups of workers *vis-à-vis* broad systemic forces operating across the whole of society. Included among these forces are changes in aggregate demand and the level of employment, the growth of new industries and products, and changes in the inter-regional balance of economic activity.

The same point may be arrived at in another way, which is crucial for the argument of this paper. The notion of skill may, of course, refer either to the requirements of the job or to the capabilities of the worker. Failure to indicate precisely which sense of the word is intended in a given context will cause an unjustifiable confusion of levels of analysis. Braverman, for example, writes as if the 'degradation of labour' and the 'deskilling of workers' were interchangeable terms, whereas in fact they are not. Even within the work place the extent to which workers are affected by job changes consequent on the reshaping of production methods is not assessed. The outcome will depend on a large number of factors, including, as we have seen, the possibility of worker resistance. But in any case workers' options are not necessarily determined solely at work-place level. Their fate will also vary according to the external availability of employment which, as has also been argued, is subject to a wide range of influences. Furthermore, if one is interested primarily in such issues as the proletarianization of the labour force or the changing composition of the working class, it is surely the total opportunity workers have to exercise their skills that is of central significance.

The distinction, then, between deskilled jobs and deskilled

workers has important implications for any theory which sets out to establish a relationship between changes in the proportion of skilled labour used in production (whether up or down) and changes in class structure as a whole. It confirms that such a theory requires the investigator to move from one level of analysis to another. Quite simply, the theory will be incomplete unless it also specifies the manner in which this analytical transition is to be made.

Now, both of the varieties of criticisms we have been considering seem to me to be pointing in the same direction. It is obvious that existing theories fail to conceptualize the factors intervening between skill and class structure very effectively, if at all. Of all the many influences that might be included under this heading, however, surely the most significant are those which stem from the so-called labour market, that is, the institutions and processes determining the exchange value of labour. All of the authors referred to above are, in one way or another, bound to acknowledge the importance of influences on the cost of skilled labour to individual employers, and this makes the cursoriness of their analysis of labour market factors in the employment of skills particularly hard to understand. If, to take the theme of the first criticism as illustration, we ask whether labour resistance to deskilling is at all important, the answer must surely include mention of contingencies which are already at least partly understood. Research into the informal fixing of output norms by workers has, for example, provided strong evidence that the occurrence of such behaviour depends on the extent to which workers' earnings and jobs are shielded from the fluctuations of the labour market and the vicissitudes of wage competition (Lupton, 1963). It is true that the introduction of more formally organized bargaining on to the shop floor greatly complicates the situation, but it would be naive to ignore the role that market factors may play in this development as well.

The second criticism, lack of systematic attention to external economic change, has arisen for an analogous reason. There is a widespread tendency in all sociology to divorce the study of work situation and labour process change from the totality of workers' economic experience and even to afford them special theoretical status. This last point is again worth stressing, since, following Braverman, there has been a reassertion of the primacy of the exploitation of the worker at the point of production and a contingent tendency to disparage interpretations which emphasize the labour market as a key factor in the class position of labour (see, for example, Crompton and Gubbay, 1977). Really, however, the antithesis is false. Ever since Baldamus wrote his study of 'effort bargaining' (Baldamus, 1961), it has surely been appreciated that the production process is itself a market process – that the labour contract is in practice being renegotiated every second of the working day (Fox, 1974; pp. 181–206; Eldridge, 1973; pp. 49–64). Is this not the fundamental reason why restrictive practices exist at all? Conversely, the form in which employers organize production and labour's effort is supervised – whether directly, by responsible autonomy (Friedman, 1977b) or by a system of sub-contracts – will play an important part in constituting and reinforcing the characteristics of the labour market as a whole. And finally, of course, the nature of the product and the demand for it will be of crucial significance in the same context.

Obviously, the so-called labour market is not a market in the ordinary sense. For present purposes it will be more convenient to regard it as a series of social 'filters' intervening between productive skill and class structure. This series should be grouped into categories defined by their relationship to each other. Let us now see how this might be achieved in the context of a key empirical issue in the analysis of deskilling and change in class structure, namely, the impact of mechanization on craft labour in Britain.

Craft labour and systemic forms of deskilling

The fate of craft labour in contemporary industrial life is obviously critical from many points of view. It has figured prominently in recent discussions about British industrial relations problems and, as the extensive literature on the labour aristocracy reveals, about long-term changes in class structure. In *Labor and Monopoly Capital* Braverman relied on a comparison of what he took to be the initial situation of the craft trades in both Britain and the USA with the impact of Taylorite systems on craft labour in the USA alone. If instead one follows through the fate of craft labour in Britain, it soon becomes apparent that Braverman's employment of the term 'deskilling' suffers from being too vague and unspecific.

In order to justify this point, I propose to borrow a well-known framework that has been developed by manpower economists and statisticians when analysing and forecasting changes in occupational structure. In such work it is usual to pick out three components, called 'effects' or 'shifts' which make up the total available amount of employment – industry, cyclical and occupational. They can be shown to be statistically independent and in need of separate causal explanation. The first two reflect what I have been referring to as systemic changes in the overall size and interdependence of labour markets in varying times and places. Whole categories of both capital and labour find themselves involved, regardless of the market decisions that individual employers or workers may have made.

The first component is industry shifts. This term is reserved for changes over time in the industry mix of an economy (or the changed weighting of subsectors within industry groups). Such changes may be classified into two kinds: (a) absolute, where new industry bypasses older products, progressively undercuts their markets and destroys related employment; (b) relative, where the growth of new industry alongside the old merely means the addition of a new sector of jobs to the total structure of employment. The second component is cyclical shifts. This concept refers to the consequences for the employment structure of both general and localized fluctuations in the level of economic activity. It represents a particularly important set of factors which must obviously be controlled before any generalizations are made about the impact of changes in labour processes.

In contrast with these systemic forms of change, the third category, occupational shifts, denotes labour market forces which operate (that is, are internal to) the point of production. But the study of occupational effects on employment still obliges one to continue to distinguish between deskilled workers and deskilled jobs. Economists and others who work in this area undoubtedly use the concept in a quantitative fashion, as a summary of the total impact on the labour market of all influences on labour utilization within the relevant unit of analysis – for example, the individual establishment, firms or industries. As such, it has many components, including not only the 'degradation of work' itself but also subtle changes in product technology and use of materials. Hence, a job may be downgraded, for example, but the resulting technical change may so expand product volume that displaced skilled workers are reabsorbed elsewhere, still performing skilled work. Does the notion of labour process change extend to such phenomena, or does it exclude them altogether? Either way, the connection between job redesign (degradation) and valorization (extraction of surplus value from the worker) must be seen as highly contingent and essentially an empirical problem.

One effect of this conceptual framework is that it reveals the looseness involved in speaking about deskilling unless the term is qualified according to the level within the labour market at which deskilling takes place. That is, a separation needs to be made between systemic (industrial and cyclical) and occupational forms of deskilling. That this is not merely a debating point but entails certain important empirical consequences may be seen by applying it to the problem of the deskilling of craft labour and the consequences for class structure of trends in craft employment.

For the sake of argument I shall, to begin with, ignore the question of what occupational labels really mean and shall merely seek to disaggregate trends in craft employment during the course of this century. In any case, the published employment statistics used below report only the existence of jobs in the form in which they are recognized, paid for and returned on official forms by individual employers. Nevertheless, what this exercise will reveal is the role of the labour market as a distributor among potential recipients of a finite, if variable, supply of occupational labels carrying a skill connotation in this sense. The consequence, as several authors have realized, is that the labour market can and often does become a source of deskilling in its own right (see, for example, Friedman, 1977a, *passim*; Littler, 1978).

The empirical material on which my findings are based is limited to four industry groupings with a well-established tradition of entry to skilled employment via apprenticeship, namely, engineering, shipbuilding, construction and printing. In these, according to various inquiries, the majority of skilled workers are, and always have been, in a formal sense at least, time-served men. (See, for example, EITB, 1975; Phelps-Brown, 1968, p. 44). Of course, various groups of craft tradesmen are employed outside these particular industries. Unfortunately, it is impossible to trace the location and distribution of the relevant workers because in industries outside those already listed the available data, mostly governmental, rarely separate the numbers of strictly time-served men from other groups loosely described as 'skilled', to whom the apprenticeship system may not apply.

For present purposes, however, it will be adequate to concentrate on the craft industries *per se*. Even here, the available sources are very imperfect. A discussion of what they do and do not reveal has been published in greater detail elsewhere (Lee, 1981). In what follows I shall concentrate on summarizing the findings which show the significance for workers in apprenticed trades of systemic modes of deskilling as against the narrow range of occupational effects considered by Braverman.

We may usefully begin by discussing industrial (as opposed to occupational) deskilling. Much of the deskilling literature gives the impression that when multi-process craft operations are given over to detail workers, the latter typically make their appearance within the same industry as that originally employing craftsmen. Why should we assume that this is the only (or even the most usual) method by which technical development occurs? It can be argued, *pace* both orthodox and Marxist economics, that the industrial capitalist is not readily prompted to innovate in response to price competition and frequently does not possess any reliable method of forward planning for manpower or machinery. Consequently, new techniques of production are developed in periods of what Schumpeter euphemistically called 'Creative Destruction', in which new enterprise bypasses ossified sectors of the economy (Schumpeter, 1976, ch. 7).

Inertia should certainly be borne in mind when one is considering the effects of technological change on the British economy and its labour force. It may explain why the history of the craft trades, in particular, provides plenty of examples of the kind of bypassing implied by Schumpeter's model. Moreover, the deskilling effect in many of these cases seems to have been relative rather than absolute. In the nineteenth century, for instance, paper-making and furniture and shoe manufacture may all be cited as examples of industries in which mechanization created new branches of the trade for the mass market but did not immediately and dramatically undermine the market for the quality products of the hand worker. During the present century the experience of the 'engineering' industry, as it is known, has undoubtedly, been similar, although few discussions of the changing position of the engineering craftsmen seem to have given the point sufficient attention. Most statistical sources and many discussions treat what is a large, amorphous and evolving agglomeration of firms as if it possessed an essential unity and comparability over time. Proceeding solely on this assumption, it would appear that the percentage of craft labour employed in engineering has declined over the century in favour of a much higher proportion of semi-skilled occupations (see Table 4). It is a tempting but false conclusion to take this as an indication of the decline of engineering skill as a result of the direct introduction of semi-skilled machining. In fact, most of the apparent trend may, in the author's view, be ascribed to *relative* industry shifts, the growth of new spheres and modes of employment. Activity in the skill-intensive general engineering sector remained at best static before the later 1930s, and investment levels were insufficient to produce a radical technological deskilling. By contrast, growth in employment and investment in, say, motor-vehicle and cycle production, electrical engineering, aircraft manufacture, though not dramatic (Buxton, 1975), would certainly have impinged on estimates of overall skill use in the industry as a whole. (Incidentally, there is a certain amount of evidence that post-war full employment, by expanding investment in all sectors, actually *increased* the relative employment of craft labour in engineering; see Department of Employment, 1965, no. 2, pp. 15–17.)

Two additional points are worth making. First, insufficient recognition is given to the fact that new industries, though they may employ large numbers of detail workers, nevertheless create in themselves a certain, often substantial, amount of new job opportunity for traditional crafts. Second, new technologies and plants can create new skills, electricians being an obvious example. (For examples within building, see Jeanes, 1966.) The growth of these must be offset against the putative deskilling of older crafts. The interesting question for the student of class structure, therefore, is not simply the issue of the 'objective' changes in the skill content of jobs brought about by the industrial locus of employment; it also involves the issue of whether worker organization is able to ensure that the new expertise is actually recognized. Before turning to the question of trade unionism, however, we must consider the other systemic mode of deskilling.

The relevance of recession and cyclical factors generally for the study of deskilling has been rather neglected, because such developments typically occur at times when the sort of labour process changes more usually associated with the term deskilling are held back in the economy in large. Down-swings are usually associated with a fall in the levels of investment necessary for the introduction of labour-saving plant and machinery. Moreover, the long-term impact of economic cycles on the composition of the working class appears to be self-cancelling. For example, the loss of total absolute employment in craft trades in Britain caused by the inter-war slump was more than compensated for by subsequent rearmament and post-war reconstruction and by simultaneous demographic changes in the working population as a whole.

It is legitimate, nevertheless, to describe the cyclical unemployment of craftsmen in recessions as a form of deskilling, for three
reasons. First, for many groups of workers the severance from skilled
work is likely to be permanent, especially if the recession has
revealed an underlying lack of competitiveness in the basic industry.
This effect may also be produced or compounded if the worker is
beyond a particular stage in his life-cycle, or if the search for
alternative employment leads him to become enmeshed in a separate
internal labour market from which it is difficult for him to revert to
his previous skilled job. Second, any process of recovery, though it
may replace the stock of jobs lost in the down-swing of the cycle, may
nevertheless fail to do so without causing substantial dislocations to
individual workers through organizational, financial and geographical shifts in the locus of employment. Third, and in consequence,
recession (and not labour process deskilling) provides the most direct
and tangible form in which the initially relatively privileged groups,
such as skilled workers, experience proletarianization. In short,
cyclical deskilling is likely to be highly relevant to an understanding
of how key groups of workers experience the unfolding of class
relationships in a society. Their response to that experience may, of
course, take some surprising forms.

There have been two major occasions during the time span
covered here when large numbers of craftsmen were effectively
deskilled as the result of cyclical factors: in the years surrounding the
slump of the 1930s and, subsequently, during the current recession
beginning in the 1970s. Only in the second of these periods were data
collected that make it at all possible to control for industry shifts by
giving the numbers of craftsmen within individual industrial groupings. Even then, the exercise is possible only over a limited period
and for three of our four industries. The results are summarized in
Table 4. The figures show a sharp decrease in the absolute number of
skilled employees between the two dates, and this wastage was, in
fact, maintained steadily over the whole period. What is more,
surveys of skilled labour shortages have indicated that skilled
tradesmen who are pushed out of jobs, especially as the result of
redundancy, are mostly lost to skilled employment completely.
(NEDO, 1977; Department of Employment, 1979). There need be
little doubt, therefore, about the deskilling effect of the recession.

It can also be seen from these data, I would argue, that the
availability of craft employment has depended far less upon changes
internal to each industry, in its use of different grades of skill, than

upon the general state of economic activity to which all workers are vulnerable. True, the percentages in the final column of the table appear to show a small to moderate fall in the relative representation of skilled workers. But there are several technical considerations which mean that this effect is largely an artefact of the data-gathering process. First, the industry aggregates involved are extremely crude and do not allow for differences in the rate of decline between subsectors or for the fact that the most depressed are also the most skill-intensive. Second, there have been adjustments to the occupational classification such that foremen, for example, were included as skilled workers at the earlier date but not the later. Finally, crude percentages are not in any case a particularly valid measure of occupational shifts. To establish their effects on a more sophisticated basis would require extensive resources, better data and the use of more mathematically based measures. We are, therefore, fortunate that in one case, engineering, such work has been carried out, and its conclusions are wholly consistent with those presented here (Wabe, 1977). In short, the recent data confirm the importance of recognizing a distinct cyclical mode of deskilling of workers.

Unfortunately, it is much harder to identify the impact of 'pure' cyclical deskilling upon craft employment before the Second World War. Statistical sources are poor, but in any case, the impact of the recession on the same industries which appear in Table 4 was more divergent. Shipbuilding and the heavier sectors of engineering underwent a rapid decline in employment. On the other hand, newer areas of engineering, with the exception of the period 1929–32, experienced a gradual growth. The building trade as a whole also

Table 4   *Recession and deskilling in three industries, 1965–75*

Industry	Year	Number of craftsmen in employment	Total employment (%)
Construction	1965	533.0	47.1
(private)	1976	344.1	44.4
All engineering	1965	969.1	37.4
	1976	716.1	30.5
Shipbuilding	1965	83.7	56.4
	1975	71.3	53.2

Source: Lee (1981).

underwent a major expansion. And we have so far failed to consider the position of the printing trade, which enjoyed a much more equable pattern of employment both before and after the Second World War. Even in these cases, however, individual groups of workers were still vulnerable to dislocation arising from quasi-cyclical factors. Taking the period as a whole, my investigations have led me to the conclusion that cyclical deskilling had a far greater effect on the availability of craft employment than did any moves towards the internal redesign of the job structure of craft industries.

In this section, then, I have been emphasizing the systemic effects (industrial, cyclical) which impinge upon the employment of craft workers. For the student of class structure and industrial relations this has important implications. The data indicate that the deskilling impact of systemic factors is often of far greater consequence for individual workers than changes in the relative usage of skilled labour at the point of production. Whether one is attempting to interpret the position of craft workers or predict the general direction of change in the class structures, the point is highly significant.

But before such a result and its relevance for theory can be accepted and considered, it is essential to examine in greater depth the relationship between the purely quantitative concept of occupational effects on employment and actual qualitative changes in skill technology and work organization.

Craft deskilling and qualitative labour process change

Naturally, the investigation of any occupational change demands much more than mere head-counting in published sources. In the craft context the major problem is to ascertain how far a surplus of spurious craft employment – in excess of technical 'requirements' – has been encouraged in British industry because of the activity of organized labour and, if so, whether this phenomenon has increased over time, especially during the period of post-war prosperity.

Conventional wisdom has been somewhat facile in its assessment of what 'technical requirements' have actually been at any given time. There is the widely quoted judgement of H. A. Turner, for example, that workers are skilled or unskilled 'according to whether or not entry to their occupations is deliberately restricted and not in the first place according to the nature of the occupation itself' (Turner 1962, p. 184). It is essential to modify the apparent extremism of this widely cited statement, which has been used to support both generalizations about the historical period in which British craft unions consolidated their control and assertions about craft control in a much wider range of historical and industrial contexts. In neither case, however, should it be accepted without careful consideration. In an important critique of the applicability of Turner's analysis to the situation of craft labour in the period 1870–1914, for example, Charles More (1980, ch. 7) makes the following points.

1 The ability of craft trade unions to socially construct was constrained by their low level of organization at that time, and they were certainly in no position generally to impose expensive overmanning and job descriptions upon reluctant employers (cf. also Zeitlin, 1979, p. 264)
2 Formal apprenticeship survived not primarily because it became a device for union entry control but because it yielded genuine returns to employers financially, technically and in terms of labour force recruitment and management.
3 The distinctive positions of craft workers rested essentially on the fact that the bulk of them possessed *real* skills, of salience to employers, which were not subject to such an extensive deskilling at that time (or even as a result of the First World War) as has been widely believed.

A comparison of More's results with the pattern of subsequent developments suggests that the above three points have continued, contrary to conventional wisdom, to shape the relationship between skill, on the one hand, and, on the other, the kind of recognition accorded to it – *such as, for example, would be likely to be reflected, albeit imprecisely, in official employment returns*. First, despite the net growth of union membership during the twentieth century, the ability of craft unions to impose controls has not necessarily become much greater. It certainly remained very precarious during the inter-war years because of unemployment. And even in the post-war period unionization of the craft labour force has been far from complete in many trades: against notorious instances – Fleet Street, for example – where it appeared to be strong, one must set the small-firm sectors of industry and examples like building, where craft unions have actually declined in strength since 1945. Quite often, too, the achievement of membership growth and the conclusion of closed-shop or productivity agreements have only been achieved by relinquishing much of the exclusive system of controls. The original justification for that system did not, in fact, lie principally in the artificial enhancement of the pay and status of the skilled worker. Its main rationale lay in the persistent oversupply of skilled labour, especially in large cities. Its survival in the post-war period was caused, as trade unionists themselves claimed, by the fact that important sectors of the craft industries continued to differ in significant ways from the image of industry projected by the full employment ethos. The enforcement of craft controls was most closely adhered to in conditions of continued employment insecurity brought about by such factors as regional decline or the casualization of the labour force, which were conducive to weakness in labour organization. But in any case, post-war prosperity, technical change and labour shortage did not make it any easier to maintain 'irrational' controls over job descriptions. As survey evidence has indicated, such factors *weaken* a union's ability to prevent dilution (see, for example, Department of Employment, 1971; Mackay *et al.*, 1971, pp. 277, 301). One must therefore remain sceptical about widespread union ability to inflate job descriptions and pay.

Secondly, the survival of apprenticeship in its traditional form provides further evidence of the limited extent of union ability to 'socially construct'. Neither at local nor at national level have craft unions been able to impinge successfully on employers' 'right to manage' industrial training or to enhance the content or status of apprenticeship (Lee, 1979). As a result, throughout this century apprentice numbers have fluctuated with the state of trade and have frequently fallen below such quotas as have been set out in union rule books. Likewise, the content of training has essentially been fixed by the immediate production needs of individual firms.

The apprenticeship system survives, in fact, not because of trade-union pressure but because it has had the tacit support of employers over the years. Above all, the craft union claim that the long period of apprenticeship still confers vital skills and experience is reflected in managerial recruitment behaviour. Though firms complain, for example, about union restrictions on the upgrading of semi-skilled workers, Mackay *et al.* (1971, p. 309) concluded that in engineering a much more fundamental hindrance to extensive upgrading has been technological limitations on the use of non-apprenticed labour in craft jobs. Similar considerations have apparently made employers reluctant to engage government trainees.

This brings us to the final issue: the continued salience of traditional craft skill. The matter is too complex to be treated adequately here. Suffice to say it has been the subject of several intensive manpower investigations, and their general drift has been that changes in the use of skill have been slower to take effect than might be thought on the basis of a reading of Braverman (R. M. Bell, 1972; Swords-Isherwood and Senker, 1978; Jeanes, 1966; Jones, ch. 10 below). Furthermore, their impact, even in cases of computerization, is to modify rather than to destroy traditional skill and to shift the locus of the manual skill requirement from production to planning and maintenance. But a surprising number of craft jobs have simply remained resistant to mechanization because of such factors as the small size and 'marginal' nature of the employing organization and the variability of production. Of course, no one can be sure about what may happen in the future. Also it is possible to point to a number of exceptional cases such as printing where the existence of union based 'social construction' is well-documented. The very peculiarity of these cases and the rather small fraction of the total craft labour force involved are, in their way, testimony to the absence of enforcement elsewhere.

Thus I would argue that provided these caveats are kept in mind, the study of 'social construction' and of the qualitative aspects of skill merely reinforces the impression given by quantitative employment analysis. Occupational changes in the position of British craft labour have been slight relative to the deskilling effect of recession and structural change in the economic system.

Summary and conclusions

I have tried to identify, by means of both conceptual analysis and an empirical case study, some key factors in the relationship between skill and class structure.

The main thrust of the conceptual discussion has been to emphasize the complexity of the social 'filters' intervening between changes in the technical content of modern work and the unfolding of class and class relationships. In order to analyse this complexity, it is essential to recognise the transition in levels of analysis involved in moving from one to the other. The inadequacies of prominent discussions of skill in orthodox and radical social science, I have argued, stem from their neglect of this problem. In particular, I have pointed to the need to distinguish between systemic and occupational forms of change in the structure of employment and hence to introduce this approach into the study of deskilling by modifying the term appropriately.

The empirical part of this paper has attempted to show the utility of such a framework. Applied to the crucial case of craft labour, it yields results that are important for understanding both the distinctive class position of this particular occupation and the determinants of the class structure of the advanced industrial societies. Under the first head, it has been possible to examine the systemic labour market forces, as against the merely occupational ingredients of 'market capacity', through which craft workers rather than craft jobs become deskilled. As for the second, the obvious implication is that technical change will have differentiating consequences for the societies of the capitalist world and the tendencies inherent in their class structures. Hence the apparent absence of marked occupational shifts in craft employment in Britain stems, I suggest, from the fact that various market factors have slowed down the pace of innovation in this country by comparison with that of the USA, and the technical, strategic and social position of craft labour has thus been less liable to change. Braverman, under the influence of Babbage and ultimately Marx, assumes too readily that the effect of price competition on individual employers will always be the same. Yet in Britain the individual capitalist has not always been a ready innovator in response to such pressures. This is a result at odds with the latent convergence thesis, which lurks behind concepts like deskilling and the degradation of work.

Finally, the case of craft skills in Britain demonstrates how important is the structure and behaviour of the labour/product market in setting out the parameters within which industrial conflict occurs. Labour in all sectors of the economy is presented with basic employment conditions as a *fait accompli*. Unions can and do conduct a guerrilla campaign against them, no doubt, but there is nothing especially new about that. In general, the evidence in support of the view that the recognition of craft skills has ever been imposed on reluctant employers by the 'social construction' practices of unions alone is, at best, highly selective in focus. It is, in fact, at least as convincing to argue, from a broad perspective on the craft labour market in Britain, in favour of the opinion expressed by J. T. Dunlop in a review of Turner's book:

technology and strategic position lead to apprenticed trades rather than the reverse. It is true that demarcations would be less sharp in the absence of apprenticeship but job classification and occupations are derived primarily from job requirements'. [Dunlop, 1964, p. 289]

It would follow from this that the presence of recognized craftsmen as a relatively stable and enduring component of the British working class reflects their continued technical and strategic capacity within both internal and external labour markets.

One cannot in any case assume, without a great deal more comparative research, that net skills in the working class as a whole are either rising or falling. I have tried to show that this is a variable whose magnitude has many complex components. Both radical and conventional theories of skill tend to equate, in a simple way, the disappearance of traditional craft jobs with the removal of all skill from modern life. This is to share the reluctance of many employers to give skill due recognition and may do a great disservice to the workers concerned.

9   The deskilling of clerical work
Rosemary Crompton and Stuart Reid

In this paper we shall examine Braverman's account of clerical deskilling. Although we would regard ourselves as in basic agreement with the major thrust of Braverman's argument – that is, that the constraints/requirements of the capitalist mode of production have resulted in the tendency increasingly to deskill work, including clerical work – in contemporary capitalist society, we would suggest that the concept of deskilling is capable of further refinement, which enhances our understanding of the empirical processes of the deskilling of particular occupations. In the first section we shall argue that deskilling involves not only the fragmentation and routinization of the clerical *labour* process, as Braverman implies, but also the progressive elimination of elements of control – or the capitalist function – from the work role of the clerk. (Similar points may also be made in respect of the deskilling of manual craft work). In the second section we shall argue that empirically Braverman (1974, p. 355) has tended to overestimate the extent to which the 'polarization of office employment and the growth at one pole of an immense mass of *wage-workers*' has occurred – at least until the comparatively recent past. In the third and fourth sections we shall examine the role of the computer in the deskilling of clerical work. An empirical case study carried out by one of the authors will be used as an example of the deskilling of the clerical labour process, thereby enhancing the polarization to which Braverman refers, and we shall, through an examination of the work of other authors, make some tentative suggestions as to the role of computer mechanization in centralizing control within the organization (and thus removing control from the lower echelons of the organizational hierarchy).

An examination of the concept of deskilling

Braverman's account of deskilling[1] focuses on the labour process, on the manner in which conception is separated from execution and capitalist control over labour thereby increased. The benchmark by which deskilling is measured is the skilled artisan. Such craftsmen – able to perform all the many tasks contributing to the manufacture of the finished article – were associated with earlier, pre-capitalist forms of production, overseen by craft and guild. Indeed, in its early stages, capitalism did no more than bring such workers together under one roof, 'and the work thus remained under the immediate control of the producers in which was embodied the traditional knowledge and skills of their crafts' (ibid., p. 59). By implication, at this stage conception and execution were still united.

However, it can be argued that the occupational role of craftsmen during earlier stages of capitalist development was not restricted to the carrying out of the labour process. Although we would not wish to enter into the debate on the nature of the 'labour aristocracy', it is clear that many craftsmen not only enjoyed personal autonomy in respect of their own work but also actively supervised the work of others.[2] Indeed, many craftsmen directly employed subordinate workers. As is discussed in Chapter 7, subcontracting was widespread during the nineteenth century and persisted until the First World War. Subcontracting acted as a means both of craft control and of control over the labour of the less skilled. To the extent that subcontractors and other craftsmen organized and supervised the labour of 'their' workers, it can be argued that they carried out the function of the employer – or capital. Therefore, given that the deskilling of craft work also incorporated the demise of the subcontracting system, the occupational role of the craftsman was stripped not only of its craft elements but of its entrepreneurial function as well.

Viewed from this perspective, deskilling has a double aspect; that is, the work role is stripped not only of individual autonomy – or control over the labour process – but also of control over the labour power of others, an aspect of the function of capital. However, the loss of control in the latter sense plays no part in Braverman's argument; the craft workers under discussion in *Labor and Monopoly Capital* are already embedded in factory production, and the concept of deskilling is developed solely with reference to the labour process. We would suggest therefore, that his account is inadequate. Although earlier generations of clerical workers were clearly not involved in subcontracting, according to Braverman, they performed 'semi-managerial' functions; they were loyal servants directly responsible to the owner, from whom they stood at little social distance. They had all the hallmarks of an 'intermediate stratum', which 'takes its characteristics from *both sides*. Not only does it receive its petty share in the prerogatives and rewards of capital, but it also bears the mark of the proletarian condition' (ibid., p. 407). That is, clerical workers were not only engaged in a labour process but also carried out aspects of the capitalist function.

In the case of the clerical worker 'carrying out the function of capital' should not necessarily be taken to mean simply the direct supervision of the work force (although in some cases, to be sure, this may well be the case).[3] In addition, we would include a control position in respect of capital, and particularly money capital and resource allocation. Clerical occupations might include, for example, much accountancy work, insurance underwriting and claims, and investment management. Clearly, we are here operating on the boundary of clerical and managerial work. It is our contention that, as Braverman implies, in the not too recent past clerical workers have carried out such functions. Indeed, this fact is recognized by Braverman, in that he describes the past generation of clerical workers as an 'intermediate stratum'.

Braverman (ibid., p. 298) also argues that clerical work, like manual work, once possessed the craft form; 'although the tools of the craft consisted only of pen, ink, other desk appurtenances, and writing paper, envelopes and ledgers, it represented a total occupation.' His account of clerical deskilling, therefore, parallels that of skilled manual deskilling; conception is separated from execution within the clerical labour process. However, as we have argued above, the clerical work role has incorporated not only the clerical labour process but also aspects of the function of capital. Therefore the stripping of the 'old' clerical stratum of 'all its privileges and intermediate characteristics' involved not only the deskilling of the clerical 'craft' but also the progressive removal of these functions from the work role.

Clerical deskilling in perspective

In emphasizing the former at the expense of the latter, Braverman's analysis of the deskilling of the clerical labour process overstates the extent to which the clerk has been reduced to the level of an operative in the 'factory-office'. Clerical workers, he states, are 'virtually a new stratum', and 'if one ascribes to the millions of present-day clerical workers . . ."middle-class" or semi-managerial functions . . . the result can only be drastic misconception of modern society. Yet this is exactly the practice of academic sociology and popular journalism' (ibid., p. 293).

Braverman's grounds for making this assertion are to be found primarily in his assessment of the success of Taylorism as a managerial strategy used to optimize clerical 'productivity' through the deskilling of work tasks. This leads him to characterize clerical workers in this century as a relatively homogeneous stratum, deprived of those 'semi-managerial functions' which once associated them (however tenuously) with management and sharing the class position of the manual worker:

The problem of the so-called employee or white-collar worker which so bothered early generations of Marxists, and which was hailed by anti-Marxists as proof of the falsity of the 'proletarianization' thesis, has thus been unambiguously clarified by the polarization of office employment and the growth at one pole of an immense mass of *wage-workers*. [ibid., p. 355]

In this statement Braverman echoes the work of Klingender (1935) who, writing in the 1930s, declared that the 'proletarianization' of clerical workers was already complete and that the clerk was as undeniably part of the mass proletariat as the factory operative. To the extent, therefore, that clerical workers failed to identify themselves with manual workers (for example, through trade-union organization) they suffered from 'false consciousness'. Klingender anticipated many of Braverman's arguments in pointing to the increased regimentation and routinization of clerical work, the relative decline in clerical earnings and the growing polarization of the office work force.

Yet, as Braverman says, academic sociology never accepted the image of the proletarian clerk and this was largely due to the characterization of the 'black-coated worker' provided by Lockwood (1958) in the late 1950s. Although clerical incomes had declined in relation to sections of the manual labour force and mechanization had brought changes to the office routine, Lockwood emphasized that the clerk still enjoyed conditions of work and employment superior to the manual worker's and that these benefits (such as shorter hours, longer holidays, better pension and sick-pay schemes) distinguished the black-coated worker's class position from that of the mass proletariat. Moreover, the clerk's location (in the office), his access to promotional channels and the status which accompanied a monthly salary, a suit and an office desk associated the clerk (in his own and other people's eyes) firmly with management. Any lack of identification with the manual working class was, for Lockwood, a result of these distinctions in conditions and status which marked the 'life-chances' of the clerk as superior to those of the manual worker. The 'class-awareness' of the clerk faithfully reflected his class position.

To the extent that the privileges of the clerk identified by Lockwood really existed (and his analysis was explicitly less applicable to women), they might be regarded as evidence of the surviving value of the clerk to his particular employer, which lay in his possession of specialized knowledge and experience of a unique set of problems, tasks or clients. Further, as we suggested at the start of this chapter, in addition to its 'craft' character, clerical work might also be seen to encompass capital functions, both resulting from, and sustaining the clerk's proximity to, management. Braverman's characterization of clerical work underestimates the extent to which, until recent times at least, it was a heterogeneous category containing many individual employees whose craft skills and control had not been removed.

The introduction of electronic data-processing (EDP) technology to office work began a new chapter in the history of the clerk, and we will argue that it has had a substantial effect on the 'craft' nature of clerical work, deskilling in both the senses previously identified. Thus while furthering the process of fragmentation, standardization and routinization already apparent in the mechanization and reorganization of clerical work, EDP also affects the allocation of decision-making in the organization and removes those elements of clerical work which we have suggested may be considered capital functions. In the next section we will look in more detail at the specific form of clerical deskilling consequent upon computerization, drawing on a case study of clerical work in a local authority treasurer's department.[4] Before the discussion of the case study material, however, we feel it is essential to locate the discussion in the context of recent technical developments.

The case study (and much of the other discussion in this chapter) describes the operation of a computerized batch system, that is, the work is prepared by clerks and sent in batches to the computer department, from where it is returned after processing. As the discussion that follows will illustrate, this temporary loss of control over the data on the part of the clerk is an important feature of clerical deskilling. However, with the more recent development of direct-entry, on-line systems, it has been suggested that this particular disadvantage (from the point of view of the clerk) of earlier batch systems is in the process of being surmounted (Mumford, 1980).

We would suggest that, as yet, it is simply too early to assert with confidence what will be the ultimate impact of these developments on the nature of clerical work. However, their introduction raises a number of possibilities to which we will return in our concluding discussion.

Clerical work in a computerized treasurer's department

The advent of office machinery, especially adding machines and the Hollerith punched-card processor, enabled employers not only to handle a greater volume of work without substantial increases in staffing levels but also to employ staff purely as machine operators or on routine tasks of form-filling and data preparation. Thus the value of the clerk of particularistic (and acquired) knowledge and skills began to be undermined.

The computer, and the other forms of EDP developed since its first commercial applications in the 1950s, both extends and transforms the trends begun with the subdivision of clerical labour and the use of mechanical forms of calculation and information processing. The first and most obvious advantage of the computer to most employers has been its potential to reduce labour costs by handling large amounts of data at unprecedented speed and with a high degree of accuracy. This has been of particular value in areas such as public service, where the years since the last war have witnessed a huge expansion in staffing, budgets and responsibilities. The computer has proved not only a vital asset in controlling labour costs but also a primary aid and stimulus to the centralization of administrative resources which has characterized the growth of the public sector.

The effects of EDP usage on clerical work have been numerous. The need for standardized documentation is universal, ensuring that raw data is translated into codes which can be entered into the computer's processing unit and memory, and that the bulk of the actual processing of data will be performed away from the department whose responsibility it is. This entails a new dependence on the performance of another department (the computer department) and its staff and equipment. For example, it introduces new deadlines, and timetables will frequently be determined by this other department. Consequently, the clerk's ability to check, correct or alter work is restricted for important periods of time. Further, the computer can be used to store quantities of information which could otherwise have been held only on manual files or in the minds of clerks themselves. The need for clerks with a detailed personal knowledge of payees; control over the pace of the labour process; to retain all information on the computer.

To illustrate some of these effects, and the reactions of clerical workers themselves to the process of computerization, we will describe the tasks of a clerk working on a local authority payroll. The whole process of her work is geared to the computer.[5] Information on the pay of council employees comes in from other departments and establishments on standard forms (varying slightly according to the nature of the employees and the mode of payment – weekly/ monthly, cash/cheque), and the clerk transfers the information from these pay sheets on to a standard Payroll Record Card, one for each employee, and despatches these, in batches, to the computer department.[6] Once the payroll data has been punched on to disk or tape and run on the computer, the clerk receives a full print-out of the data, which must then be checked for errors. To some extent, the computer's program does this itself by providing a list of any payment deviating from the normal pattern, which the clerk can then follow up. Having rectified any problems, the clerk then submits the data for a final run. The computer produces payslips and (where appropriate) the actual cheques for payees. The clerk's job then is simply to separate the computer-printed payslips and cheques and arrange for them to be dispatched. The computer also provides a weekly print-out of the total value of the payroll so that any remaining errors may subsequently be rectified. The clerk amends details and makes alterations: far from seeing the total work process, she operates on the periphery, relying almost totally on the performance of the computer. The only area of discretion remaining to her (and an acknowledged source of interest and variety) is queries from payees, but this constitutes a small proportion of the clerk's total workload.

The sense of subordination and dependence in relation to the computer was frequently expressed by the staff in this finance department. The feeling that 'the computer is running us, we're not running the computer' was common to many of the clerks and often also to their supervisors and managers. Another clerk spelt out in more detail the difficulties involved in giving work over to the computer:

to a certain extent, one becomes a slave to the computer. Also, once stuff's gone to the machine-room they won't let you touch it. So if you want to make an alteration mid-week you can't do it. Another thing is, you're governed by the timing of the computer, the program – work has to fit into it.

For employees who had worked for the county council for some years and who have lived through the mechanization and then computerization of work procedures or had had experience of non-computerized systems elsewhere, the impact was particularly striking. The element of personal contact had gone; one no longer saw through the process from beginning to end; individuals no longer possessed the wealth of specialized knowledge once needed to deal with problems. The very capability of the computer brought problems for the clerks. As one male section head said:

the computer system does everything much more quickly so you need fewer staff. However, if anything goes wrong you lose time . . . you have to make up the time you've lost. Doing it manually the time taken is more predictable. with a computer the ordinary payroll officer has a less clear idea of how pay is worked out – their job is less interesting. They put a few figures on a piece of paper for the computer and that works out everything.

Previously, the clerks had had specialized knowledge and had dealt with a particular area of work in its totality, which ensured both interest and individual expertise. The central role of the computer seemed to deny employees the chance to see the work process through from beginning to end. A male clerk in his fifties put it this way: '[Once] you knew exactly what was going on in the job. You worked hard but could see the results – that made it personal'. The clerks at the lower levels of the hierarchy saw these new jobs, accurately enough, as dead-end: there was little prospect of promotion, especially for female clerks, and no strong link between clerical workers and the professional or managerial staff in the higher strata, the latter being increasingly recruited on the basis of qualifications rather than seniority or acquired knowledge and experience. One experienced section head lamented the problems involved in motivating staff to work well when, in his words, the work 'is an interminable pattern, like a conveyor belt almost, like assembling TV sets.' Nevertheless, many respondents acknowledged the advantages of the computer, especially in terms of its ability to handle large volumes of data at great speed. The expansion and centralization of the authority's activities and resources made EDP a necessity if employees were not to be overwhelmed with work. But they acknowledged that these advantages were obtained at the cost of much that had been interesting and valued in the work: personal knowledge of payees; control over the pace of the labour process; knowledge of the whole work process, and the variation of work which accompanied this.

These changes have had serious consequences for the character of recruitment and employment in clerical work. The need for the traditionally valued knowledge and experience of the clerk is diminished: information becomes stored on the computer and is no longer the possession of a particular individual. Elements of knowledge and decision-making in the labour process, which bestow control and job interest, are removed from the employee and vested in machinery or re-allocated to technical and managerial elites. A computer specialist in the local authority recognized that this contributed to some opposition to computerization. 'Clerks', he said, 'have an antagonistic attitude when thinking is taken away from them.' Employers can recruit relatively unqualified staff to fill most of these routine clerical posts, knowing not only that the jobs require little skill or training, but also that they have little association with administrative, technical or managerial posts higher up the office hierarchy.

The process of the subdivision and mechanization of clerical labour began well before the computer and this has contributed to the increasing employment of women in low-level clerical jobs – so much so that the proportion of clerks who were female rose from 21 per cent in 1911 to almost 70 per cent by 1966 (Department of Employment, 1974, p. 22). Technological advance has not slowed this trend.[7] Married women in particular are participating in the labour force in greater numbers and are now as likely to be in paid employment as unmarried women (ibid., p. 11). One of the attractions of women workers to employers is that until recently they could be paid at lower wage rates than men; now, concentrated in the lowest grades, they can be effectively isolated from the organizational career structure. This is particularly true of married women, who are frequently regarded by managers as working not for a first income but for extras or pin-money. Younger, unmarried women are expected to work only until they marry or have a child. The management liturgy 'It's not worth promoting women, they only leave' helps to justify discrimination against female employees and, in turn, increases the likelihood of women leaving boring, dead-end jobs for a different job or domestic life.[8]

Women provide a cheap, flexible (about one-third of women work part-time) and readily available source of labour from which employers staff the lowest paid, most routine jobs. In the treasurer's department in our example of the twenty-five employees on the lowest clerical grades, nineteen were women; of the thirty-eight employees on the three grades encompassing most of the clerical staff, twenty-eight were women; more significant perhaps, of the ten top employees in the department (section heads and managers), not one was a woman. There was complete male monopoly of the higher levels of bureaucratic authority. Computerization has added new dimensions to this 'feminization' of the clerical work force, which began in earnest with the subdivision of clerical tasks and the introduction of office machinery. First, the sort of job described earlier requires neither formal qualifications nor an extensive period of training. Nor does it involve the employee in acquiring or retaining knowledge about more than one aspect of the department's total workload. Thus the employer requires neither a qualified nor an experienced employee. Second, the creation of a large stratum of employees working predominantly to a pace and to procedures governed by the computer exaggerates further the division between those executing the work and those making decisions, a division reflected in the patterns of recruitment and promotion and enforced by the predominance of female employees in the low-grade posts.[9] Third, the use of EDP technology to reduce the future demand or the current level of labour has been considerably aided by the relatively high level of turnover among female employees. Very few direct redundancies have occurred in Britain due to computerization, most staff reductions taking the form of the non-replacement of department staff. This pattern increases the convenience of female employees to the manager and employer. In addition, the occupations created in response to computerization have tended, with some exceptions, to be equally segregated along sexual lines. In the study cited (and, indeed, in all other instances known to the authors) the data-preparation operators ('keypunch girls'), who feed data from clerks on to computer disks or tape for processing, were exclusively female – predominantly young women doing a highly repetitive machine-operating job.

We have described some of the characteristics of the computerization of a clerical work process and the reactions of the employees themselves. Central to this analysis is the observation that the computer's potential as a means of storing, monitoring, processing and making available information diminishes the value of the clerk's particularized knowledge of the work process and her/his ability to exercise discretion in making decisions and in controlling the performance of work. Braverman (1974, p. 347) himself states: 'The greatest single obstacle to the proper functioning of such an office (i.e. the 'factory-office') is the concentration of information and decision-making capacity in the minds of key clerical employees.' The computer removes this obstacle by enabling information to be stored and processed away from the employees themselves. At the same time, the availability of information from the computer provides a new source of potential authority and control for senior management and poses a threat to the position of lower and middle-level personnel.

In brief, then, the process of polarization of the office work force is greatly facilitated by the use of EDP technology. The storage and processing of information relocated in the computer system robs clerical employees (and possibly lower managerial and administrative workers as well) of elements of autonomy and control of the labour process which previously distinguished their jobs from other forms of routine labour. The 'feminization' of clerical employment has marked a recognition of the creation of posts which consist of tasks overwhelmingly bound to the performance of machinery. The importance over the last two decades of formal qualifications as the basis for career mobility has further marked the separation of a trained, qualified and relatively privileged stratum of managers, professionals and technical experts from the mass of clerks performing repetitive and highly restricted tasks as 'servants' to the computer.

The centralization of control

In the previous section we argued that the introduction of the computer has enormously increased the further deskilling of the clerical 'craft'. As a consequence, a routine, 'feminized' clerical labour force has been created. We would also suggest that the introduction of the computer has the effect of further centralizing control within the organization. Here we draw not on a specific study but on the findings of a number of other authors' works.

One consequence of the development of complex hierarchies

which has accompanied the growth of capitalism is that control in respect of capitalist functions has been relatively diffused down the organizational hierarchy (Wright, 1976). To a considerable extent, of course, such control will rest with management, but, as we have suggested, the boundary between 'clerical' and 'managerial' work is not entirely unambiguous. In some cases the element of control in the clerical work role may be reasonably clear – as with the insurance clerk who decides when to pay out a claim or the wages clerk who both checks on the accuracy of information received and calculates the amount to be paid, which may include special elements such as pay advances, bonus payments, deductions for absence or lateness and so on. To be sure, the elements of control in the work role described above are themselves constrained by a series of bureaucratic rules. Nevertheless, we would stress that in uncomputerized systems such control is mediated personally through the clerk. These characteristics of clerical work, we would argue, are largely responsible for the fact that clerical work has tended to be associated historically with power and authority within the organization. However, such authority does not simply exist 'by association', as clerical work has traditionally been the bottom rung of the ladder in respect of promotion to positions of power and authority.[10]

We would suggest that the advent of the computer has served not only to deskill the clerical craft but also to centralise aspects of control which were once relatively diffused throughout the organizational hierarchy. Our point has been admirably summarized by Blau (1967, p. 465):

Although extending organizational hierarchy has administrative advantages for the top executive of a large organization, it also removes him increasingly from the operating level and makes it difficult for him directly to control operations and keep tight reins on them. This loss of close contact . . . is not such a disadvantage if top management has instituted indirect mechanisms of control and can exercise with their aid sufficient influence on operations by setting policies and formulating programs. The automation of accounting procedures through computers is just such an impersonal mechanism of control. . . .[11]

The literature on the organizational impact of computers has tended to focus on managerial rather than clerical work. Leavitt and Whisler (1958) predicted that computers would centralize power within the organization and would severely attenuate the middle levels of managerial authority. This would have the effect of reducing promotion prospects, or, even if there were no absolute decline in the number of higher-level jobs, the raising of a predicted 'control barrier' would lead to an increase in horizontal recruitment into the organization. We would suggest that a similar process may be discerned in respect of clerical work; that is, the centralization of control within the organization may reduce promotion opportunities by raising the 'control barrier'. In any case, it is likely that the routine workers remaining in clerical work as a consequence of the deskilling of the clerical craft will be considered 'unsuitable' for promotion because of the nature of the work tasks they perform.

Empirical studies (Eason *et al.*, 1977; Stewart, 1971) of the impact of the computer on the organization carried out in the wake of Leavitt and Whisler's predictions have been somewhat inconclusive. It is interesting to note, however, that those studies carried out in financial organizations – banking, insurance and the accounting departments of large companies – have tended to report an increase in the centralization of control (Whisler, 1970; Stymne, 1966). Banking and insurance clerks Lockwood (1958) argued, were once regarded as the 'artistocrats' of the white-collar world. Yet it is precisely in these areas of clerical employment that computer impact on the deskilling of clerical work has been most marked. At the very least, therefore, it would seem that some reshuffling of the clerical hierarchy is in order.[12]

Conclusion

We have argued that Braverman's account of the deskilling of clerical labour is preoccupied with the labour process to the exclusion of the potential loss of those elements of the function of capital which, together with the craft-like nature of clerical work, we have suggested contributed to both the more favourable treatment and the better terms and conditions of employment of clerical workers in the past. Clerical deskilling, therefore, involves both the process of fragmentation, simplification and standardization of work tasks and the diminution of the clerical worker's role as an 'intermediary' between management and the mass of routine workers. Consequently, the clerk's ability to make decisions or to order the work of others is diminished. The particular characteristic of the computer as office technology is its capacity to store and process information which was once the domain and possession of the clerk, and to impose internal controls on these operations (for example, checks on the accuracy and validity of data) which would once have depended on the experience and acquired knowledge of the individual worker. The clerk can no longer entertain the possibility of a 'total view' of the work process, nor exercise responsibility and discretion based on experience and delegated direct from management or employer.

We have suggested that the value of the clerk to the employer once resided both in a detailed knowledge of clerical work procedures (the clerical 'craft') and also in the fact that, to varying extents, clerical workers have exercised control on behalf of capital. Both of these features of clerical work made the clerk a 'suitable' promotion prospect, and both have been eroded. The clerk now typically performs more exclusively the functions of (deskilled) labour, being increasingly peripheral to the performance of the computer and having little or no responsibility for the co-ordination and completion of the many separate work tasks in the process as a whole. Functions of capital are relocated in the higher supervisory and managerial strata, or, progressively, in the work of those who plan, control and co-ordinate the use of the computer.

This process of transition has been reinforced dramatically by the parallel transition of clerical work from a male-dominated area of employment to one dominated by female labour. The recruitment of women workers into routine clerical and office machine-operating posts has not only been a recognition of the character of many of the jobs generated by the expansion of clerical employment but has also enabled management to construct the division of the office work force along sexual lines. This has had the advantage, for management, of creating a routine clerical work force largely cut off from access to positions of responsibility but constituting a flexible, dispensable and relatively quiescent stratum of employees. Thus the polarization of class positions through clerical deskilling, which Braverman describes in terms of the transformation of the labour process, depends also on a polarization of functions within the administrative work force, facilitated by the capacities and potential of computer technology and reinforced by a sexual division of labour.

We have suggested that Braverman's account of the degradation of work in the twentieth century has, through an excessive focus on the labour process, failed to take sufficient account of other aspects of the work role – notably the carrying out of the function of capital – which have also been significantly affected by twentieth-century developments. It may be further suggested that this emphasis is in part a consequence of the fact that the explicit model for

Braverman's account of an undivided labour process is the skilled artisan, whose method of working itself initially evolved under guild or petty commodity-production relationships. A further critical point which has frequently been made in respect of Braverman's work is that, given the benchmark noted above, his empirical account of managerial strategy with regard to labour in the era of monopoly capitalism is excessively Taylorist.[13] It can be argued that the characterization of Taylorism as the bedrock of modern capitalist labour management fails to take into consideration some of the unintended by-products – notably worker resistance – which may be manifested directly through collective resistance or, less directly, through poor motivation, labour turnover, absenteeism and difficulties with recruitment.

Braverman's discussion of the automation of clerical work relies almost entirely on earlier accounts of the introduction of batch processing (for example, Hoos, 1961). This kind of office automation was based on systems designs which themselves drew heavily on the methods of the work-study engineers who followed after Taylor (Mumford, 1980). Not surprisingly, therefore, empirical studies of such applications (including the study reported in this paper) have revealed that such automation has resulted in fragmented, repetitive work – in a word, deskilling. Equally, as the empirical study suggests, it has also resulted in problems of employee motivation, which will have negative consequences for clerical productivity.

By overlooking not only the backlash of problems raised by Taylorist techniques but also the alternative techniques adopted by management (Friedman, 1977b), Braverman considers in insufficient detail the possibility of any counterbalance or reaction to deskilling. However, as we mentioned above, different technologies may open different possibilities for work organization or may be used as means of reskilling work to counter the worst consequences of Taylorist techniques. The introduction of on-line or distributed-processing computer systems, using visual display units (and, ultimately, 'intelligent' terminals based on microprocessors), may provide the opportunity or impetus to reverse the deskilling of clerical work. In such systems, the direct link to the computer file allows the worker to interact with the machine at his or her own discretion rather than being tied to unvarying deadlines, as is the case with batch systems. It also revives the possibility that the clerk may be able to follow through the total work process by regaining direct and immediate control of the data during all parts of its processing.

As yet it is too early to judge what this second phase of automation will mean to the clerical worker. Historically, the clerk's proximity to management has limited the manager's use of Taylorist control strategies. As Lockwood pointed out in 1958, 'For a hundred years the manuals of office procedure have suggested that you do not get the best out of your clerks by ordering them about bluntly' (p. 79). It is possible that the poor motivation and recruitment problems brought about, in large part, by the introduction of batch computer systems as tools of deskilling may be countered by a reassertion of the managerial strategy of 'responsible autonomy', giving discretion back to the employee.

To the extent that alternative strategies of managing the labour force are discussed by Braverman (1974) – 'human relations' or 'self-actualization', for example – they are dismissed as mere manipulation, employed simply to habituate the worker to the capitalist mode of production. Such strategies may indeed be manipulative, ultimately geared to increasing productivity whilst retaining the commitment of the workforce. Nevertheless, if they are successful, they may have important consequences both for the individual and for the particular forms of development of trade-union and class-consciousness.

10 Destruction or redistribution of engineering skills? The case of numerical control[1]

Bryn Jones

A certain current in Marxism, seeking to elaborate the concept of the labour process has been influential in representing changes in types and scale of new production technology as effects of necessary and general 'tendencies' or 'laws' of capitalist exploitation and accumulation.[2] The object and orientation of these laws is proposed primarily as the subordination of the autonomy of manual production workers through simultaneously decreasing the level of skill in production tasks and increasing managerial control over their execution.

In contrast (but not necessarily in overt opposition) to these theories are alternative Marxist arguments stressing the role of economic class struggle (Lettieri, 1976; Coombs, 1978; Friedman, 1977b) as an effective check and as a force that modifies capitalist objectives and principles in the organization of work around new technologies. The very notion of the inherent and unilateral power and motivation of capital to subordinate production workers has been criticized by Cutler (1978) for its abstractedness *vis-à-vis* the conditions of financial calculation, composition of product demand, technical constraints and labour markets. All of these conditions may vary between industries and enterprises and will therefore preclude any universal order of priorities and mode of calculation in capitalist production. This critique also points out the incommensurability between, on the one hand, classification of skills according to a composition by categories of conception and execution and, on the other hand, capacities for *actual* tasks required for particular instances of mechanized production.

There are, therefore, grounds for rejecting a unilateral motivation and capacity to deskill on the part of capitalist management. It can be argued that the forces working to determine the skill composition of an enterprise's or an industry's labour force cannot be deduced from inherent tendencies to generate inferior forms of skills. The question that arises then is how particular non-deterministic conditions can be defined. Three features of a production enterprise seem pertinent. In the first place, there are the traditions, strengths and strategies of the trade unions concerned and their relationship with relevant labour markets. There are historical exemplars, principally in the textile spinning and weaving industries instanced by Turner (1962, pp. 106–68), to show that the aggregation or fragmentation of task skills as occupational categories can derive from union strategies either to hierarchize or to generalize wage rates. The dangers with this kind of explanation are that it may, if generalized, relapse into a Weberian 'conflict of interests', within which particular economic and technical influences are simply objects of rational calculation by contending parties.[3] A second constraining influence on the allocation of task skills to new production technology might clearly be the market for a firm's or industry's product and, allied to this, the physical characteristics of that product. Bright (1958), for example, compared levels of mechanization in the electric light bulb industry, which achieved 'higher' levels of automation than the shoe industry. Light bulbs were saleable as standardized products made of materials which lent themselves to a high degree of automatic machining. Footwear designs changed frequently as a result of fashion changes, and production was variegated in terms of sizes and composed of materials that were difficult to adapt to automatic or semi-automatic machining operations.

These influences do not however, rule out a third determinant. The structure of occupations and production organization inside particular firms need not simply represent a proliferation of 'environmental' constraints. One of Joan Woodward's (1966) principal findings was that management organization across a variety of industries varied according to whether production jobs were concerned with the equipment appropriate to either process forms of production manufacture of single units or large or small batches of products. (One plausible inference could therefore be, as Braverman has claimed, that different production technologies reduce task skills which allow autonomy for workers, replacing these with co-ordination by managerial organization and control.) Hence it could be conceded that there is not a universal category of 'conception' in technique-specific skills, which can be fragmented and incorporated into a system of management control. Yet it might still be claimed that where production technologies *are* similar with respect to batch sizes produced and materials worked, skill fragmentation/centralization then becomes amenable to determination by similar structures of managerial control. One problem for this latter deduction, however, concerns the status of categories of technician and technical management, whose role in Woodward's cases appears to increase with the extension of automatic production operations. It could not therefore be proposed that there is a universal deskilling of their production functions as well as those of manual production workers, unless the technical staff are lumped into a general category of 'management' which is a classification many Marxists, let alone other writers, would find hard to justify.

A more detailed counter-demonstration to deterministic and universalistic conceptions of the direction and nature of skill changes is therefore called for, together with a more precise definition of the relationship between the three conditions of trade-union strategy in relation to labour markets, product market and composition and machine-management control systems.[4] An examination of a particular case of technological advance in a specific industrial sector may be valuable, since it avoids the dangers of over-generalization and provides indicators for comparison with other industries and forms of work organization. This rationale underlies my own research into the constraints and consequences of the introduction of numerical control (NC) machine tools into sectors of the British engineering industry for the organization of job tasks and hence 'levels' of skill.

The rest of this paper is divided into an examination of (i) the pertinence of NC machine tools for both theories of deskilling and employment in British engineering; (ii) the existing evidence on the impact of NC on the utilization of skills in the engineering labour force; (iii) a selective interpretation of some preliminary results of interview material from my own investigation of NC use in small-batch engineering firms in Wales and the south-west of England.

The central concern here is with the *distribution* of task skills to different occupational categories through the varying influence of the three conditions outlined above. It will be argued, at least in the case of numerical control, that particular cases of the redistribution of skills can best be understood not on the assumption of a unilateral subdivision of production skills and tasks coupled with their centralization by management, but in terms of the constraints on their divisibility. The organization of NC machines in small-batch engineering requires a distribution between planning/computer programming tasks and metal-machining tasks of 'skills' of metal cutting (as perceptual knowledge) and computer coding of plans and drawings (as conceptual analysis). The precise division of these skills into the tasks of machining occupations and programming occupations is shown to vary in accordance with differences in, and interrelationships between, trade union positions, product markets and pre-existing systems of management control.

Numerical control and its implications

In describing the application of NC machine tools to small-batch engineering, Braverman claims that it is worth considering in detail, as a prime instance of the managerial use of machinery in the capitalist mode of production, and of how this affects the worker and the labour process (Braverman, 1974, p. 197). The automation of production such as work with machine tools affects the worker and labour process, according to Braverman, by destroying craft knowledge, cheapening and fragmenting labour functions and separating the task skills of execution from those of conception, effectively reducing the knowledge of any of these new occupations.

In support of this contention, Braverman describes the content of the new occupational tasks involved in machining by NC on the basis of engineering literature[5] and his own experience. He describes the job of what is known as 'part-programming' (of the machining instructions from drawings into instructions for a computer) as limited in the technical knowledge required, and the machining tasks as virtually stripped of all their former skill content. Braverman concedes that there is nothing in NC technology to preclude, for example, 'the unity of this process in the hands of the skilled machinist . . . since the knowledge of metal-cutting practices which is required for programming is already mastered by the machinist' (ibid., p. 199).

The reasons for the non-appearance of this form of work are, of course, the necessities of fragmentation and cheapening of jobs 'dictated by the tendencies of the capitalist mode of production' which 'inhere in each capitalist firm'. In support of his arguments Braverman cites the relatively impartial evidence of the management specialist J. R. Bright (1958, 1966), who has argued against the rather simplistic thesis that automation generally requires a higher level of skill than the preceding levels of technology. By deploying the evidence of his extensive surveys of manufacturing industry, Bright showed 'more evidence that automation had reduced the skill requirements of the operating work force' (Braverman, 1974, p.

220). Bright's work however, must be considered with more care than Braverman accords it. Bright himself takes pains to describe how automation (as the mechanization of categories of human actions in the co-ordination and operation of industrial production) may either reduce or *increase* the level of skills in the area that is 'automated' (Bright, 1958, pp. 189–97).

To illustrate the latter possibility, consider an example from the part of mechanical engineering which uses skilled labour to prepare, operate and monitor a machine tool and unskilled labour to provide materials and tool pieces. With the introduction of a machine tool which can perform several types of machining operation rather than the one or two of the previous machine, the unskilled transfer and handling work is reduced, and as a result the ratio of skilled to unskilled labour increases. This example points to two important features of automation developments. The effect on skill levels has to take some account of the numbers of occupations involved and the distribution of job tasks among those occupations. If, in this example, the operator had been responsible for his own 'unskilled' handling requirements, then the 'raising' of skills would be specific to the one occupation.

The scale of mechanization of production activities constructed by Bright to assess the extent of the elimination or augmentation of skills has also been criticized. In the context of a study of technological change and employment in the engineering industries Bell (1972) has pointed out that Bright's scale cannot differentiate between different characteristics of the mechanization of an allegedly uniform function. For example, within Bright's categories 1 and 2 the man–machine relationship has the man as the initiating control source, a variable machine response, and a manual source of power with hand or hand tool actions. Bell points out that it could be argued that into such 'levels' could be fitted human operations on both motor-car assembly lines and assembly lines of limited batches of specialized machinery, yet quite different types of both labour and equipment would be associated with these two forms of production.

This heterogeneity of technology within specific levels of Bright's scale leads Bell to propose that the relationship between automation and labour characteristics be analysed in terms of various *systems* responsible for three different functions of production:

    (i) The system which carries out the function of transforming a material or object 'the transformation process itself'.

(ii) The system which *transfers* materials through the transformation process.
(iii) The system responsible for the function of controlling systems i and ii.[6]

The common principle behind the range of NC machine tools which have succeeded each other in levels of sophistication over the past twenty years is, in Bell's terms, that the system of control has been automated. The information necessary for the termination and initiation of different machining movements by different tools on the same machine has to be put into precise and unambiguous computer codes away from the machine, on (in most types of machines) paper tapes which are placed in the machine's control cabinet and which activate the mechanical movements by signals through electronic circuitry. The tape largely takes the place of written instructions to the operator and completely eliminates the need for any interpretation of drawings by him.

Of the technical advantages of these machines, claims are made most frequently for standardization or repeatability (even on very small batches it is important that dimensions and finish are identical) and accuracy or precision (the elimination of the possibility of faulty execution between the information input and its mechanical transmission). As a result of these characteristics, overall quality is enhanced and scrap rates reduced. In addition, several metal-removal techniques, such as milling or drilling, can now be concentrated on one machining unit ('machining centres'), thus reducing handling and transfer time. Braverman also claims that another facet of this automation (which my interviews confirm) is that variability in machining can also be viewed as having been eliminated through more rigid control of those operations over which the machine operator previously had discretion. However, this is now control of machine motions and not of the remaining human actions, which are in many cases as uncontrolled as before. To the extent that machine operations still require certain human actions, these are still dependent upon human volition.

In the twenty-odd years since its own transformation of metal-machining NC technology has in turn benefited from subsequent developments in micro-electronics and computers. These advances have led to new forms of processing the machining information and the articulation of the machine tool(s) to the information control system. The first-phase NC machines receive their information from the paper tape, which is itself a product of the programming of the relevant information through a computer facility linked to the plant's planning department. The tape has to be transferred to the machine tool before it can be checked for errors in this system, and any subsequent modifications require that it be taken back to the programming section.

The second wave of NC computer-controlled (CNC) machines have a computer facility built into their control cabinets. New instructions to the machine can be put into the control system directly via a keyboard, and, where necessary, these instructions can then modify the existing tape to produce, in effect, a new tape. The latest, and possibly final, stage in this articulation of the machining and information control systems is referred to as Direct Numerical Control (DNC). Apart from a few of these systems that are claimed to be operational in Japan,[7] DNC were until recently only in the developmental stage. Their advance consists in linking a number of separate machining systems to a central computer, located off the shop floor, which has the capacity and flexibility to control and instruct the most diverse machining processes without the medium of the paper tapes. Sufficient programs are contained in its memory for new instructions to be put in by programming staff or, with other favourable developments, for the central computer itself to modify instructions after feedback on any necessary modifications made by the machining units.

In the firms I have studied the standard or 1960s vintage NC machines were in the majority and several had between two and four CNC machines. DNC, it may be comforting to know, was not used by any of the firms and in several was not even contemplated. DNC was not only not in use, but in most firms not even thought appropriate because of the organizational and financial costs involved. Some management respondents had only a hazy idea of what was meant by DNC.

Machine tool and NC usage in Britain

Although many published and some purpose-designed statistics pose severe problems of interpretation for a disaggregated analysis, the case studies by myself and others need to be placed in the more general context of British engineering employment and capital investment patterns. Engineering Industry Training Board estimates show that in the year ending April 1966 there were a total of 787,751 craftsmen employed in non-shipbuilding and non-foundry engineering. This had declined to 594,750 by the year ending April 1974 (EITB, 1975, p. 8).

It is difficult to distinguish changes within the general craftsmen category in order to calculate numbers in machining-related crafts because of changes in Department of Employment samples and occupational classifications. (The new 1973 classification, on advice from the engineering industry, lumped skilled machine-tool makers, setters, operators, and other non-maintenance and non-electrical occupations into one 'mechanical engineering craftsman/production' category.) Between 1969 and 1972, however, numbers of machining-related craftsmen remained stable at around 270,000. The new, more heterogeneous category of machining-related crafts showed a small decline in numbers, from 357,600 in 1973 to 329,990 in 1977. In the aerospace sector of engineering the proportion of all craftsmen in the sector's total employment remained fairly constant at around 27 per cent in the period 1968–9 to 1978, according to the Engineering Industry Training Board.[8] If NC and related forms of automation have contributed to a decline in numbers of craftsmen, this decline has not been sufficient to show up in the overall magnitudes of craft employment.

In view of the growth of NC use, however, it would hardly be plausible to assume that NC had had no impact at all on employment patterns, given the machine-manning options it provides for firms. NC as a proportion of all metal-cutting machine tools has doubled from 0.65 per cent in 1971 to 1.32 per cent in 1976.[9] On the assumption used by Bell and Tapp (1972) that one NC machine replaces the capacity of three conventional machine tools, the total of 9725 machines now estimated to be in use in Britain might have reduced machine-operating jobs by about 19,500 since 1966 or 9530 since 1971.[10] These hypothetical numbers might be greater if it were assumed that whereas NC machines are always worked on double and sometimes treble shifts, conventional machines may not be.

Bearing in mind that NC may be worked with either craft or non-craft or skilled or semi-skilled tasks, it cannot be estimated which category these 'lost' jobs have reduced most. On the other hand, the total of jobs affected may well be higher than the numbers given above, if note is taken of the increased sales of machining centres. The latter combine several machining functions, such as milling, drilling and boring, on one single machine. Over the past five years 1735 of these machines have been installed, so that machining centres now form almost one-third of all NC. The principal labour saving from these machines would be in unskilled transferring work and in skilled tool-setting duties. 26 per cent of the 1970s' sales have automatic or 'indexing-turret' tool-change facilities.

NC usage is not now simply a feature of large or even medium-sized plants. Establishments in the size band 10 to 499 employees now hold 60 per cent of all NC stock, and those in the lowest size category, 10 to 49 employees, now hold 21 per cent of the total, as against the 12 per cent of the plants in the 500–999 category. (Notice that these establishments may or may not be coterminous with companies.) NC installation is thus growing at a faster rate and is penetrating all plant sizes, with the most labour-saving types of machine assuming the largest sales. NC as a proportion of all machine tools is probably higher in Britain than in the USA. The distribution of NC within sectors of engineering is both uneven and changing.

Although it is not increasing NC installations as fast as previously, aerospace (from which case-study material is given below) still has the largest proportion of the total for the industry (2.9 per cent), closely followed by the metal-cutting machine tool sector. In aerospace production and related establishments, which formed four of the five firms described beow, there were 1037 NC machines of all types, of which 24 per cent were multi-function machining centres. The aerospace firms investigated in the following study held about 9 per cent of the total NC stock of this sector.[11]

Bell and Tapp (1972) apply the automation classification given above to the pattern of occupational skills and job functions in machine-related occupations. They (correctly, in my view) isolate the third system, the control of the information process, as the one currently being modified by automating small-batch machining.[12] Hence the human capacities to be changed are those relevant to information, not, for example, those of system 1 (manual dexterity). In the seventeen firms in the Bell and Tapp study the total number of craftsmen employed was estimated to be about 22 per cent less on NC than on comparable conventional machines with the same batch size. However, within the craftsmen category there were differences between firms as to both usage of their craftsmen and the type of craftsmen involved.

The specialized or less versatile craftsmen tended, on the whole, to be used less in NC machining, whereas the number of versatile craftsmen (competent on, and familiar with, different types of machine) tended to be greater on NC than on conventional machines. A further determinant of the skill distribution was the division of functions. Where operators continued to do their own tool-setting they were men from a high skill category – frequently craftsmen. Where the setting duties were made into a separate occupation the overall level of skills, especially on machine-operating functions, tended to fall. In other words, separate the machine-setting from the machine-operation job, and the overall skill level falls; increasing skills 'off' the machine (setting and supervising) means decreasing skills on the machine operation. Bell and Tapp were unable to isolate correlations between quality of work and skill composition/distribution, but in general the longer the run of components produced in a machine shop – that is, the larger the batch size – the more likely were specialized setting-up jobs and less skilled operators. Conversely, where small batch sizes prevailed, so did a combination of setting and operating tasks in one machining occupation and, therefore, a wider range of skills in the occupation.

Large firms tended to use less craft-trained labour, and it was suggested that these firms, because of their size, had the resources to train up their own labour. To explain the relative persistence of higher craft levels than might be expected for NC work, Bell and Tapp (1972) suggest non-technical factors: union pressures to check deskilling; management inertia inhibiting creation of training programmes for semi-skilled labour; the location of NC machines within shops composed largely of conventional machines – the manning levels and employment patterns of NC being strongly influenced by the arrangements for the conventional machines. Concluding, Bell and Tapp (1972, p. 111) state:

If anything, the data support the view that there is nothing inherent about the nature of NC machines that requires a particular employment pattern. We take the argument further to suggest that once a pattern which is relatively intensive in the use of more skilled labour is established, there are a number of forces at work to maintain that pattern.

An investigation of skill redistribution for NC machining

Braverman's description of NC has the universalistic and deterministic character described above. The conception–separation thesis leads him to describe programming positions as devoid of metal-cutting experience, and machining jobs as stripped of a knowledge of tool control. Yet these *lacunae* in job knowledge must, in his terms, also be considered conducive to production efficiency. It is difficult to see how this could be achieved by such a double deskilling since (as will be shown below) some tool knowledge is required on the shop floor during machining operations and metal-working experience is required in advance of machining by part-programmers. Bhattacharyya *et al.* (1976, p. 10) found, in a survey of NC users, that in about 90 per cent of their cases setter-operators had 'to make sure that the correct tooling was available when required for the right components . . .'. Since in few cases was it *solely* the programmer who selected tool types, the authors concluded that 'most programmers do not have sufficient production engineering experience'.

In other words, where operations are pre-planned and programmed, if all the relevant knowledge cannot be incorporated into one occupation (here programming), it has to be utilized in another. This is another way of posing the problem of skill distribution. Similarly, Bell and Tapp conceded that no strict conclusion regarding the redistribution of, or reduction in, specific skills could be drawn from their work, partly because their frame of reference included only technical personnel who were engaged in the material processes of machine preparation and operation. Given the greater involvement of planning workers in NC tasks, this last omission is of some importance. The Bell and Tapp study had other limitations: it relied on statistical inferences and was confined to areas and engineering sectors which might not be radically affected by the implications of NC methods. Omitted altogether were Wales and the south-west of England and the aerospace sector. My study was, hence, aimed at a qualitative investigation of aspects of NC organization and social and economic characteristics, as these influenced skill distribution, in particular small-batch engineering firms in Wales and the south-west of England.

In-depth interviewing of works management, supervisors, shop-floor workers and planning and programming staff has so far been undertaken at five firms in south-west England and South Wales regions. A more detailed study was made of one of the larger of these establishments, with extra interviews being conducted with training staff, maintenance service staff, tooling managers and computer organizers. Interviews with works management and engineers at two smaller firms were also held, principally to gain some impression of the situation of NC use in the small firm. Some information was also obtained from trade union officials and shop stewards. This latter is principally preparatory material for the second part of the research (in progress at present), which seeks to contrast union perceptions of the situations in the five firms with accounts from management. The trade union interviews are also aimed at clarifying the role of the relevant unions and their shop-floor representatives in past and future advances in the acquisition and use of NC-type machinery.

Of these five firms, two were concerned exclusively with parts and equipment for aerospace. Another produced, partly for aerospace and partly for other users, a variety of 'environmental control systems', such as air-pressure devices. A fourth establishment produced a range of components for other sections of its division of the company, which in turn concentrated on the production of control systems for rail-based transportation systems. The fifth establishment was a medium-sized specialist subcontractor working mainly for the aerospace industry. It was notable because it was set up as a separate firm within a holding company and was devoted solely to subcontracting NC machining work. It was anticipated that the effects of NC on production organization would be more advanced in aerospace than in other sectors of engineering. NC had been used in aerospace almost since it first became available. It was also known to be an industry in which NC was being used to advance high-quality machining work and hence was encroaching upon some of the highest craft skills. It was also thought that the close connection between the industry and government defence contracts shielded the industry from market vicissitudes and allowed levels of investment in which other sectors of British engineering are notorious for lagging behind.

The preliminary evidence from this research project is organized into five sections in order to deal with the problems posed at the outset of this paper. These problems were an assessment of the separate and reciprocal influences of product and market constraints, internal management–organizational structures and trade-union strategies *vis-à-vis* the labour market, on the division of production task skills between pre-planning (in these cases, programming) occupations and machine operation/supervision. These factors in this process are discussed first with reference to management plans for their NC investment, and then in relation to supervisory and control procedures and the allocation of skilled production labour. The final sections discuss the determination of task division, and hence 'skills', between programmers and machinists in relation to the varying influences of trade unions and their labour markets.

Criteria in NC investment decisions

Only in the new firm specifically set up in 1970 as an NC sub-contractor was there any clear-cut case of investment which was planned solely in terms of the requirements and benefits of NC working. Even here half the machines were conventional (for finishing work), with the usual complement of craftsmen operators. This firm had also adopted the customary form of line management and was heavily reliant upon well qualified and experienced programming staff for co-ordination between shop floor and customer requirements. In all the other firms, even where NC formed 50 per cent of total machine stock, NC machines had been installed in ones or twos as finances allowed or to replace obsolete conventional machines. In most cases NC machines were scattered among the conventional machines and were not seen as part of a separate NC strategy.

Although I was not able to interview all those involved in investment decisions, no one cited labour costs as an influence in buying NC, even when pressed on this issue. More frequently cited were the reductions in between-machining or 'floor-to-floor' time. NC was often thought to produce quality work which could not even be envisaged with conventional work. Repeatability of items was frequently mentioned – it was thought that standardization of components was something that could never be achieved with even the best craftsmen on conventional machines. With one exception all management groups mentioned the scarcity of highly skilled labour as a factor influencing the decision to buy NC. In the one firm where multiple interviews were carried out, another facet of the capital-investment process was revealed as it was clear that the chief engineer's department was messianically in favour of NC and looked forward to the paradise of DNC. That this was not the view of senior management was apparent from grumbles that the latter did not really understand NC. Other managerial departments voiced their disquiet over such a total NC policy. Since the existing NC complement were widely accepted as failing to match the promised cost reductions, scepticism about wholesale commitment to NC investment appeared to be quite genuine.

A general objection to all this evidence might be that it is disingenuous to accept managerial statements that labour costs are not a prime reason for NC installation. This objection would presume that management is hardly likely to boast to a sociologist that NC is its way of cutting wage costs. Clearly labour costs influence investment decisions but it is not necessarily the case that they determine the decision to introduce NC and to purchase particular machines. At least one technical manager interviewed said that he might be prepared to argue in terms of labour costs in order to win over a financial director to NC purchase. This manager himself thought that cost reductions were only indirectly related to wage savings. The inquiry into production engineering efficiency with NC by Birmingham University (Bhattacharyya *et al.*, 1976) showed the minor importance of labour costs in NC purchases. Similarly, Piore's (1968) case studies of new capital investment in several US industries showed that the labour costs related to new technology were only assessed in the most haphazard manner. No definite conclusion on the weight of any particular objectives in a machine-tool purchase can be reached until evidence is produced from an actual decision-making procedure. This is a level of business decision which social scientists have not yet been invited to witness or have succeeded in entering.[13]

Supervisory controls and communication systems

Technical literature on NC often exhorts management to take on NC as a total system and transform its structures of command and shop organization accordingly. At no firm I visited had such revisions been attempted. The traditional line management of shop manager – supervisors – foremen was still the main form of control over production, even though a new chain of communication is necessitated by NC (and is described below) between machine-tool setters and operators on the one hand and with the programming/planning department (or with individual programmers) on the other hand. In varying degrees this passage of information cuts across the line-management hierarchy as an 'informal' mechanism. In two of the larger firms, however, where it was felt shop referrals to planners were diverting the latter from programming work, renewed insistence on passing up machine complaints/queries to planning was executed. A rigid reintroduction of the line form of communication up to shop management and across to planning heads was reasserted.[14] This was regarded as time-wasting and inefficient by operating staff and as reducing their job satisfaction by programmers.[15] It appears to demonstrate the intransigence of organizational forms designed for pre-NC methods – it certainly did not appear to enhance the planner's control of machining. It is worth noting, however, that (possibly with an eye to future computerized information systems) in two firms an attempt has been made to create forms of 'group technology'. In these, supervision and machining time is allocated to limited types of components or 'families' according to, for example, similar dimensions rather than machining requirements (cf. G. A. B. Edwards, 1971).

Skill levels and skill composition of machining labour

Of the five firms studied, two maintained a strict distinction between setters and operators. Both claimed that this related to the scarcity of skilled labour. When one notices that from the early 1970s onwards the intake of new apprentices was substantially reduced on a national scale, there may be a perverse truth in this statement.[16] As a consequence, both firms had also organized their own operator-training schemes. In these two firms, however, the stratification of skills differed. Although both had their own training schemes for non-apprenticed school-leavers (and these took up to three years to complete), one firm had placed its setters (principally craftsmen) on staff status (giving them white coats with gold collars to symbolize this). Below these men were Grade 1 operators, mainly experienced in a limited number of conventional and NC machines. Grade 1 men were often products of the machinist training scheme mentioned above. Below these were Grade 2 men, responsible to a setter and exclusively working NC machines after just one month's training. This category was being expanded from twenty to around thirty or forty per shift. Setting, Grade 1 and Grade 2 categories were also ranked in that order for wage rates.

The reason given for the shift in skill composition was that new orders coming 'on stream' were long runs of relatively uncomplicated components, replacing a mish-mash of separate and diverse components produced over the past few years. In other words, skills were compressed 'off the machine', while required levels on the machine were reduced because of changes in the composition of the product. Of the three other firms, one used a combination of setter-operators and setters with operators. There were little or no supervisory duties here for setters and almost certainly 50 per cent of the operators were craftsmen. Consistent with Bell and Tapp's findings, however, was the fact that longer runs of some components were on those machines which had the lowest proportion of craftsmen. The two remaining firms were similar, as each had setter-operators with no separate setting category. They were different, however, in as much as one (a medium-sized, purpose-built NC subcontracting firm) had no craftsmen on NC, whereas the other firm's NC operators were predominantly craftsmen. These differences were reflected in the division of tasks between machinists and programmers and were conditioned by trade-union and labour-market factors.

Divison of tasks between programmers, planner-programmers and machinists

Braverman's description of the tasks of programmers and NC machinists makes no reference to the intersection of their different duties, other than claiming that machinists have a knowledge of metal-working which is denied to technical planners, but, according to him, machinists are themselves denied knowledge of tool actions and capacities.[17] Part-programming is, however, *contra* Braverman, a peculiarly composite task. It requires certain levels of numeracy and mathematical competence to calculate dimensions and to envisage three-dimensional effects from paper. Also required are a knowledge of metal-cutting tools and the materials worked, even with automatic machines of the NC kind, and an appreciation of the limitations and idiosyncracies of particular machines. Many of my respondents, actually involved in planning/programming work and its supervision, were doubtful whether computerization via Computer Aided Design and data storage on tools and materials would eliminate these qualities of programmers. In many cases each element in the combination of materials, contours, tool tips and tool movements was thought to be unique to that particular job and could not be transferred to new work. There was much distrust, for example, of tool manufacturers' standardized specifications of tool capacities. The paradox of NC use is that part-programming presupposes a knowledge of tooling performance and metal qualities which in many cases is only acquired through shop-floor experience and therefore resides with setters and the more experienced operators.

This hiatus is crucial, moreover, for examining the division of responsibilities between programmers and machinists and their input of skills to particular functions. Figure 2 shows the progress of a typical piece of NC machining work. There are two crucial junctures.

First at the 'prove-out' stage[18] the efficacy of the program calculated in the planning office is put to the test by a trial run on the production machine. The part-programmer is normally present by the machine at this stage, making observations of the accuracy of his specifications of tool feeds, speeds and dimensions. (Union constraints already occur, however, since in no firm I visited would the programmer activate the automatic sequences or switch to manual control.) Flaws may mean revisions either by the operator using a manual override mechanism or by a literal 'return to the drawing-board'.

Hold-ups occur because programmers are disinclined, or forbidden by their union (the Technical and Supervisory Section of the AUEW–TASS), to work the shifts or times put in by machinists. Often there are only about four hours in the day when both employees are jointly available and this causes pressures when some large jobs have a machining cycle of about ten hours each. The shift disjunction is even more significant when modification to tapes (or 'editing', as it is sometimes known) becomes necessary. In several firms it is common practice for operators to use the manual override devices to overcome a hold-up on night shifts. (It was also pointed out to me several times that operators must have sufficient machining experience to detect a change in the noise pitch that signified tool wear and so prevent an expensive scrapping of tool, component or both. Often a craftsman or machinist with long experience is the only available category of worker to operate machines for this check.)

Tape modifications were an even more delicate issue with the latest NC control systems (the CNC machines referred to above). Given the above disjunctures between programming and operating duties, it is quite feasible, and even conducive to efficiency, for machine operators to make use of the memory-adaptation and tape-editing facility on CNC machines. Firms that object to these facilities being directly available to operators have to arrange the non-inclusion of the editing facility when they order, or the blanking-off of the relevant adaptation and editing controls. Hence in one firm the controls bore the legend 'In no circumstances must this cabinet be unlocked.'

In three firms the obstacles of programmer availability and gaps in tool and metal knowledge were overcome and the programmer was loaded with full responsibility for 'editing' the tape in very much the same fashion as at the 'prove-out'. Two of these firms had CNC with the editing function blanked off. In the third there was some ambiguity as to whether operators might invade this facility on a night shift or when machining problems became acute. The main reason given for refusal to cede editing to operators was the lack of any adequate information facility! The tapes could be modified on the shop floor but the record of the change might remain hidden in the computers' memory, or the planning department's master tape might remain unchanged.[19]

Another obstacle to operator control of tape-editing was said to be the huge cost of some components, which could not be entrusted to many operators. The metal-knowledge hiatus also appears to have had the paradoxical effect of removing apprentice-qualified crafts-men from the machine shop, where their skills are still needed after 'prove-out', for monitoring and so on into the drawing and planning offices. Most firms preferred programmers to be ex-apprentices with machining experience. This was often the only way to secure knowledge of tool-cutting and other processes. Standardized data from makers was thought unreliable. This 'internal labour market' strategy of recruiting from production workers who already had such 'background' knowledge and experience does not, of course, overcome the communication problems on shift work.

Union strength and labour markets

The metal-tool knowledge hiatus has not (yet) been overcome through auto-detection and correction of flaws and errors by the machines themselves. In using NC, therefore, firms make decisions, or have decisions forced upon them, about the extent to which either direct production or planning workers should extend their basic tasks (setting/monitoring and initial programming, respectively) into the grey area of modification of records and machine instructions about metal-cutting, changing tool types, modifying speeds. However, in only one company were the operators taking over the responsibility, which their knowledge of metals gave them, to modify the com-puter's instructions through the CNC facility.[20]

Because access to this facility allows operators to change the program as they see fit, it seems appropriate to consider this arrangement as a return of operator 'skills'. There appeared to be three reasons for this case of the 'clawing back' of skills. The operators were predominantly craftsmen: the firm's labour market stretched as far as the north-west of England. The AUEW branch appeared to be strong, well-staffed and with clear-cut policies. By contrast, the TASS membership in the planning office was said to be

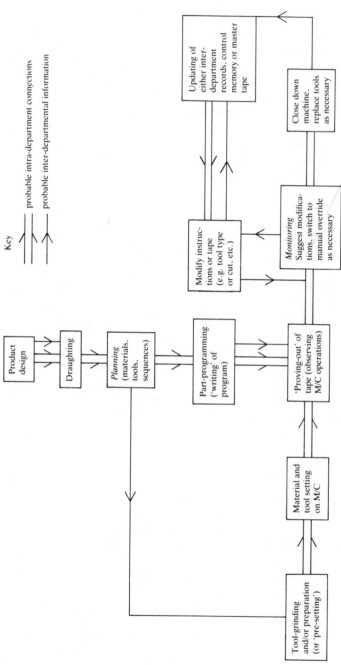

Figure 2 *Stages of tasks in production by NC machining*

weakly organized. Third, the head of planning was intent on concentrating his programming staff on strictly engineering problems rather than what he considered to be routine discrepancies. Mis-matches between machine tapes and master tapes were not thought to be a problem since master tapes were revised after five orders.

By contrast, tape modifications by operators were ruled out in the other firms for different reasons. In one, because of the lack of craft knowledge among the operators; in a second, because the operators were on piece rates and could be expected to violate the job content to get faster output times; in the third, there was a strong TASS section, assertive in its definition of programmer responsibilities, and the hierarchical management ethos was opposed to a merging of computing and operating spheres referred to above. Another argument put to me in this firm (in which some CNC machines were specially bought *without* the editing facility) was that tape preparation was made in 'high-level' computer languages which were difficult to translate into simple modifying codes. It was thought that it would be difficult to familiarize operators with the high-level languages. However, at least one AUEW steward interviewed there saw CNC as a wedge to 'claw back' operator responsibilities. Finally, the fourth firm – the specialist NC plant, although it had no CNC – was probably correct in predicting antipathy to operator editing when CNC was acquired. The union certainly did not have the coherence or strategy to make it an objective, while the expensive nature of components and expansive role of the programming staff were expected to preclude its consideration.

Conclusion

The evidence presented here further contradicts even modified theses about general and inherent tendencies to deskill because of 'laws' of capitalist exploitation and accumulation.[21] Even in a very small sample, mainly from one sector of engineering, there was sufficient variation among enterprises to confirm the decisiveness of product and labour markets, organizational structures and trade-union positions as independent influences on the forms of skill deployment. There is nothing 'inherent' in the hardware of NC or its concept that would allow for the deskilling and control and surveillance assumed by both theorists of the labour process and publicists for NC installation. This is not to deny that such motivations exist among manufacturing management. It merely reasserts that management calculation cannot be concerned solely with labour costs and utilization. Similarly, management cannot construct, *de novo*, the conditions under which labour is to function.

It was seen above that conflicting principles of labour management may be woven into the structure of the firm. The departmentalized (Taylorist) system of control could not simply be dismantled to allow control by the information controls of a computerized system, despite the 'efficiency' claimed for the latter. Indeed, the conventional system reasserted itself at the expense of efficiency. The departmentalization of a function was a bar to efficient machine use and hence to intensity in the performance of direct labour. The hiatus in metal and tool knowledge arose because of a distribution of skills between occupations in planning departments and the shop floor. This division was sometimes accentuated by trade-union policy.

Hence the precise divisibility of task skills, while technically constrained, was determined by combinations of these organizational and trade union influences. On the other hand, the material character of the product and the effect (at different times within one firm) of the composition of demand (size of orders) was also a crucial influence on the deployment of machine-related skills. At all times the relative supply of skilled labour influenced this deployment. So managements were caught in the contradictory position of still needing a level of metal-machining skills for NC but accentuating this shortage by installing NC machines that craftsmen need not, and often would not, work.

It was these kinds of consideration which appeared to lead to both specialized craftsmen setters and to sub-apprentice training systems, rather than a unilateral deskilling strategy. However, just as management was unable to articulate and execute a coherent NC strategy because of competing objectives and inherited structures, so trade unions were unable to act as rational strategists. TASS and the AEUW operated with separate objectives and in different spheres of interest (hence limiting any joint strategy on job automation). But their different tactics, paradoxically, had advantageous effects. The TASS ban on shift working threw the shop floor on to its own resources when programmers were not available and hence preserved some independence of machine modification for operators. Similarly, the AUEW principle of 'one man, one machine' designed to preserve numbers employed, created boredom for long stretches of machining time. However, because operators now had 'spare capacity', they could not be so easily 'specialized' as monitors of several machines. As a result, the arrival of CNC has given them the quite unexpected possibility of an increment to their range of task skills in tape-editing functions.

Any general development towards deskilling in the organization of contemporary industrial work could only be confirmed if it were possible to aggregate the skills used by particular enterprises in particular industries. However, this exercise would depend upon there being a compression of skills within particular units of production such that, for example, technical management monopolized knowledge relevant to the task functions required in production, possibly through automation of information/control functions. The evidence from NC machine-tool use in the above cases suggests that the relevant control function of part-programming demands a combination of skills which, even if these occupations were considered to be mainly managerial or unproductive (as some of the theories criticized here would argue), cannot be compressed into one such controlling position or category of positions.

In this chapter I have concentrated on the market, organizational, trade-union and technical factors which have been shown to have varying influences upon the distribution of the task skills associated with different functions and responsibilities among managerial, technician, and production workers. I am not suggesting that the influence of these different factors is random. But the evidence from the areas of engineering examined here indicates that their precise effects on skill distribution – and therefore upon the level of skills employed – varies from enterprise to enterprise. Since the influence of these factors is also likely to vary in other industries, it follows that no process of a general reduction of skills can be said to be taking place. It also follows that varieties of Marxism which adduce necessary or general reductions in skills from characteristics of some concept of capitalist-production-in-general are operating with a fundamental misconception of the organization of capitalist production in specific economies and industries.

Notes

Chapter 1 Introduction

1 Braverman is not alone in doing this. Drucker (1955, p. 247–9), a management theorist, assumes scientific management is the ultimate managerial practice and that the history of management theory has reached its summit.

2 The important studies are Burawoy (1979), Elbaum and Wilkinson (1979), Friedman (1977a) and Zeitlin (1979). For empirical studies which attempt to support the central tenets of Braverman's argument, see Zimbalist (1979).

3 In rejecting a crude social construction thesis, there is a danger of throwing the baby out with the bath water, for the significance it attaches to the bargained nature of job and wage structures is important. Accordingly, 'real' skills may be seen as one means by which skilled status is achieved, and the key question is whether these skills provide a basis for worker organization. It is thus possible, in cases where they do not, that groups of workers may trade real skills which provide little bargaining power for less autonomy combined with higher wages (cf. Rubery, 1978).

4 As Jill Rubery has suggested to me, perhaps the basic reason why literacy is forgotten is that it is now a universal and general skill and thus fails to differentiate workers or to provide them with a basis for bargaining.

Chapter 2 Braverman, capital accumulation and deskilling

1 This paper is a shortened version of an article that first appeared in *Capital and Class*, vol. 7 (1979), pp. 58–99. The main omissions from the present version are discussions of work by the Brighton Labour Process Group, Palloix, Stone and Mandel, and comments on Braverman's treatment of the reserve army of labour. Earlier versions of the paper were read at the 1977 CSE Annual Conference, at a BSA Industrial Sociology Group conference on 'Skill and the labour process', and at the Nuffield Deskilling Conference held in Windsor in 1978. Bill

Schwarz, John Humphrey and the members of the Warwick CSE and Trade Unionism groups all provided valued advice and support.

2 Early reviews of Braverman concentrated on exposition of his analysis, while more recent reviews have developed more critical assessments. Among the major reviews are Heilbroner (1975); Davies and Brodhead (1975); de Kadt (1976); *Monthly Review* (1976); Young (1976); Jacoby (1977); Schwarz (1977); Lazonick (1977); Nichols (1977); Coombs (1978); Cutler (1978) and MacKenzie (1977)

3 Among examples of this criticism, see in particular Schwarz (1977); Jacoby (1977); Coombs (1978); Nichols (1977); Palmer (1975); Friedman (1977a) and MacKenzie (1977).

4 See in particular Schwarz (1977); Lazonick (1977); Jacoby (1977); Coombs (1978) and Palmer (1975).

5 Braverman's (1974, pp. 150–1) discussion of economism is underpinned by the assumption that capital in the monopoly sector can finance wage gains out of monopoly superprofits. This is clearly related to the position of Baran and Sweezy.

6 At one point in *Labor and Monopoly Capital* Braverman recognizes working-class self-activity outside production only to counterpose to it the total domination secured by capital through and within production:

This working class lives a social and political existence of its own, outside the direct grip of capital. It protests and submits, rebels or is integrated into bourgeois society, sees itself as a class or loses sight of its own existence, in accordance with the forces that act upon it and the moods, conjunctions and conflicts of social and political life. But since, in its permanent existence, it is the living part of capital, its occupational structure, modes of work, and distribution through the industries of society are determined by the ongoing processes of the accumulation of capital. It is seized, released, flung into various parts of the social machinery and expelled by others, not in accord with its own will or self-activity, but in accord with the movement of capital. [ibid., p. 378]

7 The analysis developed by Marx (1976, appendix) makes explicit the theorization of the transformation of the labour process from its inherited form to a form appropriate to capital accumulation – from 'formal' to 'real' subordination of the labour process to capital – in a manner hardly visible in *Capital* itself. However, it is only in *Capital* that the transformation of the labour process is effectively related to the limits and contradictions besetting specific phases of valorization and accumulation.

8 This is implied in Marx's caution concerning the ideological and organizational features of skill within the developed capitalist labour process:

The distinction between higher and simple labour, 'skilled labour' and 'unskilled labour' rests in part upon pure illusion, or, to say the least, on distinctions that have long since ceased to be real, and that survive only by virtue of a traditional convention; in part on the helpless condition of some sections of the working class, a condition that prevents them from exacting equally with the rest the value of their labour power. Accidental circumstances here play so great a part that these two forms of labour sometimes change places. [Marx, 1976, p. 305, note]

9 Some commentators (for instance, Mandel in his introduction to Marx, 1976, p. 944), identify real subordination with mechanization and modern industry, while manufacture is identified with formal subordination. While Marx clearly considers modern industry as the culmination of 'real subordination' it is also clear that the manufacturing division of labour represents a form of 'real subordination' (see in particular Marx, 1976, pp. 1024, 1034, 1054–5). This conceptualization underlines the central significance of scale and development of a complex apparatus of collective labour as well as machinery in Marx's analysis of the mystification of the capital relation arising through the real subordination of labour and the labour process to capital.

10 The specific place of the 'intensification' of labour in the analyses of absolute and relative surplus value is ambiguous in some respects, but must primarily be located as an element of relative surplus value production.

11 In this context Marx's celebrated discussion of the contradictions between specialization and the flexible development of human competences in modern industry (Marx, 1976, pp. 614–19) cannot be interpreted only as a contrast between capitalist reality and potential forms of the organization of labour in a socialist society, nor only as a contrast between forced specialization of labour powers within the capitalist factory and the crippling obsolescence of such specialization when the labourer is thrown out of employment, but also as a contradiction besetting the capitalist organization of the labour process itself in relation to the pursuit of valorization.

12 See Sweezy (1942); Baran and Sweezy (1968) and Sweezy (1974).

13 For critiques, see Mandel (1978), especially ch. 17; Gamble and Walton (1976), chs. 3–4; and also Rowthorne's (1976) critique of Mandel, which underlines the point that the critics should not and need not rest their case on a *mechanical* invocation of rising organic composition/falling rate of profit arguments (see also Fine and Harris, 1976). It is worth adding that these strictures do nothing to undermine the emphasis Baran and Sweezy place on the increasing centrality of advertising and marketing strategies for oligopolistic capitalism, or Braverman's related analysis of the elaboration of this part of the corporate apparatus and personnel, in *LMC*, ch. 12.

14 For a vivid account of the realities of subordination inherent in the reorganization of craft work under the auspices of capitalist manufacture, see McKendrick (1961).

15 It should be obvious that I agree with Stedman-Jones that the notion of

the 'labour aristocracy' does not, in itself, constitute an analysis but is rather a label for a nexus of interrelations between labour process, phases of accumulation and working-class politics and culture. Moorhouse (1978) provides a hostile assessment of attempts to develop an analysis of the 'labour aristocracy', which usefully summarizes the problems and emphasizes in particular (a) the number of different accounts of this nexus on offer, and (b) the problematical character of the relation between working-class politics and developments in the labour process. However, on the basis of this argument he seeks to absorb the debate into general analyses of working-class sectionalism and the cultural hegemony of capital in a manner which denies the evident significance of vertical divisions between skilled and quasi-skilled workers and non-skilled workers as a basis for cultural and political divisions. Field (1979) offers a more sympathetic assessment but pinpoints similar issues.

16 In addition, Burgess (1975) provides a useful account of the phases of development over the whole of the second half of the nineteenth century.

17 Since this was written Lazonick (1979) has provided a detailed account of the development of the social division of labour in cotton. From my point of view he offers an exemplary analysis as first, he criticizes Marx for accepting Ure's account of the power of the machine to suppress worker resistance, second, he analyses the interplay between valorization strategies and the strengths and weaknesses of worker organization, and third, he focuses on the manner in which the social division of labour articulates with sexual divisions.

18 See Wilkinson (1977) on Britain; Stone (1974), who discusses the pattern of American developments but overstates the purely ideological character of hierarchization following the thorough defeat of craft organization; Rubery (1978), who comments on the theoretical issues raised by Stone and by Wilkinson; and, especially, Elbaum and Wilkinson (1979) for a comparison of British and American development.

19 Though lack of space precludes further discussion, it should be noted that a valuable aspect of Braverman's analysis of Taylorism is his account of the development of a corporate apparatus of planning and control (*LMC*, especially chs. 5, 15, 18). However, it is doubtful whether the notion of a shrinking elite of conceptualizers counterposed to a mass of deskilled clerical labourers constitutes an adequate basis for the analysis of that apparatus.

20 Palmer's discussion of Braverman has been characterized by de Kadt (1976) in terms of the distinct levels of analysis at which they have worked: Braverman at the most general level of the logic of capital, and Palmer at the more particular level of specific forms of worker

resistance and diverse employers' strategies. Palmer (1976) seems to accept this characterization and to equate it with the distinct preoccupations of political economists (laws of motion) and social historians (resistance and struggle of the 'losers'), adding only that the latter constitutes a countervailing logic which qualifies the former. However, this concedes too much, both in general and in relation to aspects of Palmer's argument: the bases and forms of resistance must themselves be theorized in relation to the dynamic of accumulation if class struggle is to be analysed as integral to the laws of motion of capital and not be merely tacked on at the end. For further discussion of rival analyses of 'scientific management', see Elger and Schwarz (1980).

21 Rubery (1978) offers a useful analysis of the bases of bargaining leverage among semi-skilled workers in mechanized production. She emphasises that:

> the development of capitalism not only presents problems for worker control and organisation, inducing defensive tactics on the part of existing trade union organisations, but also offers new opportunities for organisation. Thus the development of machine technology may to some extent have undermined the skilled union's basis for organisation and control but, by transforming much unskilled labour into semi-skilled labour or, rather, by increasing the proportion of the labour force directly involved in the mechanized production process, it increased the bargaining power of a large section of the labour force. Semi-skilled workers were now in control of a greater volume of production, and further represented a threat to some skilled workers as the real skill differential declined, thus forcing some skilled unions to recruit semi-skilled workers, whilst in other industries organisation of semi-skilled workers proceeded independently. [ibid., p. 30]

Friedman (1977a and b) uses a similar argument as his point of departure for a discussion of the centrality of non-Taylorist, concession-making, co-optive management strategies in the post-war period, though he relies most heavily upon the limitation of the reserve army of labour in explaining the strength of worker resistance.

Chapter 3 The sexual division of labour and the labour process

1 Various friends and colleagues over a long time provided the stimulus to my writing a paper on Braverman, and Angela Coyle, Tony Elger, Simon Frith, Richard Hyman and Bill Schwarz discussed my ideas with me and/or read sections of the manuscript. I am extremely grateful to them all for their help and support.

2 These arguments would also apply to the paper by Baxandall, Ewen and Gordon (1976), whose notion of 'craftswomanship' is also romanticized.

3 It is, in my view, mistaken to draw oversimple parallels between institutions like the family and the education system and the labour

process, arguing that they are all subject to the same tendencies within capitalist society. This problem besets a number of American Marxist works: see, for example, Bowles and Gintis (1976) and a number of the revisionist historians of education for discussion of the parallels between the education system and the labour process.

4   Marx discusses this in his appendix to *Capital*, vol. 1.

5   Thompson (1979) elaborates upon these arguments. While correctly emphasizing the formalistic, ahistorical approach which abstracts different levels of analysis from the social totality, Thompson ends up criticizing all forms of abstraction for failing to analyse experience.

6   The notion of class as process, as social relation and as an historical concept is elaborated by Thompson (1968, preface).

7   Jean Gardiner develops some of these arguments in a different way (Gardiner, 1977, p. 162), where she argues that women's relationship to the class structure has two aspects: a relationship to class which is mediated by the family and by men and a direct involvement in the social labour process.

8   There is a sense in which some of the debates about Eurocommunism are concerned less with 'reading off' a political analysis from an analysis of the class structure than with searching for a theory of class which would justify a particular political strategy.

Chapter 4   Taylorism, responsible autonomy and management strategy

1   Taylor's technical contributions were not therefore simply by-products, as Braverman (1974, p. 110) suggests, but necessary preconditions for raising and maintaining labour productivity; see Kelly (1982).

2   Equally 'monolithic' accounts of Taylorism derive from the practice of privileging a particular text as the clearest expression of Taylorism as a whole; cf. P. S. Taylor (1979), Sohn-Rethel (1978), Bendix (1974) and Drucker (1976).

3   Problems of implementation are also discussed in R. Edwards (1979) and Palmer (1975), both of which are useful correctives to Braverman. Fridenson (1978) illustrates, through the use of Taylorism in France, how managements may adapt the system to meet their own particular needs.

4   A similar distinction is implicit in R. Edwards (1979) and Palmer (1975).

5   For a discussion of the implementation of a job-enrichment scheme that highlights the differential responses of work forces, see Roberts and Wood (1982).

Chapter 5   Skilled manual workers in the labour process, 1856–1964

1   Many people have assisted me with this research. I should like to thank especially my two thesis supervisors, Gavin MacKenzie and Michael

Mann, and my colleagues at Lancaster and in the 'State and economy' BSA study group. I would also like to thank Tony Elger, David Lee, Tony Manwaring and Rosemary Crompton, who commented on earlier drafts of this paper.

2 I am distinguishing here between mechanized and automatic factory production. This is a difference of degree. The hand-mules in spinning and early lathes like Maudslay's in engineering were not automatic and required considerable intervention by operatives. Automatic looms and machinery in the cardroom required far less, as did automatic mules. The degree of intervention by operatives on lathes is a variable and is strongly influenced by the relative strength of skilled manual workers in the local labour market.

Chapter 7   Deskilling and changing structures of control

1 I would like to thank Ronald Dore, Andrew Friedman, Patrick Fridenson, Howard Gospel and Stephen Wood for their criticism and help in the development of this chapter. Some of the arguments have been presented in the context of a Japanese comparison (see Littler, 1980).

2 Considerable confusion surrounds the notion of subcontract because of the failure to distinguish between external subcontract and internal contract. The continuance of internal contract through the nineteenth century reflected inside the factory the continuance of petty workshop production outside. Nevertheless, external subcontract or outwork, which merges into ordinary commercial relationships, does not represent a cohesive structure and is not relevant to the gist of this paper.

3 See Emanuel Lovekin's account of his career as a butty master and 'sinker' between the 1840s and 1899 (in Burnett, 1977, pp. 289–96). His autobiographical account revolves around his personal relationships with colliery owners.

4 Stedman-Jones claims that the use of the idea of a 'labour aristocracy' has always been vague and ambiguous:

> Its status is uncertain and it has been employed at will, descriptively, polemically or theoretically, without ever finding a firm anchorage . . . the term has often been used as if it provided an explanation. But it would be more accurate to say that it pointed towards a vacant area where an explanation should be. [Stedman-Jones, 1975, p. 65]

5 There was some internal contract within the 'sweated' trades, but typically such trades were based on small workshops whose very size precluded extensive internal contract.

6 For the details of the Richard, Johnson and Nephew struggle, see Littler (1981).

7 This pattern was also repeated in France (letter to the writer from Patrick Fridenson, 13 August 1979).

8   For more detailed comparisons of Britain and the USA, see Littler (1981). I do not wish to imply that Braverman's description of the development of the American labour process is correct. His account is partly right and partly wrong.

Chapter 8   Beyond deskilling: skill, craft and class

1   This is a revised and shortened version of a paper published in *Sociology*, vol. 15 (1981), pp. 56–78.

Chapter 9   The deskilling of clerical work

1   It is interesting to note that although the concept of deskilling has become synonymous with Braverman's work, he himself does not use the term.

2   See Foster (1974) for a 'strong' statement of this perspective. A recent bibliography may be found in Hobsbawm (1978).

3   Following Carchedi (1975b), we would make a distinction between the co-ordination necessary to any complex labour process and the control necessary to ensure that labour works consistently, avoids waste and so on – in short, necessary to maintain the rate of extraction of relative surplus value. The former is an aspect of the labour process, the latter an aspect of the function of capital. Given that complex labour processes have been developed entirely within the constraints of capitalist relations of production, control and co-ordination are fused – as in, for example, the work role of the foreman.

4   For a fuller discussion of this case, see S. Reid, 'The Computer and White-Collar Proletarianisation: a Case Study of Local Government', Ph.D thesis submitted to Faculty of Economics and Politics, University of Cambridge, 1980. Although we have spoken so far of labour and capital, the case material is drawn not from the private sector but concerns a public organization. For two reasons we feel this is less problematic than it may at first seem. First, the example focuses on changes in the labour process which illustrate Braverman's thesis of the separation of conception and execution, irrespective of the organization of the institution. Second, the rigid financial constraints on the public sector produce accounting procedures, management techniques and a concern for productivity comparable in many respects with those of the business firm.

5   The feminine is used as the majority of the clerks in the study from which the example is drawn were women.

6   The possibility of using direct entry terminals (VDUs) had been considered in this department but had not yet been implemented. These would enable the clerk to enter data directly into the computer, but the

potential effects on clerical job content were not clear. Such a development was regarded by the management as a means of further reducing labour costs by cutting clerical and data-preparation staff.

7 Other factors (for example, low pay, full employment policies and changing social attitudes to women's employment have also made major contributions to this trend.

8 On women's orientations to work and the vicious circle of their dual role at home and work, see Garnsey (1978); Beechey (1977); Barron and Norris (1976); Bland *et al.* (1978); Beynon and Blackburn (1972).

9 Of the male clerks on the lowest grades, there were only two for whom promotion was a real possibility, as they were both young and undertaking further study through day-release schemes. The remainder were older men who had failed to gain promotion earlier in their careers or who had moved, relatively recently, into routine clerical work from other occupations. Age and their lack of appropriate qualifications ruled out the prospect of career mobility for them.

10 The promotion opportunities associated with clerical work (as compared with both skilled and unskilled manual work) have long been singled out as an important feature contributing to the enhanced 'life chances' of the clerk and, more particularly, acting as a constraint on 'militant' behaviour and increasing a managerial identification. See Lockwood (1958); Parkin (1972); Sykes (1965).

11 The centralization of control, it should be noted, is a hotly debated issue; see Blau *et al.* (1976); Leavitt and Whisler (1958); Whisler (1970); Stymne (1966).

12 We hope to explore this issue (among others) in the course of our current research, 'The Contemporary Work Situation of Clerical Employees' (sponsored by the SSRC).

13 Friedman (1977b, p. 49) has described Taylorism as a 'direct control' strategy which 'tries to limit the scope for labour power to vary by coercive threats, close supervision, and minimizing individual worker responsibility'.

Chapter 10 Destruction or redistribution of engineering skills?

1 This paper is based upon preliminary interpretations of a project sponsored by the SSRC. Since the time of writing, the project has been completed after further fieldwork. It is hoped that a more comprehensive statement of the theoretical and substantive implications of the manner of adoption of computer-controlled machine tools by British engineering firms may be offered in a subsequent publication. Thanks are due to members of departmental seminars at Bristol University (Sociology Department) and Manchester University (Department of Liberal Studies in Science) and to Peter Senker of the Science Policy

Research Unit, University of Sussex, for critical comments on earlier versions of this paper.

2   The most prominent expressions of this position are Braverman (1974) and various contributors to the journal *Capital and Class*, the most articulate among the latter being the Brighton Labour Process Group. Deskilling is also implicitly assumed as a tendentious principle of capitalist production by many other writers, who do not see it as a manifest feature in the same way as the first-named authors (cf., *inter alia*, Noble, 1978, and Friedman 1977b).

3   This deficiency in Weber's theory of economic relations and latter-day Weberians is analysed in Jones (1977).

4   Friedman (1977a) has provided a severe challenge to the Marxist assumption of unilateral managerial power by examining the shifts in control between management and unionized workers in terms of the product cycle of the British motor-car industry. His alternative to this single power is to posit a dual management strategy. When worker resistance is weak, direct control is exercised by management, more or less as Marx and, more explicitly, Braverman propose. When workers organize checks to this type of strategy, then 'responsible autonomy' is ceded, with management retaining indirect overall control. This dualism is essentially a simple categorization. It discounts the variety of constraints and conditions on both management decision-making and labour strategies. A study which more successfully relates labour organization and successes to different kinds of constraint upon managers and owners of capital is that of Lazonick (1979). He reappraises the impact of the re-equipment of the nineteenth-century Lancashire cotton industry with the automatic spinning mule.

5   Braverman appears to rely heavily on a text by Leone (1967), the significance of which is dealt with below. Another Marxist commentary on the introduction of NC in the USA which, unlike Braverman's analysis, is informed by a survey of firms operating NC is that of Noble (1978). His characterization of the process of utilization of NC consists principally of a counterposition of managerial motives for NC usage (to control labour) to various means of workers' adaptations of NC in order to resist controls. Variations in conditions are however, scarcely discussed.

6   It should be noted that Braverman (1974, p. 195) mistakes automation of the transfer function (on a conveyer line) for a mechanization of control, an error which further obfuscates the significance of this term.

7   Bell (1972, ch. 21). This was true at the time of writing. Operationalization and diffusion will probably proceed apace within the next two or three years.

8   EITB (1975, p. 11), plus provisional estimates supplied privately to the

author. The figures in the preceding paragraph are from the Department of Employment's *Gazettes*, 1970–8.

9   All the following figures on NC numbers are derived from the 1977 *Metalworking Production* machine-tool survey (Iredale, 1977).

10   It is worth noting that the total stock of all kinds of Britain's metal-working machine tools has, since 1966, declined by an estimated 250,000 (Iredale, 1977, p. 21). This latter figure puts the importance of NC for job elimination into a more modest perspective.

11   Bhattachryya *et al.* (1976) argue that NC use in Britain is held back because research and development on NC tools is 'too much concentrated on the sophisticated end of the market which is primarily catering for the minor aerospace industry' (p. 15).

12   Defined in Bell and Tapp's study as units machining one to twenty components, where these batches form at least half of the work undertaken.

13   Since it was frankly admitted by the same managers that control over the variability of machine operators' performance was among their objectives in NC purchase, any secrecy over wage costs would be puzzling. Interpretation of interview statements suggests to me that wage-cost reductions are seen in a more general context of total costs per successfully machined item. The question must, of course, be more clearly specified of whether individual categories of labour's wages are the target, or whether it is the total wage bill, including overtime.

14   This reassertion was, however, inserted into a relatively new division and allocation of the shop and engineering service departments to particular 'product centres'. The hierarchical principles remain in force with respect to planning and programming.

15   The Birmingham University study by Bhattacharyya found communications to be equally prolonged and segmented, having to go via a planning department and a central computing section.

16   Cf. EITB (1975, p. 14). The cut-back in apprentice training coincides with the onset of the recession in 1972–3. These 'lost' apprentices would, of course, have been qualifying in the past year or so.

17   Braverman's (1974, pp. 200–3) principal authority for these job descriptions appears to be machine-tool advertisements and the introductory text by W. C. Leone (1967). The latter, as an executive of the Ex-cell-O NC manufacturing company, might be expected to underestimate the demands NC makes on skilled manpower. Just as Taylor represents for Braverman the explicit verbalization of the capitalist mode of production, so it appears that NC salesman express the truth of employment with computer-directed machines.

18   Bhattacharyya *et al.* (1976, p. 6). In the aerospace industry and in the precision end of the market the average time (out of total production time) for proving and setting was 35 per cent.

19   The inappropriateness of NC technology for its actual use is commented upon by Noble (1978). His discussion of the factors inhibiting greater operator control over information inputs is notable for its omission of the problem of effective storage and retrieval of operators' innovations to the program.

20   The trade press (for example, *Machinery and Metalwork Production*) refers to several other examples of operator involvement with CNC editing.

21   A counter-argument in defence of overall tendencies might be that the evidence here is merely a snap-shot and that eventually the deskilling process will be accomplished. To arrive at this situation, however, would require the elimination not only of the particular constraining conditions detailed here but also of the very production conditions of these forms, such as the departmentalization of management. This would be a somewhat more radical transformation of capitalism than is contained in the theoretical position criticized here.

Bibliography

AITKEN, H. G. J. (1960), *Taylorism at Watertown Arsenal: Scientific Management in Action 1908–1915*, Cambridge, Mass.: Harvard University Press

ALDRIDGE, A. (1976), *Power, Authority and Restrictive Practices*, Oxford: Blackwell

Amalgamated Engineering Union (1968), *Report of National Committee*, London: AEU

Amalgamated Society of Engineers (1898), *The Engineering Trade Lockout*, London: ASE

American Federation of Labour (1935), 'AFL report on the Bedaux System', *American Federationist*, vol. 42, pp. 936–43

ASHWORTH, J. H. (1915), *The Helper and American Trade Unions*, Baltimore, Md: Johns Hopkins University Press

Athenaeum (1917), 'Industrial reconstruction: an employer's view', no. 4615, March, pp. 134–7

BABBAGE, C. (1971), *On the Economy of Machinery and Manufactures*, Fairfield, NJ: Kelley (first published 1835)

BAILES, K. E. (1977), 'Alexei Gastev and the Soviet controversy over Taylorism, 1918–24', *Soviet Studies*, vol. 29, no. 3, July, pp. 373–94

BAIN, G.S. (1970), *The Growth of White Collar Unionism*, Oxford: Oxford University Press

BALDAMUS, W. (1961), *Efficiency and Effort*, London: Tavistock Press

BARAN, P., and SWEEZY, P. (1968), *Monopoly Capital*, Harmondsworth: Penguin

BARRON, R. D., and NORRIS, G. M. (1976), 'Sexual divisions and the dual labour market', in D. Barker and S. L. Allen (eds.), *Dependence and Exploitation in Work and Marriage*, London: Longman, pp. 47–69

BAUDOUIN, T., COLLIN, M., and GUILLERM, D. (1978), 'Women and immigrants: marginal workers?', in C. Crouch and A. Pizzorno (eds.), *The Resurgence of Class Conflict in Europe since 1968*, vol. 2, *Comparative Analysis*, London: Macmillan, pp. 71–99

BAXANDALL, R., EWEN, E., and GORDON, L. (1976), 'The working class has two sexes', *Monthly Review* (special issue on 'Technology, the labor process, and the working class'), vol. 28, no. 3, pp. 1–9

214   *Bibliography*

Bedaux Archives (1926–39), Microfilms 1–27

BEECHEY, V. (1977), 'Some problems in the analysis of female wage labour in the capitalist mode of production', *Capital and Class*, no. 3, Autumn, pp. 45–66

BELL, D. (1973), *The Coming of Post-Industrial Society*, New York: Basic Books

BELL, R. M. (1972), *Changing Technology and Manpower Requirements in the Engineering Industry*, Watford: Engineering Industry Training Board

BELL, R. M., and TAPP, J. (1972), 'Automation and the structure of employment in machine shops', unpubl. report for Engineering Industry Training Board, Science Policy Research Unit, University of Sussex

BENDIX, R., ed. (1974), *Work and Authority in Industry*, Berkeley: University of California Press

BEYNON, H. (1973), *Working for Ford*, Harmondsworth: Penguin; reprinted in 1975 by EP Publishing

BEYNON, H., and BLACKBURN, R. M. (1972), *Perceptions of Work*, Cambridge: Cambridge University Press

BHATTACHARYYA, et al. (1976), 'Penetration and utilisation of machine tools in British industry', unpubl. report for Manufacturing Systems Unit, Department of Production, University of Birmingham

BLACKBURN, R. M., and MANN, M. (1979), *The Working Class in the Labour Market*, London: Macmillan

BLAND, L., et al. (1978), 'Women "inside and outside" the relations of production', in Women's Studies Group Centre for Contemporary Cultural Studies, *Women Take Issue: Aspects of Women's Subordination*, London: Hutchinson, pp. 35–78

BLAU, P. M. (1967), 'The hierarchy of authority in organisations', *American Journal of Sociology*, vol. 73, no. 3, pp. 453–67

BLAU, P. M. et al. (1976), 'Technology and organization in manufacturing', *Administrative Science Quarterly*, vol. 21, no. 1, pp. 20–40

BLAUNER, R. (1964), *Alienation and Freedom*, Chicago: University of Chicago Press

BLOOR, T. (1965), 'Trade union job control through apprenticeship training', unpubl. MA thesis, University of Manchester

Board of Trade, UK (1915), 'Report of an enquiry into the conditions of apprenticeship and industrial training in various trades and occupations of the UK', unpubl. report, London

BOSQUET, M. (1972), 'The prison factory', *New Left Review*, no. 73, May–June, pp. 23–34

BOWLES, S., and GINTIS, H. (1976), *Schooling in Capitalist America*, London: Routledge & Kegan Paul

BRANSON, N. and HEINEMANN, M. (1973), *Britain in the 1930s*, London: Panther

BRAVERMAN, H. (1974), *Labor and Monopoly Capital*, New York: Monthly Review Press

BRAVERMAN, H. (1976), 'Two comments', *Monthly Review* (special issue on 'Technology, the labor process, and the working class'), vol. 28, no. 3, pp. 119–24

BRIGHT, J. R. (1958), *Automation and Management*, Cambridge, Mass.: Harvard University Press

BRIGHT, J. R. (1966), 'The relationship of increasing automation and skill requirements', in National Commission on Technology, Automation and Economic Progress, *The Employment Impact of Technological Change*, vol. 2, *Technology and the American Economy*, Washington, DC: Government Printing Office, pp. 203–21

Brighton Labour Process Group (1976), 'Production process of capital and capitalist labour process', paper given at CSE Conference, Coventry

Brighton Labour Process Group (1977), 'The capitalist labour process', *Capital and Class*, no. 1, Spring, pp. 3–26

British Printing Industries Federation (1976), *Employment in Print*, London: BPIF

BROWN, G. (1977), *Sabotage: a Study in Industrial Conflict*, Nottingham: Spokesman Books

BURAWOY, M. (1978), 'Towards a Marxist theory of the labour process', *Politics and Society*, vol. 8, nos. 3–4, pp. 247–312

BURAWOY, M. (1979), *Manufacturing Consent*, Chicago: University of Chicago Press

BURGESS, K. (1969), 'Technological change and the 1852 lockout in the British engineering industry', *International Journal of Social History*, vol. 14, no. 2 pp. 215–36

BURGESS, K. (1975), *The Origins of Industrial Relations in Great Britain*, London: Croom Helm

BURNETT, J., ed. (1977), *Useful Toil*, Harmondsworth: Penguin

BURNHAM, J. (1941), *The Managerial Revolution*, New York: Day

BURNS, T., and STALKER, G. M. (1961), *The Management of Innovation*, London: Tavistock Press

BUTTRICK, J. (1952), 'The inside contract system', *Journal of Economic History*, vol. 12, no. 3 pp. 205–21

BUXTON, N. K. (1975), 'The role of the new industries in Britain during the 1930s – a reinterpretation', *Business History Review*, vol. 49, no. 2, Summer, pp. 205–22

CARCHEDI, G. (1975a), 'Reproduction of social classes at the level of production relations', *Economy and Society*, vol. 4, no. 4, pp. 361–417

CARCHEDI, G. (1975b), 'On the economic identification of the new middle class, *Economy and Society*, vol. 4, no. 1, pp. 1–86

CARR, E. H. (1966), *The Bolshevik Revolution*, vol. 2, Harmondsworth: Penguin

CHILD, J. (1967), *Industrial Relations in the British Printing Industry*, London: Allen & Unwin

CLARKE, A. (1968), *Working Life of Women in the Seventeenth Century*, London: Cass

CLARKE, J. F. (1966), 'Labour relations in engineering and shipbuilding on the north-east coast in the second half of the nineteenth century', MA thesis, University of Newcastle

CLARKE, R. O. (1957), 'The dispute in the British engineering industry 1897–8: an evaluation', *Economica*, vol. 24, no. 94, May, pp. 128–37

CLEGG, H., FOX, A., and THOMPSON, P. (1964), *A History of British Trade Unions since 1889*, Oxford: Oxford University Press

COLE, G. D. H. (1928), *The Payment of Wages*, London: Allen & Unwin

COLE, G. D. H. (1939), *British Trade Unionism Today*, London: Allen & Unwin

COLEMAN, D. C. (1958), *The British Paper Industry 1494–1860*, Oxford: Oxford University Press

COLLINSON, W. (1913), *The Apostle of Free Labour*, London: Hurst & Blackett

CONANT, E. H., and KILBRIDGE, M. D. (1965), 'An interdisciplinary analysis of job enlargement: technology, costs and behavioural implications', *Industrial Labour Relations Review*, vol. 18, no. 3, April, pp. 377–95

CONNELLY, T. J. (1960), *The Woodworkers*, London:Amalgamated Society of Woodworkers

COOMBS, R. (1978), 'Labour and monopoly capital', *New Left Review*, vol. 107, January–February, pp. 79–96

COPLEY, F. B. (1923), *Frederick Taylor: Father of Scientific Management*, 2 vols., New York: Taylor Society

CORIAT, B. (1980), 'The restructuring of the assembly line: a new economy of time and control', *Capital and Class*, no. 11, Summer, pp. 34–43

CORLEY, T.A. (1966), *Domestic Electrical Appliances*, London: Jonathan Cape

CORRIGAN, P., et al. (1978), *Socialist Construction and Marxist Theory: Bolshevism and its Critique*, London: Macmillan

CRESSEY, P., and MACINNES, J. (1979), 'Voting for Ford: industrial democracy and the control of labour', paper given at CSE Conference, Leeds

CROMPTON, R. (1979), 'Trade unionism and the insurance clerk', *Sociology*, vol. 13, no. 3, September, pp. 403–26

CROMPTON, R., and GUBBAY, J. (1977), *Economy and Class Structure*, London: Macmillan

CROZIER, M. (1964), *The Bureaucratic Phenomenon*, London: Tavistock

CUCA, J. R. (1977), 'Industrial change and the progress of labour in the English cotton industry', *International Review of Social History*, vol. 22, part 2, pp. 241–55

CUTLER, T. (1978), 'The romance of "labour"', *Economy and Society*, vol. 7, no. 1, pp. 74–9

CUTLER, T., *et al.* (1978), *Marx's Capital and Capitalism Today*, London: Routledge & Kegan Paul

DAVIES, M., and BRODHEAD, F. (1975), 'Labour and monopoly capital: a review', *Radical America*, vol. 9, no. 2, pp. 79–94

DE KADT, M. (1975), '"Management and labor" review of Braverman', *Review of Radical Political Economy*, vol., 7, no. 1, pp. 84–90

DE KADT, M. (1976), 'The importance of distinguishing between levels of generality', *Review of Radical Political Economy*, vol. 8, no. 3, pp. 65–7

Department of Employment (1965), *The Metal Industries*, Manpower Studies no. 2, London: HMSO

Department of Employment (1970), *Printing and Publishing*, Manpower Studies no. 9, London: HMSO

Department of Employment (1971), *Skilled Engineering Shortages in a High Demand Area*, Manpower Paper no. 3, London: HMSO

Department of Employment (1974), *Women and Work: A Statistical Survey*, Manpower Paper no. 9, London: HMSO

Department of Employment (1979), 'Skill shortages in British industry', *Employment Gazette*, vol. 87, May, pp. 433–6

DEVINAT, P. (1927), 'Scientific management in Europe', *International Labour Office Studies and Reports*, series B, no. 17, Geneva: ILO

DOBB, M. (1963), *Studies in the Development of Capitalism*, London: Routledge & Kegan Paul (first published 1948)

DOERINGER, P., and PIORE, M. (1971), *Internal Labour Markets and Manpower Analysis*, Lexington, Mass.: Heath Lexington Books

DRUCKER, P. (1955), *The Practice of Management*, London: Heinemann

DRUCKER, P. (1976), 'The coming rediscovery of scientific management', *Conference Board Record*, vol. 13, no. 6, pp. 23–7

DUNLOP, J. T. (1964), 'Review of Turner', *British Journal of Industrial Relations*, vol. 14, no. 2, pp. 287–9

EASON, K. D., *et al.* (1974), *A Survey of Man–Computer Interaction in Commercial Applications*, Loughborough: Department of Human Sciences, Loughborough University of Technology

EASON, K. D., *et al.* (1977), *Case Studies in the Impact of Computer Based Information Systems of Management*, Loughborough: Department of Human Sciences, Loughborough University of Technology

EDWARDS, G. A. B. (1971), *Readings in Group Technology*, Brighton: Machinery Publishing

EDWARDS, R. (1975), 'The social relations of production in the firm and labor market structure', *Politics and Society*, vol. 5, no. 1, pp. 83–108

EDWARDS, R. (1979), *Contested Terrain*, London: Heinemann

ELBAUM, B., and WILKINSON, F. (1979), 'Industrial relations and uneven development: a comparative study of the American and British steel industries', *Cambridge Journal of Economics*, vol. 3, no. 3, pp. 275–303

ELDRIDGE, J. E. T. (1973), *Sociology and Industrial Life*, London: Nelson

ELGER, A. (1979), 'Valorisation and deskilling – a critique of Braverman', *Capital and Class*, no. 7, Spring, pp. 58–99

ELGER, A., and SCHWARZ, B. (1980), 'Monopoly capitalism and the impact of Taylorism: notes on Lenin, Gramsci, Braverman and Sohn-Rethel', in T. Nichols (ed.), *Capital and Labour: A Marxist Primer*, London: Fontana, pp. 358–69

Engineering Industry Training Board (1975), *The Craftsmen in Engineering*, Watford: EITB

FIELD, J. (1979), 'British historians and the concept of the labor aristocracy', *Radical History Review*, vol. 19, Winter, pp. 61–85

FINE, B., and HARRIS, L. (1976), 'Controversial issues in Marxist economic theory', in R. Miliband and J. Saville (eds.), *Socialist Register*, London: Merlin Press, pp. 141–78

FLANDERS, A. (1964), *The Fawley Productivity Agreements*, London: Faber

FLANDERS, A. (1970), 'Trade unions and the force of tradition', Fawley Foundation Lecture 1969; reprinted in A. Flanders, *Management and Unions*, London: Faber, pp. 277–94

FONG, H. D. (1930), *Triumph of the Factory System in England*, Tientsin: University Committee on Social and Economic Research, Klankai University

FOSTER, J. (1974), *Class Struggle and the Industrial Revolution*, London: Weidenfeld & Nicolson

FOX, A. (1955), 'Industrial relations in nineteenth-century Birmingham', *Oxford Economic Papers*, vol. 7, part 1, no. 1, pp. 57–70

FOX, A. (1958), *A History of the National Union of Boot and Shoe Operatives*, Oxford: Blackwell

FOX, A. (1974), *Beyond Contract*, London: Faber

FRASER, W. H. (1974), *Trade Unions and Society*, London: Allen & Unwin

FRIDENSON, P. (1978), 'Corporate policy, rationalisation and the labour force: French experiences in international comparison; 1900 to 1929', paper given at Nuffield Deskilling Conference, Windsor

FRIEDMAN, A. (1977a), *Industry and Labour*, London: Macmillan

FRIEDMAN, A. (1977b), 'Responsible autonomy versus direct control over the labour process', *Capital and Class*, no. 1, Spring, pp. 43–57

FRIEDMAN, A. (1978), 'Worker resistance and Marxian analysis of the capitalist labour process', paper given at Nuffield Deskilling Conference, Windsor

FYRTH, H. J., and COLLINS, H J. (1959), *The Foundry Workers*, Manchester: Amalgamated Union of Foundry Workers

GALBRAITH, J. K. (1969), *The New Industrial State*, Harmondsworth: Penguin

GALLIE, D. (1978), *In Search of the New Working Class*, Cambridge: Cambridge University Press

GAMBLE, A., and WALTON, P. (1976), *Capitalism in Crisis*, London: Macmillan

GARDINER, J. (1975–6), 'Women and unemployment', *Red Rag*, no. 10, Winter, pp. 12–15

GARDINER, J. (1977), 'Women in the labour process and class structure', in A. Hunt (ed.), *Class and Class Structure*, London: Lawrence & Wishart, pp. 155–63

GARNSEY, E. (1978), 'Women's work and theories of class stratification', *Sociology*, vol. 12, no. 2, pp. 223–44

GIDDENS, A. (1973), *The Class Structure of the Advanced Societies*, London: Hutchinson

GILLESPIE, S. C. (1953), *A Hundred Years of Progress – the Record of the Scottish Typographical Association, 1833–1952*, Glasgow: Maclehose

GOFFEE, R. E. (1977), 'The butty system and the Kent coalfield', *Bulletin of the Society for Study of Labour History*, no. 3, Spring, pp. 41–55

GOLDTHORPE, J., et al. (1968), *The Affluent Worker: Industrial Attitudes and Behaviour*, Cambridge: Cambridge University Press

GOODRICH, C. L. (1975), *The Frontier of Control*, London: Pluto Press (first published 1920)

GORDON, D. M. (1972), *Theories of Poverty and Underemployment*, Lexington, Mass.: Lexington Books

GORDON, D. M. (1976), 'Capitalist efficiency and socialist efficiency', *Monthly Review*, (special issue on 'Technology, the labor process, and the working class'), vol. 28, no. 3, pp. 19–39

GORZ, A., ed. (1976), *The Division of Labour*, Brighton: Harvester Press

GOSPEL, H. (1982), 'The development of management organization in industrial relations – an historical perspective', in K. Thurley and S. Wood (eds.), *Management Strategy and Industrial Relations*, Cambridge: Cambridge University Press

GOTTSCHALCH, V. H., and OHM, C. (1977), 'Kritische Bemerkungen zur Polarisierungsthese bei Kern und Schemann', *Soziale Welt*, vol. 28, no. 3, pp. 340–63

GOULDNER, A. W. (1954), *Patterns of Industrial Bureaucracy*, New York: Free Press

GOWLER, D. (1970), 'Sociocultural influences on the operation of a wage-payment system: an exploratory case study', in D. Robinson (ed.), *Local Labour Markets and Wage Structures*, London: Gower, pp. 100–26

GRAMSCI, A. (1971), *Selections from Prison Notebooks*, London: Lawrence & Wishart

GREEN, J. (1974), 'Comments on Montgomery', *Journal of Social History*, vol. 7, no. 4, pp. 530–5

HABER, S. (1964), *Efficiency and Uplift: Scientific Management in the Progressive Era*, Chicago: University of Chicago Press

HART, R. A., and MACKAY, D. I. (1975), 'Engineering earnings in Britain, 1914–68', *Journal of the Royal Statistical Society*, series A, vol. 138, part 1, pp. 32–50

HECKSCHER, C. (1980), 'Worker participation and management control', *Journal of Social Reconstruction*, vol. 1, no. 1, pp. 77–102

HEILBRONER, J. (1975), 'Men at work', *New York Review of Books*, vol. 21, nos. 21 and 22, January, pp. 6–8

HILTON, J. (1935), *Are Trade Unions Obstructive?*, London: Gollancz

HINTON, J. (1971), 'The Clyde workers' committee and the dilution struggle', in A. Briggs and J. Saville (eds.), *Essays in Labour History*, London: Macmillan, pp. 152–84

HINTON, J. (1973), *The First Shop Stewards' Movement*, London: Allen & Unwin

HIRST, P. (1977), 'Economic classes and politics', in A. Hunt (ed.), *Class and Class Structure*, London: Lawrence & Wishart, pp. 125–54

HOBSBAWM, E. J. (1964), *Labouring Men,* London: Weidenfeld & Nicolson

HOBSBAWM, E. J. (1978), 'The aristocracy of labour reconsidered', in M. Flinn (ed.), *Proceedings of the Seventh International Economic History Conference*, Edinburgh: International Economic History Association, pp. 457–66

HOOS, I. R. (1961), *Automation in the Office*, Washington, DC: Public Affairs Press

HOPWOOD, E. (1969), *A History of the Lancashire Cotton Industry and the Amalgamated Weavers' Association*, Manchester: Amalgamated Weavers' Association

HOWARD, N. P. (1973), 'The strikes and lockouts in the iron industry and the formation of the ironworkers' union, 1862–1869', *International Review of Social History*, vol. 18, part 3, pp. 396–427

HUNT, A. (1977), 'Theory and politics in the identification of the working class', in A. Hunt (ed.), *Class and Class Structure*, London: Lawrence & Wishart, pp. 81–111

HUNTER, L. C. (1978), *Labour Shortages and Manpower Policy*, Manpower Studies no. 19782, London: Manpower Services Commission

HYMAN, R. (1971), *The Workers' Union*, Oxford: Oxford University Press

IREDALE, R. (1977), *'Metalworking Production': the Fourth Survey of Machine Tools and Production Equipment in Britain*, London: Morgan Grampian

JACKSON, C. (1909), *Report on Boy Labour*, Royal Commission on the Poor Laws and Relief of Distress, *British Parliamentary Papers*, vol. 44, London: HMSO

JACOBY, R. (1977), 'Review of Braverman', *Telos*, no. 29, Autumn, pp. 199–207

JEANES, R. (1966), *Building Operatives' Work*, Building Research Station, London: HMSO

JEFFERYS, J. B. (1946), *The Story of the Engineers*, London: Lawrence & Wishart

JEFFERYS, M., and JEFFERYS, J. B. (1947), 'The wages, hours and trade customs of the skilled engineers in 1861', *Economic History Review*, vol. 17, no. 1, pp. 27–44

JENKINS, M. (1974), 'Time and motion strike – Manchester, 1934–7', *Our History Pamphlet*, no. 60, London: British Communist Party

JEWKES, J., and GRAY, E. M. (1953), *Wages and Labour in Cotton Spinning*, no. 242, Manchester: University of Manchester Publications

JONES, B. (1977), 'Economic action and rational organisation in the sociology of Weber', in B. Hindess (ed.), *Sociological Theories of the Economy*, London: Macmillan, pp. 28–65

KELLY, J. E. (1977), 'Scientific management and work "humanisation"', paper read at BSA Industrial Sociology Group Conference, London School of Economics and Political Science

KELLY, J. E. (1982), *Scientific Management, Job Redesign and Work Performance*, New York: Academic Press

KERR, C., *et al.* (1964), *Industrialism and Industrial Man*, Harmondsworth: Penguin

KLINGENDER, F. D. (1935), *The Condition of Clerical Labour in Great Britain*, London: Martin Lawrence

KNOWLES, K. G. J. C., and ROBERTSON, D. J. (1951), 'Differences between the wages of skilled and unskilled workers, 1880–1950', *Bulletin of the Oxford Institute of Statistics*, vol. 13, no. 4., April, pp. 109–27

KYNASTON-REEVES, T., and WOODWARD, J. (1970), 'The study of managerial control', in J. Woodward (ed.), *Industrial Organization: Behaviour and Control*, London: Oxford University Press, pp. 37–56

LALOUX, P. (1951), *Le système Bedaux de calcul des salaires*, Paris: Editions Hommes et Techniques

LANDES, D. S. (1969), *The Unbound Prometheus*, Cambridge: Cambridge University Press

LAYTON, E. (1974), 'The diffusion of scientific management and mass production from the United States in the twentieth century', *Proceedings of the 16th International Congress in the History of Science, Tokyo*, vol. 4, pp. 377–86

LAZONICK, W. (1977), 'The appropriation and reproduction of labor', *Socialist Revolution*, no. 33, pp. 109–27

LAZONICK, W. (1979), 'Industrial relations and technical change: the case of the self-acting mule', *Cambridge Journal of Economics*, vol. 3, no. 3, pp. 231–62

LEAVITT, H. J., and WHISLER, J. L. (1958), 'Management in the 1980s', *Harvard Business Review*, vol. 36, November–December, pp. 41–8

LEE, D. J. (1972), 'Very small firms and the training of engineering craftsmen – some recent findings', *British Journal of Industrial Relations*, vol. 10, no. 2, pp. 240–55

LEE, D. J. (1979), 'Craft unions and the force of tradition – the case of apprenticeship', *British Journal of Industrial Relations*, vol. 17, no. 1, pp. 34–49

LEE, D. J. (1981), 'Skill, craft and class: a theoretical critique and a critical case', *Sociology*, vol. 15, no. 1, pp. 56–78

LENIN, V. I. (1965a), 'Taylorism: man's enslavement to the machine' (first published 1914), in V. I. Lenin, *Collected Works*, vol. 20, London: Lawrence & Wishart, pp. 152–4

LENIN, V. I. (1965b), 'The immediate tasks of the Soviet government: raising the productivity of labour' (first published 1918), in V. I. Lenin, *Collected Works*, vol. 27, London: Lawrence & Wishart, pp. 235–77

LEONE, W. C. (1967), *Production, Automation and Numerical Control*, New York: Ronald Press

LETTIERI, A. (1976), 'Factory and school', in A. Gorz (ed.), *The Division of Labour*, Brighton: Harvester Press, pp. 145–57

LIEPMAN, K. (1960), *Apprenticeship — an Enquiry into its Adequacy under Modern Conditions*, London: Routledge & Kegan Paul

LINDLEY, R. M. (1975), 'The demand for apprentice recruits by the engineering industry 1951–1971', *Scottish Journal of Political Economy*, vol. 22, no. 1, pp. 1–24

LITTERER, J. (1961), 'Systematic management: the search for order and integration', *Business History Review*, vol. 35, no. 4, pp. 461–76

LITTLER, C. R. (1978), 'Understanding Taylorism', *British Journal of Sociology*, vol. 29, no. 2, pp. 185–202

LITTLER, C. R. (1980), 'Internal contract and the transition to modern work systems: Britain and Japan', in D. Dunkerley and G. Salaman (eds.), *Organisational Studies Yearbook, 1980*, London: Routledge & Kegan Paul, pp. 157–85

LITTLER, C. R. (1981), *Control and Conflict: The Development of Modern Work Systems in Britain, Japan and USA*, London: Macmillan

LIVINGSTONE, P. (1969), 'Stop the stopwatch', *New Society*, vol. 14, no. 354, July, pp. 49–51

LOCKWOOD, D. (1958), *The Blackcoated Worker*, London: Allen & Unwin

LUPTON, T. (1957), 'A sociologist looks at work study', *Work Study and Industrial Engineering*, vol. 1, February, pp. 43–8

LUPTON, T. (1963), *On the Shop Floor*, Oxford: Pergamon Press

MACCARTHY, W. (1964), *The Closed Shop in Britain*, Oxford: Blackwell

MACKAY, D. I., *et al.* (1971), *Labour Markets under Different Employment Conditions*, London: Allen & Unwin

MCKENDRICK, N. (1961), 'Josiah Wedgwood and factory discipline', *Historical Journal*, vol. 4, no. 1, pp. 30–55

MACKENZIE, G. (1977), 'The political economy of the American working class', *British Journal of Sociology*, vol. 28, no. 2, pp. 244–52

MCKERSIE, R. B., and HUNTER, L. C. (1973) *Pay, Productivity and Collective Bargaining*, London: Macmillan

MAIER, C. S. (1970), 'Between Taylorism and technocracy: European ideologies and the vision of industrial productivity in the 1920s', *Journal of Contemporary History*, vol. 5, no. 2, pp. 27–61

MANDEL, E. (1978), *Late Capitalism*, London: New Left Books

MARSH, A. I. (1965), *Industrial Relations in Engineering*, Oxford: Pergamon Press

MARX, K. (1972), *Capital*, vol. 3, London: Lawrence & Wishart

MARX, K. (1976), *Capital*, vol. 1, with appendix, 'Results of the immediate process of production', Harmondsworth: Penguin

MEDICK, H. (1976), 'The proto-industrial family economy: the structural function of household and family during the transition from peasant society to industrial capitalism', *Social History*, no. 3, October, pp. 291–315

MICKLER, O., MOHR, W., and KADRITZKE, U. (1977), *Produktion and Qualifikation*, Gothingen: Bundesinstitut für Bernfsbilburg

MILES, C. (1968), *Lancashire Textiles*, Cambridge: Cambridge University Press

MILKMAN, R. (1976), 'Women's work and economic crisis: some lessons of the Great Depression', *Review of Radical Political Economics*, vol. 8, no. 1, pp. 73–97

Ministry of Labour, UK (1965a), *The Construction Industry*, London: HMSO

Ministry of Labour, UK (1965b), *The Metal Industries: A Study of Occupational Trends in the Metal Manufacturing and Metal Using Industries*, Manpower Studies no. 2, London: HMSO

Ministry of Munitions, UK (1922), *History of Munitions*, vol. 4, *The Supply and Control of Labour 1915–16*, London: HMSO

MONTGOMERY, D. (1974), 'The new unionism and the transformation of workers' consciousness in America, 1909–1922', *Journal of Social History*, vol. 7, no. 4., pp. 509–29

Monthly Review (1976), special issue on 'Technology, the labor process, and the working class', vol. 28, no. 3, pp. 1–24

MONTMOLLIN, M. DE (1974), 'Taylorisme et anti-Taylorisme', *Sociologie du Travail*, vol. 16, no. 4, pp. 374–82

MOORHOUSE, H. (1978), 'The Marxist theory of the labour aristocracy', *Social History*, vol. 3, no. 1, pp. 61–82

MORE, C. (1978), 'Deskilling in historical perspective', paper presented at Nuffield Deskilling Conference, Windsor

MORE, C. (1979), 'The degree of skill in the British industrial labour force', unpubl. research report, London School of Economics and Political Science

MORE, C. (1980), *Skill and the English Working Class 1870–1914*, London: Croom Helm

MORROW, L. C. (1922), 'The Bedaux principle of human power measurement', *American Machinist*, vol. 56, no. 7, pp. 241–5

MUMFORD, E. (1980), 'Participative system design: practice and theory', mimeo, Manchester Business School

NADWORNY, M. (1955), *Scientific Management and the Unions 1900–1932*, Cambridge, Mass.: Harvard University Press

NAKASE, T. (1979), 'The introduction of scientific management in Japan and its characteristics', in K. Nakagawa (ed.) *Labor and Management*, Tokyo: University of Tokyo Press, pp. 171–202

National Economic Development Office (1977), *Engineering Craftsmen: Shortages and Related Problems*, London: National Economic Development Office Publications

NELSON, D. (1975), *Managers and Workers: Origins of the New Factory System in the United States 1880–1920*, Madison, Wis.: University of Wisconsin Press

NICHOLS, T. (1969), *Ownership, Control and Ideology*, London: Allen & Unwin

NICHOLS, T. (1977), 'Review of Braverman's *Labor and Monopoly Capitalism*', *Sociological Review*, vol. 25, no. 1, pp. 192–4

NICHOLS, T., and BEYNON, H. (1977), *Living with Capitalism: Class Relations and the Modern Factory*, London: Routledge & Kegan Paul

NOBLE, D. F. (1978), 'Social choice in machine design: the case of automatically controlled machine tools, and a challenge for labour', *Politics and Society*, vol. 6, nos. 3 and 4, pp. 313–47

OKUDA, K. (1972), 'Managerial evolution in Japan', *Management Japan*, vol. 6, no. 1, pp. 28–37

OSTERUD, N. (1977), 'Letter to *History Workshop*', *History Workshop*, no. 4, Autumn, pp. 242–3

PALLOIX, C. (1976), 'The labour process: from Fordism to neo-Fordism', in CSE Pamphlet 1, *The Labour Process and Class Strategies*, stage 1, London: Conference of Socialist Economists, pp. 46–67

PALMER, B. (1975), 'Class, conception and conflict: the thrust for efficiency, managerial views of labor, and the working class rebellion, 1903–1922', *Review of Radical Political Economics*, vol. 7, no. 2, pp. 31–49

PALMER, B. (1976), 'Political economists, historians and generalisation', *Review of Radical Political Economics*, vol. 8, no. 3, pp. 68–9

PARKIN, F. (1972), *Class Inequality and Political Order*, London: Paladin

PARKIN, F. (1974), *The Social Analysis of Class Structure*, London: Macmillan

PAYNE, P. L. (1974), *British Entrepreneurship in the Nineteenth Century*, London: Macmillan

PELLING, H. (1968), 'The concept of the labour aristocracy', in H. Pelling (ed.), *Popular Politics and Society in Late Victorian Britain*, London: Macmillan, pp. 37–61

PHELPS-BROWN, E. H. (1968), *Report of the Committee of Enquiry under Professor E. H. Phelps-Brown into Certain Matters Concerning Labour in Building and Civil Engineering*, Cmnd 3714, and research supplement, Cmnd 3714–I, London: HMSO

PHILLIPS, A., and TAYLOR, B. (1978), 'Sex and class in the capitalist labour process', paper presented at Nuffield Deskilling Conference, Windsor

PICHIERRI, A. (1978), 'Diffusion and crisis of scientific management in European industry', in S. Giner and M. S. Archer (eds.), *Contemporary Europe*, London: Routledge & Kegan Paul, pp. 55–73

PIGNON, D., and QUERZOLA, J. (1976), 'Dictatorship and democracy in production', in A. Gorz (ed.), *The Division of Labour*, Brighton: Harvester Press, pp. 63–99

PIORE, N. H. (1968), 'The impact of the labour market upon the design and selection of productive techniques within the manufacturing plant', *Quarterly Journal of Economics*, vol. 82, no. 4, pp. 435–49

POLLARD, S. (1968), *The Genesis of Modern Management*, Harmondsworth: Penguin

POLLARD, S. (1969), *The Development of the British Economy 1914–1967*, London: Edward Arnold

POLLARD, S., and ROBERTSON, P. (1979), *The British Shipbuilding Industry, 1870–1914*, Cambridge, Mass.: Harvard University Press

POULANTZAS, N. (1975), *Classes in Contemporary Capitalism*, London: New Left Books

POULANTZAS, N. (1977), 'The new petit bourgeoisie', in A. Hunt (ed.), *Class and Class Structure*, London: Lawrence & Wishart, pp. 113–24

RICHARDSON, H. W., and ALDCROFT, D. H. (1968), *Building in the British Economy between the Wars*, London: Allen & Unwin

RICHARDSON, J. H. (1954), *An Introduction to the Study of Industrial Relations*, London: Allen & Unwin

ROBERTS, B. C., LOVERIDGE, R., and GENNARD, J. (1972), *Reluctant Militants*, London: Heinemann

ROBERTS, C., and WOOD, S. J. (1982), 'Collective bargaining and job redesign' in J. Kelly and C. W. Clegg (eds.), *Autonomy and Control at the Workplace: Contexts for Job Design*, London: Croom Helm

ROBERTS, G. (1967), *Demarcation Rules in Shipbuilding and Ship-repairing*, Cambridge: Cambridge University Press

ROLLIER, M. (1979), 'Taylorism and the Italian Unions', in C. Cooper and E. Mumford (eds.), *The Quality of Working Life in Western and Eastern Europe*, London: Associated Press, pp. 214–25

ROLT, L. T. C. (1971), *Landscape with Machines*, London: Longman

ROSDOLSKY, R. (1977), *The Making of Marx's 'Capital'*, London: Pluto Press

ROSE, M. (1979), 'Treatment of the labour process in French industrial sociology with special reference to recent studies', mimeo, University of Bath

ROWE, J. W. F. (1928), *Wages in Practice and Theory*, London: Routledge & Kegan Paul

ROWTHORNE, B. (1976), 'Late capitalism', *New Left Review*, vol. 98, July–August, pp. 59–83

ROY, D. (1952), 'Quota restriction and goldbricking in a machine shop', *American Journal of Sociology*, vol. 57, no. 3, pp. 427–42

ROY, D. (1954), 'Efficiency and the fix', *American Journal of Sociology*, vol, 60, no. 3, pp. 255–66

Royal Commission on the Employment of Children (1843), *Inquiry into the Employment and Conditions of Children in Mines and Manufacturies*, appendix to second report, *British Parliamentary Papers*, nos. 431 and 432, vols. 14 and 15

Royal Commission on Trade Unions and Employers' Associations, 1965–1968 (1968), *Report*, Cmnd 3623, London:HMSO

RUBERY, J. (1978), 'Structured labour markets, worker organisation and low pay', *Cambridge Journal of Economics*, vol. 2, no. 1, pp. 17–36

RYRIE, A. C. (1976), 'Employers and apprenticeship', research note, *British Journal of Industrial Relations*, vol. 14, no. 1, pp. 89–91

SADLER, P. (1970), 'Sociological aspects of skill', *British Journal of Industrial Relations*, vol. 8, no. 1, pp. 22–31

SAMUEL, R., ed. (1977a), *Miners, Quarrymen and Salt Workers*, London: Routledge & Kegan Paul

SAMUEL, R. (1977b), 'The workshop of the world: steam power and hand technology in mid-Victorian Britain', *History Workshop*, no. 3, Spring, pp. 6–72

SAUL, S. B. (1967), 'The market and the development of the mechanical engineering industries in Britain, 1860–1914', *Economic History Review*, 2nd series, vol. 20, no. 1, pp. 111–30

SAVILLE, J. (1960), 'Trade unions and free labour: the background to the Taff Vale decision', in A. Briggs and J. Saville (eds.), *Essays in Labour History*, London: Macmillan, pp. 317–50

SCHLOSS, D. F., ed. (1898), *Methods of Industrial Remuneration*, London: Williams & Norgate

SCHUMPETER, J. A. (1976), *Capitalism, Socialism and Democracy*, 5th edn, London: Allen & Unwin

SCHWARZ, B. (1977), 'On the monopoly capitalist degradation of work', *Dialectical Anthropology*, vol. 2, no. 2, pp. 159–67

SCOTT, W. H., *et al.* (1956), *Technical Change and Industrial Relations*, Liverpool: Liverpool University Press

SEYMOUR, W. D. (1967), *Industrial Skills*, London: Pitman

SHEPARD, J. (1971), *Automation and Alienation*, Cambridge, Mass.: MIT Press

SIMON, H. A. (1948), *Administrative Behaviour*, New York: Free Press

SISSON, K. (1975), *Industrial Relations in Fleet Street*, Oxford: Blackwell

SMELSER, N. (1959), *Social Change in the Industrial Revolution*, London: Routledge & Kegan Paul

SMITH, H. L., and NASH, V. (1889), *The Story of the Dockers' Strike, 1889*, London: Cedric Chivers

SOHN-RETHEL, A. (1976), 'The dual economics of transition', in CSE Pamphlet 1, *The Labour Process and Class Strategies*, stage 1, London: Conference of Socialist Economists, pp. 26–45

SOHN-RETHEL, A. (1978), *Intellectual and Manual Labour*, London: Macmillan

STARK, D. (1980), 'Class struggle and the transformation of the labour process', *Theory and Society*, vol. 9, no. 1, pp. 89–130

STEARNS, P. N. (1975), *Lives of Labour*, London: Croom Helm

STEDMAN-JONES, G. (1975), 'Class struggle and the Industrial Revolution', *New Left Review*, no. 90, March–April, pp. 35–69

STEWART, R. (1971), *How Computers Affect Management*, London: Macmillan

STINCHCOMBE, A. (1959), 'Bureaucratic and craft administration of production', *Administrative Science Quarterly*, vol. 4, no. 2, pp. 168–87

STONE, K. (1974), 'The origin of job structures in the steel industry', *Review of Radical Political Economy*, vol. 6, no. 2, pp. 113–73

STORM-CLARK, C. (1977), 'The two faces of coal', *New Society*, vol. 4, no. 769, June, pp. 649–51

STYMNE, B. (1966), 'EDP and organisational structure', *Swedish Journal of Economics*, vol. 68, no. 2, pp. 89–116

SWEEZY, P. (1942), *Theory of Capitalist Development*, New York: Monthly Review Press

SWEEZY, P. (1974), 'Some problems in the theory of capital accumulation', *Monthly Review*, vol. 26, no. 1, pp. 38–55

SWORDS-ISHERWOOD, N. B., and SENKER, P. J. (1978), 'Technical and organisational change in machine shops', report to the Engineering Training Board, May mimeo, Science Policy Research Unit, University of Sussex

SYKES, A. J. M. (1965), 'Some differences in the attitudes of clerical and manual workers', *Sociological Review*, vol. 13, no. 3, pp. 297–310

Bibliography

TAYLOR, A. J. P. (1960), 'The subcontract system in the British coal industry', in L. S. Presnell (ed.), *Studies in the Industrial Revolution*, London: Athlone Press, pp. 215–36

TAYLOR, F. W. (1906), *On the Art of Cutting Metals*, New York: American Society of Mechanical Engineers

TAYLOR, F. W. (1919), *A Piece-Rate System* (first published 1895), in F. W. Taylor, *Two Papers on Scientific Management: A Piece-Rate System; Notes on Belting*, London: Routledge & Sons, pp. 31–126

TAYLOR, F. W. (1947), *Scientific Management*, New York: Harper & Row

TAYLOR, P. S. (1979), 'Labour time, work measurement and the commensuration of labour', *Capital and Class*, no. 9, Autumn, pp. 23–38

TAYLOR, R. (1978), *The Fifth Estate*, London: Routledge & Kegan Paul

THOMPSON, E. P. (1968), *The Making of the English Working Class*, Harmondsworth: Penguin

THOMPSON, E. P. (1979), *The Poverty of Theory and Other Essays*, London: Merlin Press

THURLEY, K., and WOOD, S., eds. (1982), *Managerial Strategy and Industrial Relations*, Cambridge: Cambridge University Press

Trades Union Congress (1910), *TUC Joint Committee Report on the Premier Bonus System*, London: TUC

Trades Union Congress (1933), *The TUC Examines the Bedaux System of Payment by Results*, inquiry instituted by the 1932 Congress, report issued 1933, London: TUC

TRAUB, R. (1978), 'Lenin and Taylor: the fate of "scientific management" in the (early) Soviet Union', *Telos*, no. 37, pp. 82–92

TURNER, H. A. (1952), 'Trade unions, differentials and the levelling of wages', *Manchester School*, vol. 20, no. 3, pp. 227–82

TURNER, H. A. (1962), *Trade Union Growth, Structure and Policy*, London: Allen & Unwin

TURNER, H. A., *et al.* (1967), *Labour Relations in the Motor Industry*, London: Allen & Unwin

VENING, M., FRITH, O., and GRIMBLEY, C. (1975), *The Craftsmen in Engineering: An Interim Report*, Watford: Engineering Industry Training Board

WABE, S. (1977), *Manpower Changes in the Engineering Industry*, Watford: Engineering Industry Training Board

WARBURTON, W. H. (1939), *The History of Trade Union Organization in the North Staffordshire Potteries*, London: Allen & Unwin

WATSON, W. F. (1935), *Machines and Men: An Autobiography of an Itinerant Mechanic*, London: Allen & Unwin

WEBB, S., and WEBB, B. (1909), *The Public Organization of the Labour Market: Being Part II of the Minority Report of the Poor Law Commission*,

Royal Commission on the Poor Laws and the Relief of Distress, London: Longman

WEDDERBURN, D., and CROMPTON, R. (1972), *Workers' Attitudes and Technology*, Cambridge: Cambridge University Press

WEINBAUM, B., and BRIDGES, A. (1976), 'The other side of the pay check: monopoly capital and the structure of consumption', *Monthly Review* (special issue on 'Technology, the labor process, and the working class'), vol. 28, no. 3, pp. 88–103

WEST, J. (1978), 'Women, sex and class', in A. Kuhn and A. Wolpe (eds.), *Feminism and Materialism*, London: Routledge & Kegan Paul, pp. 220–53

WHISLER, T. (1970), *The Impact of Computers on Organisations*, New York: Praeger

WIGHAM E. (1973), *The Power to Manage: A History of the Engineering Employers' Federation*, London: Macmillan

WILD, R. (1975), *Work Organisation: A Study of Manual Work and Mass Production*, London: Wiley

WILKINSON, F. (1977), 'Collective bargaining in the steel industry in the 1920s', in A. Briggs and J. Saville (eds.), *Essays in Labour History*, London: Croom Helm, pp. 102–32

WILLIAMS, A. (1915), *Life in a Railway Factory*, London: Duckworth

WILLIAMS, G. (1958), *Recruitment to Skilled Trades*, London: Routledge & Kegan Paul

WOOD, S. J. (1980), 'Corporate strategy and organizational studies', in D. Dunkerley and G. Salaman (eds.), *Organizational Studies Yearbook 1980*, London: Routledge & Kegan Paul, pp. 52–71

WOOD, S. J. and KELLY, J.E. (1978), 'Towards a critical management science', *Journal of Management Studies*, vol. 15, no. 1, pp. 1–24

WOODWARD, J. (1958), *Management and Technology*, London: HMSO

WOODWARD, J. (1966), *Industrial Organization: Theory and Practice*, London: Oxford University Press

WOODWARD, J., ed. (1970), *Industrial Organization: Behaviour and Control*, London: Oxford University Press

WRIGHT, E. D. (1976), 'Class boundaries in advanced capitalist societies', *New Left Review*, no. 98, July–August, pp. 3–4

YATES, M. L. (1937), *Labour Conditions in British Engineering*, London: MacDonald & Evans

YOUNG, B. (1976), 'Review of Braverman', *Radical Science Journal*, vol. 4, pp. 81–93

ZEITLIN, J. (1979), 'Craft control and the division of labour: engineers and compositors in Britain, 1890–1930', *Cambridge Journal of Economics*, vol. 3, no. 3, pp. 263–74

ZIMBALIST, A., ed. (1979), *Case Studies on the Labour Process*, New York: Monthly Review Press

Index

234   *Index*